Motivation in Organisations

Motivation in Organisations: Searching for a Meaningful Work-Life Balance extends the current motivation models in business education to include motives of human behaviour that have been neglected for decades. It debunks some of the myths about human motivation (self-interest as the dominant factor, amorality and non-spirituality) and explains why this approach to teaching business is erroneous and leads to wrong and harmful practices in many organisations.

In a very personal and engaging style, the author presents a "map of motivations", based on a humanistic approach to management. This includes the latest findings of Abraham H. Maslow supported by sound philosophical reflections and modern research. He also presents specific ways of putting the framework into practice, sharing stories from students and professionals of how this framework has helped them better understand their own motivations and look at their daily work in a much more meaningful way.

The book is highly relevant to students and researchers in humanistic management, people management, organisational behaviour, business ethics, corporate social responsibility and sustainability. In short, this text will be truly inspiring to anyone who wants to reflect on motivation in organisations and how to achieve a better work-life balance.

Manuel Guillén is Associate Professor of Management, Organisational Behaviour and Professional Ethics at the University of Valencia (UV), Spain, and specialises in the area of leadership and trust in organisations. He is Founder and Director of the Institute for Ethics in Communication and in Organizations (IECO) and Director of the IECO-UV Chair of Business Ethics. For eight years, he has been the General Secretary of the Spanish branch of the European Business Ethics Network (EBEN-Spain). He is also Co-Founder of the International Humanistic Management Association Center Consortium. Guillén is a regular visiting researcher at Harvard University, where he is currently Representative of the University of Valencia Grants Programme.

Humanistic Management
Series Editors: Michael Pirson, Erica Steckler,
David Wasieleski, Benito Teehankee,
Ricardo Aguado and Ernestina Giudici

Humanistic Management draws together the concepts of social business, sustainability, social entrepreneurship, business ethics, conscious capitalism and cooperative capitalism to present a new humanistically based research paradigm. This new paradigm challenges the prevailing neo-liberal 'economistic' approach that dominates twentieth-century management theory and practice, and instead emphasises the need to protect human dignity and wellbeing as well as economic drivers.

Aesthetics, Organization, and Humanistic Management
Edited by Monika Kostera and Cezary Wozniak

Motivation in Organisations
Searching for a Meaningful Work-Life Balance
Manuel Guillén

For more information about this series, please visit: www.routledge.com

Motivation in Organisations
Searching for a Meaningful
Work-Life Balance

Manuel Guillén

LONDON AND NEW YORK

First published 2021
by Routledge
2 Park Square, Milton Park, Abingdon, Oxon OX14 4RN

and by Routledge
52 Vanderbilt Avenue, New York, NY 10017

Routledge is an imprint of the Taylor & Francis Group, an informa business

© 2021 Manuel Guillén

The right of Manuel Guillén Parra to be identified as author of this work has been asserted by him in accordance with sections 77 and 78 of the Copyright, Designs and Patents Act 1988.

All rights reserved. No part of this book may be reprinted or reproduced or utilised in any form or by any electronic, mechanical, or other means, now known or hereafter invented, including photocopying and recording, or in any information storage or retrieval system, without permission in writing from the publishers.

Trademark notice: Product or corporate names may be trademarks or registered trademarks, and are used only for identification and explanation without intent to infringe.

British Library Cataloguing-in-Publication Data
A catalogue record for this book is available from the British Library

Library of Congress Cataloging-in-Publication Data
Names: Guillén, Manuel (Guillén Parra) author.
Title: Motivation in organisations : searching for a meaningful work-life balance / Manuel Guillén.
Description: New York : Routledge, 2021. | Series: Humanistic management | Includes bibliographical references and index.
Identifiers: LCCN 2020026233 | ISBN 9780367322106 (hardback) | ISBN 9780429317293 (ebook)
Subjects: LCSH: Employee motivation. | Organizational behavior. | Work-life balance.
Classification: LCC HF5549.5.M63 G85 2021 | DDC 658.3/14—dc23
LC record available at https://lccn.loc.gov/2020026233

ISBN: 978-0-367-32210-6 (hbk)
ISBN: 978-0-429-31729-3 (ebk)

Typeset in Sabon
by Apex CoVantage, LLC

For Mum and Dad, my first teachers, for so many things

Contents

List of figures xii
Foreword by Dr Donna Hicks xiv
Preface xvi
Acknowledgements xx

PART I
Mapping the territory of human motivations 1

1 Human motivation theories: Are they really human? 3
   Understanding Herzberg's extrinsic and intrinsic motivations 3
   Revisiting Maslow's hierarchy of needs 7
   Building a map of motivations 10
   Using the map of motivations 14
   Some practical tips 17
   Some questions for reflection 18
   A final critical thought on why the map is not yet accurate enough 19
   References 20

2 The *extrinsic moral motivations*: Human yearning for dignity 21
   Human motivation theories neglecting the moral dimension 21
   Inviting Aristotle to join the conversation with Maslow and Herzberg 22
   Comparing Maslow's hierarchy with Aristotle's conceptions of good 25
   Recovering the neglected moral dimension in human motivation theories 29

viii Contents

    Extrinsic moral motivation founded on human dignity and source of trust 33
    The crucial role of moral motivation to rebuild trust 35
    Some practical tips 36
    Some questions for reflection 39
    A final critical thought on why the map is not yet accurate enough 39
    References 40

3 **The *intrinsic moral motivations*: Aiming to do the right thing**   42
    Revisiting Maslow's latest ideas on the moral dimension of motivations 42
    Maslow's and Aristotle's common ideas on human nature and moral goodness 44
    Intrinsic moral motivations: *The human desire to do good, honouring our own dignity 47*
    Moral motivations *are higher than* useful *and* pleasant *motivations 49*
    Intrinsic moral motivations *shape our moral virtues and our moral conscience 55*
    Intrinsic moral motivations *demand free moral character 57*
    Intrinsic moral motivations *are a manifestation of our human ideals 59*
    Some practical tips 62
    Some questions for reflection 64
    A final critical thought on why the map is not yet accurate enough 64
    References 65

PART II
Exploring the region of higher human motivations   67

4 **The *transcendent motivations*: Human readiness to give**   69
    Overcoming a self-centred vision of human motivations 69
    Transcendent motivations: *Human willingness to give 71*
    Transcendent motivations *or human generosity in debate among academics 74*
    Transcendent useful motivations: *Human willingness to give useful good, to serve 78*

Transcendent pleasant motivations: *Human willingness to give pleasant good, to please* 80
Transcendent moral motivations: *Human willingness to give moral good, to do good* 83
Transcendent motivations' *presence in ordinary and professional life* 85
Some practical tips 88
Some questions for reflection 90
A final critical thought on why the map is not yet accurate enough 90
References 91

5 The *spiritual motivations*: Human aspiration for the highest goods   93
   The neglected spiritual motivations 93
   Spiritual motivations *in pursuing the highest human goods* 95
   Spiritual motivations *in Maslow's latest enquiries* 97
   Spiritual motivations' *different conceptions* 99
   Spiritual motivations: *Worthy of universal recognition and respect* 103
   Extrinsic spiritual motivations: *The willingness to receive spiritual good* 106
   Intrinsic spiritual motivations: *The willingness to acquire spiritual good* 109
   Transcendent spiritual motivations: *The willingness to give spiritual good* 111
   Evidence of spiritual motivations 112
   Some practical tips 113
   Some questions for reflection 116
   A final critical thought on why the map is not yet accurate enough 116
   References 117

6 The *religious motivations*: Human longing for God's Love   120
   Religious motivations: *A human reality* 120
   Religious motivations: *A personal relationship with God* 121
   Religious motivations: *Discovering God's Love* 124
   Religious motivations: *It is all about love* 127

x *Contents*

    Religious useful motivation: *Willing to return useful good to God* 130
    Religious pleasant motivation: *Willing to return pleasant good to God* 133
    Religious moral motivation: *Willing to return moral good to God* 134
    Religious spiritual motivation: *Willing to return the spiritual good to God* 136
    Evidence of religious motivations 139
    Some practical tips 142
    Some questions for reflection 144
    A final critical thought on why having a map is not enough 144
    References 145

PART III
Using the map of motivations: Towards higher meaningful work   147

7   The map coordinates for motivations: The logic of love in organisations   149
    The logic of love *in life and work* 149
    The logic of love *in the human sciences* 151
    The logic of love *in human organisations* 153
    Receiving *truly human good in organisations* 157
    Achieving *truly human good in organisations* 161
    Giving *truly human good in organisations* 166
    Returning *truly human good in organisations* 169
    The order of love *and the* order of loves 172
    Some questions for reflection 176
    A final critical thought on why having a map is not enough 176
    References 177

8   The *compass* for motivations: Searching for a meaningful work-life balance   179
    Meaning in life and motivations 179
    The meaning of work and motivations 181
    The meaning of work as a job 183
    The meaning of work as a career 186
    The meaning of work as a calling 188

The meaning of work as a higher calling 192
Searching for a meaningful work-life balance 195
Some questions for reflection 198
A final critical thought on why having a map is not enough 198
References 199

9   **The roadmap for motivations: Always searching for higher meaningful work**   201
Searching for higher meaningful work 201
From the logic of fear to the logic of love 203
In search of a higher meaning in a job *205*
In search of a higher meaning in a career *208*
In search of a higher meaning in a calling *212*
In search of a higher meaning in a higher calling *217*
In search of higher meaningful work and life 219
Some questions for reflection 222
References 224

Index   226

Figures

1.1	Comparing Maslow's and Herzberg's motivation theories	11
1.2	A different way of comparing Maslow's and Herzberg's motivation theories	12
1.3	Comparing Maslow's, Herzberg's and other authors' motivation theories	13
1.4	Using the 2x2 map: Diagnosis of students' motivations	15
2.1	Philosophical distinction between motives and motivations	24
2.2	Comparing Maslow's hierarchy with Aristotle's types of human good	26
2.3	Definition of motivations based on Aristotle's types of human good	28
2.4	Definition of moral motivation based on Aristotle's types of human good	32
2.5	Examples of the extrinsic moral motivation	37
3.1	Defining intrinsic moral motivation	47
3.2	The hierarchical order of human nature and human goods	53
3.3	Examples from participants' intrinsic moral motivations or ideals	61
4.1	Defining transcendent motivations	72
4.2	Mapping the territory: The transcendent useful motivation	79
4.3	Mapping the territory: The transcendent pleasant motivation	81
4.4	Mapping the territory: The transcendent moral motivation	84
4.5	Examples from participants' transcendent motivations	88
5.1	The spiritual good defined	95
5.2	Mapping the territory of motivations: The spiritual motivations	105
5.3	The extrinsic spiritual motivations	107
5.4	The intrinsic spiritual motivations	109
5.5	The transcendent spiritual motivations	113
5.6	Examples of spiritual motivations	114
6.1	Love as the summary of human motivations	128
6.2	The religious human motivations	129
6.3	The religious useful motivations	132

6.4	The religious pleasant motivations	133
6.5	The religious moral motivations	135
6.6	The religious spiritual motivations	137
6.7	Examples of the religious motivations	140
7.1	Love as the summary of human motivations in organisations	150
7.2	Disciplines involved in understanding human motivations	152
7.3	The logic of love in human organisations	156
7.4	Receiving love at work	158
7.5	Achieving love at work	162
7.6	Giving love at work	168
7.7	Returning love at work	170
7.8	Map coordinates for motivations: The order of love and order of loves	175
8.1	The map of motivations and the meaning in life	180
8.2	The map of motivations and the meaning in work	182
8.3	The meaning of work as a job	185
8.4	The meaning of work as a career	186
8.5	The meaning of work as a calling	190
8.6	The meaning of work as a higher calling	194
8.7	Searching for a meaningful work-life balance: Compass for motivations	196
9.1	The logic of fear: A map of negative motivations	204
9.2	Fostering higher meaningful work as a job	208
9.3	Fostering higher meaningful work as a career	210
9.4	Fostering higher meaningful work as a calling	214
9.5	Fostering higher meaningful work as a higher calling	218
9.6	Roadmap for motivations: Searching for higher meaningful work	220
9.7	Content of the book: A "map of the map"	222

Foreword by Dr Donna Hicks

Motivation in organisations: Searching for a meaningful work-life balance

What could be more important than understanding what motivates us to do the things we do? Since we are all human beings, we have the capacity to rise above our involuntary, hardwired instincts and make decisions for ourselves and others that are consciously driven, as well as thoughtfully and deliberately chosen. The problem is, the process of moving from instinctive behaviour to carefully thought-through decisions, is not something that comes naturally. It has to be learnt.

What Professor Guillén has done in this remarkable book is created a roadmap for anyone interested in reflecting on and engaging in that learning process. In so doing, he has given us tools to achieve more complex and insightful ways of realising our potential as human beings as well as engaging in the kind of meaningful work most of us are seeking. He has also clarified what the literature on meaningful work means by "work". Is it understood as a job, a career, a calling, or a higher calling?

In order to create the roadmap, Professor Guillén has shone a bright light on the limitations of the current theories of motivation and has addressed the gaps in the literature that have ignored some of the most profound reasons for what motivates us and what gives our lives and work meaning. He has added another dimension to the classical and traditional motivation theories that espouse only extrinsic and intrinsic reasons for why we do what we do (humans' desire to achieve and receive "good"; that which is either pleasant or useful). He argues that humans also have a passionate desire for "moral" good (this includes extrinsic and intrinsic moral motivation). Integrated throughout the moral dimension is an appreciation for the role dignity plays in achieving this kind of good.

From a dignity perspective, we seek extrinsic moral good with the desire to be treated with dignity by others and our organisations. On the other hand, when we treat others with dignity, we achieve intrinsic moral good because we know it is the right thing to do. All human beings have inherent value and worth and deserve to be treated as such.

Foreword by Dr Donna Hicks

The matter of dignity plays out in the rest of the book by suggesting something that I have been talking about for decades, that treating others with dignity and receiving dignity from others are acts of love. What better way to create meaning in your life and work than by recognising the inherent worth in yourself, others, and the greater purpose of the organisation? If you love your work, then you are likely receiving and giving dignity. You are likely to feel that the purpose of the organisation is also dignity driven. With those three connections – to your own dignity, to the dignity of others, and the dignity of something greater than yourself – your goal of achieving a meaningful and fulfilling work-life balance is within reach.

I said in the beginning of this foreword that the items in the map Professor Guillén has created to help us navigate the challenging task of figuring out why we do what we do, are things that don't come naturally; we have to learn how to reflect on these issues. Fortunately, Professor Guillén has answered his highest calling by thinking deeply about the topic of human motivations and has done it with such loving intent. His commitment to love and dignity, and, for him, a connection to a Higher Power, is what motivated him to write this important book. He has given us the tools to learn how to create meaning, purpose and a life of fulfilment, not only for ourselves but also for the organisations that enable us to *do what we love*. Thank you, Manuel, for this invaluable contribution to our understanding of what it means to be human.

Donna Hicks, PhD
Associate, Weatherhead Center for International Affairs
Harvard University

Preface

I had just led a one-day seminar on human motivations in organisations for a group of corporate executives in Valencia, Spain, when one approached me and said, "Before you go, I would like to thank you for the discussion we had today, it was priceless for me". I thanked her for the positive feedback and, curious about what had caused her encouraging appraisal, I asked her which particular aspect of the day's discussion, if any, she had found most helpful.

She looked at me and said:

> "This is something quite personal . . ."
>
> ". . . I left my former employer a year ago. It was a tough decision because I was part of senior management and, if you are a woman, it is quite difficult to access such positions. Most people could not understand why I was leaving the company but, somehow, I knew it was time to go. It was a decision that came from the heart, and I knew I had to make it, even though I was not a hundred per cent sure it was the right thing".

She continued, "It was only today, during your seminar, that I finally realised why I quit and what drove me to that decision. Finally, I could define the motivations behind my determination to quit and, even though it sounds weird, I now know that I did the right thing. Again, thank you very much for your message; I am glad I was able to attend your seminar".

I wish I could say more about her and her job, but the company she left is well known in Spain, and I must respect her privacy. Nevertheless, I will share one last thing she told me that day: "You should write a book about your expanded framework on human motivations. If you write such a book, I believe you will help many people". Even now, I remember that conversation in full, and have not stopped thinking about writing this book since. That woman did not give me many reasons, but the one she mentioned – "you will help a lot of people" – was enough to give me my motivation.

A few months after that seminar in Valencia, I presented the same theory of motivations in organisations to a group of business management professors at other European universities. At the close, one attendee said to me, "You have just awoken our consciences. We cannot return and keep teaching motivation related to management in the way we used to. We must be frank with our students – tell them about the findings of your research, and how wrong we have been". This person asked me if I had considered writing a book to explain this new way of understanding human motivations.

More recently, now in the US, I was again surprised by the positive reactions when presenting my research to business professionals in Boston. Almost everyone approached me after the presentation to enquire about further readings and opportunities to learn more about *higher* human motivations; they were eager for more. It was evident that the academic article I gave them was simply not enough. Since then, wherever I present this theory of human motivations in organisations, be it at Harvard University where I spend half of the year, or back in Europe where I teach for the other half, I always get the same message from students, colleagues and practitioners: "If you write a book, you will help many people". Had I not been made aware of the value people have placed on the findings of my research, I would not be devoted to what I teach to then go on and share it with a wider audience.

The ideas you are about to explore come from over twenty years of passionate discussion with my students at the University of Valencia in Spain and also from seminars with professionals from almost every sector at the Harvard Kennedy School of Government.[1] In the beginning, I used to say to the undergraduates attending my lectures: "I'm sorry, but the theories of motivation I will be teaching you are wrong, but I have nothing better to offer you right now, so please help me become better. Let's do some research together".

If you were to ask any of my former students, they would tell you that this is exactly how frank I was with them. I worked with them for years to find a way of explaining human motivations in organisations in a manner that was open to aspects of motivation that, for decades, were entirely neglected by most major business schools and management textbooks. Unfortunately, we have been explaining the model of a person as self-interested, amoral and non-spiritual.

After a few years of discussion and research with the students, and with help and input from researchers at the institute I founded – the Institute for Ethics in Communication and in Organizations (IECO)[2] – we introduced a first version of an expanded taxonomy of motivations. The resulting "map of motivations" was the product of inclusive dialogue between social scientists and philosophers.

As I explain in further detail in the book, the definitive version of this *map* was produced partly due to a correction by an MBA student at Harvard and partly due to another year working with other colleagues. In 2015, the full version was published, co-authored together with my colleagues Ignacio Ferrero and Michael Hoffman, in the *Journal of Business Ethics*.[3]

The book you now hold in your hands is a *humanistic*, methodical and more comprehensive exploration of the theories of motivation. Parts I and II describe a new *map of human motivations* based on the most recent empirical findings of the social sciences, in dialogue with the humanities. Part III is then devoted to explaining how to use the *map*, offering you its *coordinates*, a *compass* and a *roadmap*.

A *map* is most helpful when you want to know where you are and to get to your destination. Similarly, having a map of our drives and desires might help us to better understand where those wishes, interests and ideals reside and to decide where we want to take them in our work and our lives.

This *map* might be useful for students who do not have clear criteria on which to base their professional future. It can help young professionals who are overwhelmed, who suffer from stress at work, who find tension between their work and personal life, or who do not even find meaning in their work. The *map* can be also especially useful for more mature people in the midst of a mid-career crisis. In fact, it can help us all better understand our motivations and the meaning we are giving to our work. In short, this conceptual framework allows us to reflect on how to achieve a better work-life balance.

Given the complexity of human nature, I am fully aware that attempting to build a *humanistic map of human motivations* risks oversimplification. This is why all my research is grounded in the works of some of the most renowned researchers in the field. I am also very aware that every theory is just that, a theory, with its limitations. I expect revisions and corrections to come about as more colleagues engage with this material, but, until then, I offer you the result of a long and honest search to better understand human nature and our motivations in the workplace, in particular, and our lives in general.

Clearly and simply, this book is the story of a management professor who knew he was wrong, asked for help and ended up devising a framework that may guide people to a more meaningful work-life balance. A professor who has gained a lot more from it than he had expected. A professor who has learnt much more about the complexities of human behaviour as well as its grandeur and dignity.

Students, managers and practitioners in general say that this new framework is much more relatable and easier to remember than existing theories of motivation. More importantly, they found the framework quite useful in better understanding their own motivations, to order their minds and help them make better decisions. I hope everyone who teaches human motivations can learn from the findings of this work, with a further focus on managers and practitioners. I believe we all need a more *humanistic* understanding of our motivations and, for those whose work is managing people, they will be further enlightened in knowing how to manage motivation in others.

I believe this reflection is worthy of your time, as many people around the world have commented that it could help them a lot. I hope this work serves you in understanding your personal motivation and your *purpose* in work and in life. Throughout the book, I will present the results of years of research and share many stories from students and professionals about how this framework has helped them look at their daily work in a more meaningful way and how it helped them transform their lives. My desire is that this book will lead you to reflect on your ideals and help you discover your true and profound motivations, with the ultimate goal of balancing your work and life.

As I finish writing this book, locked away at home in Boston, the entire world is engulfed in this coronavirus pandemic. During these days, I have been receiving news from Spain about the death of several co-workers and good friends. One feels great pain and helplessness at not being able to be near them and their families in such difficult times. These are difficult times for everyone. If you feel powerless in this situation, you can only pray, if you are a person of faith; in any case, we all need to look for meaning in this situation that we have never experienced before.

At this time, I have been able to see that the book by Victor Frankl, *Man's Search for Meaning*, is one of the most cited when reflecting on the COVID-19 crisis. Frankl explained that what really distinguishes man from other beings is not the will to pleasure (Freud), or the will to power (Nietzsche), but the will to meaning, to finding meaning in life, which is the first motivating force of the human being. He also said that "when we are no longer able to change a situation, we are challenged to change ourselves".

What I have tried to do in this book, while standing on the shoulders of giants like Victor Frankl, Abraham Maslow, Aristotle, Augustine and Aquinas, is to reflect on the search for meaning at work, an essential part of our lives. I hope I have been faithful to the ideas of such brilliant thinkers, and my desire is that this book helps you as much as it has helped me.

Notes

1 As the representative of the University of Valencia Grants Program at Harvard, I have been invited for several years as an occasional lecturer by the Harvard New England Alumni Association of the Leadership Survival Skills Program at the Harvard Kennedy School of Government. This program focuses on developing the skills and strategies needed to address leadership challenges.
2 IECO's mission is to promote dialogue between the social sciences and philosophy based on a holistic view of the person. It also develops tools to assess organisations from an ethical approach. www.iecoinstitute.org/en/
3 See Guillén, M., Ferrero, I. & Hoffman, W. (2015). The neglected ethical and spiritual motivations in the workplace. *Journal of Business Ethics*, 128(4), 803–816.

Acknowledgements

My gratitude starts with two people: Danilo Petranovich, the Director of the Abigail Adams Institute in Cambridge, Massachusetts, and Desmond Conway, who was an LLM student at Harvard Law School when I first met him. I would not have written this book had it not been for the insistence, support and friendship of both.

Two other people have been key in reviewing the first drafts of this book: Alejandro Cañadas and Jean Pierre Peinado, who read the early versions of the manuscript and gave me valuable comments. They made sure I was consistent and comprehensible throughout the book. In recent months, a third person, Sergio Castellano, began to read the drafts of each chapter, and his comments and advice have helped me enormously in the final writing of the text. Cristiana Nicoli de Mattos, a psychiatrist and good friend, was the final person to review the manuscripts and contributed invaluable comments.

Many thanks to the anonymous reviewers who gave their approval for this book to be published in the special Humanistic Management series by Routledge (Taylor & Francis). Special thanks to Michael Pirson, who encouraged me to publish the book in this series. Many thanks to Brianna Ascher and Naomi Round, my principal editorial contacts at Routledge, for their permanent spirit of service.

For his skills and guidance, I'm especially indebted to Ian Nicol, who edited every single word of the final manuscript with extraordinary professionalism, and who turned my English into easily readable prose that conveys the ideas that were originally in my head. Nevertheless, any errors in this book are mine alone, but the book itself would not exist without the help of every person I named before.

Most themes in the book had their genesis in my classes at the University of Valencia, and in many of the classes and talks I gave over the years throughout Europe and the US. I should thank each one of my former students for so many wonderful hours shared learning together. I must thank in a special way all those people that I name in the book without making explicit mention of their full names. Thanks to them, I have been able to better understand and explain many of the concepts and ideas that I propose throughout the text.

Much of the content was developed while preparing several leadership seminars I have lead that were organised by the Harvard Kennedy School's New England Alumni Association, so very special thanks to Madeline Snow and Karen M. Kingsbury, who put their trust in an unknown Spanish professor after hearing me speak once in a talk at RCC-Harvard.

Very special thanks to Rita Jácome and Luis Pérez, the IECO management team, for their friendship and unfailing support. Were it not for Rita and Luis, I would have given up; they set me straight along the way. I am also indebted to all the members of the IECO advisory board, starting with Donna Hicks, who wrote the foreword of this book. God surprises us by putting superb human beings along our path; Donna has been one of those people. She has been my Harvard mentor and counsellor, and she has always trusted me more than I ever trusted myself. Above all, I want to thank Donna and Rick, her husband, for their love and friendship.

Special thanks to the rest of the IECO Advisory Board for their commitment to IECO's work over the last decade, thanks to Ignacio Gil, Ginés Marco, Ignacio Bel, Joaquín Aldás, Rafael Juán, William (Bill) Bowman and William (Bill) English. Also, to all the former and current IECO Fellows: Alexis Bañón, Tomás Baviera, Alejandro Cañadas, Lourdes Canós, Fernando Chust, Esther Galdón, Antonio García, Tomás González, Álvaro Lleó, Enrique Marrades, Santiago Martínez, Borja Moragues, Carlos M. Moreno, Jean Pierre Peinado, Marco Robles and Pablo Ruíz. All of them colleagues in this exciting world of research and education and truly great friends. Also, special thanks to my doctoral supervisor, Professor Domènec Melé.

For their wisdom and guidance all this time, I am very grateful to the three businessmen who support the IECO-UV Chair of Business Ethics: Vicente Ruiz (RNB), Raúl Royo (RGIB) and Fidel García-Guzmán (Guzman Global). From them, their companies and their management teams, I have learnt many of the humanistic management principles and practices that you will read about in this book.

Particular appreciation for her confidence goes to the Rector of the University of Valencia, Mavi Mestre, who appointed me the representative of our institution in the exchange programme with Harvard University, through the RCC-Harvard. Thanks also to Guillermo Palao and Carles Padilla, the former and current Vice-rectors of International Affairs at the University of Valencia, two wonderful people with whom I have been fortunate to work in recent years.

Many thanks to David Kennedy, Director of the IGLP at Harvard Law School, for his invitations over the last four years as visiting researcher at Harvard University. Special thanks to Tyler VanderWeele, founder of the Human Flourishing program at Harvard, and to Matthew T. Lee, the programme's Director of Empirical Research for their help and collaboration with IECO researchers and their invaluable advice about much of this book's content. Special thanks also to Nien-hê Hsieh at the Harvard Business

School, for his invitation to attend all his classes and his support in promoting a Humanistic Management approach and in writing this book. Thanks to all the Harvard professors who have supported me over the years.

I also would like to make a very special mention of three people who, unfortunately, have already left us but without whom this book would never have seen the light. Juan José Renau Piqueras, my teacher, first mentor and Dean of the School of Economics at the University of Valencia; Dr Ángel Saenz-Badillos, Director of the Real Colegio Complutense (RCC) at Harvard University; and W. Michael Hoffman, who passed away a year ago and was a member of the IECO's Advisory Board. The three of them were renowned academics, great people and very good friends. I have fond memories of the entire team at the W. Michael Hoffman Center for Business Ethics at Bentley University: Mary Chiasson, Bob McNulty & Gail Sands. A million thanks for so many things.

I cannot but thank my American "family", all the residents of Elmbrook and Chestnut Hill, who have supported me for six months each of these last years living with me. Thank you all, and sorry for so many hours of absence that I had to dedicate to writing the book. Thanks to my Valencian family, the residents of Altet and Colegio Mayor la Alameda, for their patience with me.

I have been raised in an exceptional family, so I cannot finish without mentioning my sisters Yoya, Piedad, Ecarna and my brothers Antonio and Pepe for every minute they have shared with me, and their example, and for having given me nine wonderful nieces and nephews. Much of the content of this book is the result of a shared life.

Finally, this book is dedicated to the memory of my parents. I thank God for His generosity, His teaching, and His example. Although I have written the book alone, the previous two sentences show the real "culprits" for this book being written.

Part I
Mapping the territory of human motivations

1 Human motivation theories
Are they really human?

Understanding Herzberg's extrinsic and intrinsic motivations

Back in 2008, I delivered a presentation at Harvard University.[1] The title of this talk was "Human Motivation Theories: Are They Really Human?" I presented an analytical review of some of the most renowned theories on human motivations in organisations and justified why a majority of those theories seem not so human somehow. The lecture room was packed, and many of those in attendance conveyed their positive reaction and consideration to the basis of the talk. Among the participants was a Spanish MBA student who approached me and said, "I think your ideas are quite innovative and definitely on the money, but I think there is still something missing".

I was surprised by this observation from the Harvard student, and it definitely piqued my interest. He followed up on his comment by agreeing that the framework of motivations I had presented was an improvement on others he had studied, especially when referring to the human perspective, but he insisted that a piece of the puzzle was still missing.

Because of those comments, I undertook a journey of development, which meant another year of research to produce the definitive Map of Human Motivations (Guillén et al., 2015), which is at the core of this book. I make the case in this book that, unless some of the most well-known past theories of motivation are reviewed and improved, they could lead to inappropriate and detrimental practices in organisations as predicted years ago, referring to the subjacent assumptions of many of the management theories that have been taught in business schools in recent decades (Ghoshal, 2005).

Let's start this expedition together: imagine you are a business student and your management lecturer asks you what your motivations are. To begin with, why are you attending this class? The first answer from most students is quite simple: they want to pass the course and get the credits. This is an almost universal motivation for any student, no matter what they study. Even though you may find students interested in getting an A+ or just a C, what is clear is that every student in the world wants to pass the exams and, ultimately, the class.

4 *Mapping the territory of human motivations*

As human beings, we do what we have to do in order to get a particular set of results, or to obtain items we consider good, as something essential, convenient, or just satisfying, and students are no exception to this. In fact, if you ask them to provide other reasons for passing the course, among their motivations they will include all kinds of rewards they may get from their parents if they pass their exams. For instance, money or presents such as a motorbike, a car, a holiday, etc.

At this point, it is logical to ask them if they have motivations other than external rewards. The answers, however, will probably depend on how much they care about the content of your course and which parts they are specifically drawn to, but it will also have a lot to do with their personal interests. Occasionally, you may have a good student saying that they are attending the class simply in order to learn. However, the reactions to this from the rest of the class might be quite diverse, including disbelief.

Young students, especially adolescents, are not typically enthusiastic about recognising their noble desires, or even talking about them in public, exposing themselves to the risk of being embarrassed. Then again, what is true, is that the desire for learning is a universal motivation, and one that is not contingent upon *what you receive* from someone, such as your lecturer or your boss, but of *what you accomplish* while in class or at work.

Learning is something that you attain through effort, your own effort. It's a deeply personal engagement. Thus, when learning is the primary reason why students go to class, their interest is certainly higher than when their only motivation is just passing the course. This may seem obvious, but it is something that has always helped me explain the difference between our *extrinsic* and *intrinsic motivations* to my students. The former come from the outside (such as rewards), whereas the latter originate on the inside (such as learning).

It is at this point I like to ask them if they know who popularised such distinction. The reason for this is that, when I teach, I love to move seamlessly from common experience to general theories. Unfortunately, even though these two categories of *intrinsic* and *extrinsic* motivations are almost common knowledge, only a few recognise the individual responsible for them.

It was the American psychologist Frederick Irving Herzberg, one of the most influential names in business management, who first distinguished between what he called *hygienic factors* (extrinsic) and *motivator factors* (intrinsic) (Herzberg, 1968). The former refers to doing something because it leads to a distinct outcome, some external value that you expect to receive (like a good grade); the latter refers to doing something because it is inherently interesting or enjoyable, that is, it results in an internal reward (like learning something new).

You can distinguish *intrinsic* motivation when you gaze at the bright, attentive eyes of your students, looking at you, eager to know more about the topic. *Intrinsic* motivations are those reasons that move us to do things for their own sake, because we care about what we are doing, like learning something new. I must point out that, in an ideal world, learning should be the main motivation for any student.

As you almost certainly know, though, real life is always different and not so perfect. It seems that in real-world situations, students mostly care about passing the course, at least at the start of the academic year. Furthermore, such motivations are mainly *extrinsic*, meaning those reasons that move us to do things to obtain something from the outside.

What Herzberg found with his studies in organisational working environments was that *extrinsic factors* do not properly motivate an individual when they are present. Nevertheless, when these factors are absent, they can easily lower motivation. For many students, passing the course is an extrinsic factor but not a motivator. The possibility of not passing would surely produce dissatisfaction, but just passing only for the sake of passing would not be a factor in explaining a higher interest or motivation for taking the course or paying more attention to their lecturers.

Equally, in the opposite direction, Herzberg found that *intrinsic factors* do not necessarily lower motivation when they are absent, but they can be responsible for increasing motivation when present. If students are keen on studying in general, or the topic you are teaching is interesting or challenging, this will unquestionably lead to greater motivation.

It is a universal truth that to keep the attention of young undergraduates, you have to manage not only their *extrinsic motivations* but also their *intrinsic*. If you want to hold their attention, you need to ensure the class is interesting, challenging and worth their presence and effort.

That is precisely why, when teaching about human motivations, I try to challenge students by asking about their personal motives. I make an effort to present the topic in a way that engages them, starting a basic and real "conversation" with them. Accordingly, to check their understanding of the two-factor theory, I ask them to give me examples of these two kinds of motivations. For this exercise, I normally tell them to apply the theories to third parties, for instance, using their lecturers as examples.

I enquire about the kind of *extrinsic motivation* that a professor or lecturer could get from lecturing. The answer may vary depending on the group, but usually they all end up with one or all of three reasons: to make money, to get a better job or to move into a higher position at the university. Sometimes, they also suggest that we lecture to gain acknowledgement or a lasting interest from them, the students.

This is the moment when I tell them that these are really good examples of *extrinsic motivations*. I also ask them if they have ever asked their lecturers about their motivations or if they have just assumed them. This issue is quite relevant for management students; asking and listening is important when referring to the motivations of others, as we will consider again in Chapter 7.

The good news about their responses is that they really understand what *extrinsic motivation* implies. Their replies are genuine and sincere, and they are all reassuring reasons for teachers and educators to keep working how they do. This is not dissimilar to any job or organisation; *extrinsic motivations* are always related to receiving some type of external reward or appreciation from others, but these are not necessarily the main or only reasons why we teach.

Consequently, if you press the students further to tell you more about other teachers' motivations, they will probably reach the conclusion that some just love teaching; they thoroughly enjoy it. In other words, some teach because, while doing so, they feel good in themselves and with what they do. This is definitely a great example of *intrinsic motivation* and is intrinsic because the reason you keep doing something is the positive effect that activity produces within yourself. While doing this activity, in this case teaching, you feel good.

I always feel regret when most students do not see *intrinsic motivations* as a main driver for some of their lecturers' undertakings. That is a story for another time, though. The motivations of lecturers are not the important issue to reflect on right now, it just became part of the ongoing conversation with the students about human motivations in general.

The next question is usually, "If you had to choose, would you prefer lecturers motivated by *extrinsic* or *intrinsic motivations*?" As you can imagine, if they had to choose, they would rather have lecturers with strong *intrinsic motivations*. But why? Mainly because they feel that lecturers who love their job are regularly more fun, seem more knowledgeable and deliver their classes with exceptional ability.

Again, this observation from students is likely to be true for every profession. For some reason, when you perceive someone's enthusiasm, you also become an enthusiast. I remember when I was young, the reason I originally wanted to study chemistry was the passion my chemistry teacher had for the subject. *Intrinsic motivations* seem to be contagious, but why would that be? Students don't normally know how to answer that question directly, which is why I suggest they give it some thought and discuss it among themselves or in class later. We will explore this idea further in Chapter 7.

Afterwards, I tend to go further and ask them a new question: Would you rather lecturers be motivated only by *intrinsic motivations*, or also by the *extrinsic*? As you may guess, their answer is always the same; the more motivations, of any kind, they exhibit, the better. In fact, receiving a monthly salary is something you expect, but getting appreciation, interest and affection from your students is also very gratifying (both *extrinsic motivations*).

Moreover, if the lecturer loves teaching and learning from the interaction with the students (*intrinsic motivations*), motivation multiplies exponentially. Therefore, common sense seems to suggest that the greater the number and intensity of motivations at stake, especially intrinsic, the more motivated the person doing that job will be in any organisation.

Revisiting Maslow's hierarchy of needs

Now that the students understand the importance of having lecturers motivated by both *extrinsic* and *intrinsic* factors (Herzberg, 1968), it is time to return to their motivations. They have just established that they prefer having lecturers with both motivation types, so I then tell them that, as a lecturer, I also prefer having students moved by all positive motivations. If anyone is capable of doing their job better and more productively because there are more motivations at stake, then it makes sense that students will also do their "job" (studying, completing assignments, performing well in tests) better if there are more incentives involved.

It is therefore fair to say that, just as students love to have highly motivated teachers, we also care greatly about having highly motivated students. The logical conclusion is that students and lecturers alike should work together to improve our frame of mind. This undeniably presents a win-win opportunity and one that requires joint effort, not just to pass a class but because it positively affects our work and lives and is worthy of understanding and doing.

When I prompted this fundamental conversation asking about reasons why students attended classes, it was clear that the first reason was mainly extrinsic: to pass their courses and to get their degrees and certificates, and there is nothing wrong with that. Without a degree in management, the probability of them being able to get a job as managers is considerably lower.

Likewise, without employment, they will probably find it hard to live a regular and fulfilling life. In fact, it seems obvious that *extrinsic motivations* are universal, and many of them are essential and even basic to human endeavour. We all need food, drink and somewhere to live. This is precisely what the American psychologist Abraham Harold Maslow, in the middle of the twentieth century, defended in his popular hierarchy of human needs (Maslow, 1943).

Every time I mention Maslow, I see some students looking at me with a face of complicity and understanding since almost everyone has some knowledge of him. However, the truth is that most only remember some part of his theories and conclusions. I find this same phenomenon happening almost every time I ask about Maslow in my seminars, regardless of the audience's origin and background.

Most people remember that he proposed a hierarchical order of human needs that has been immortalised as a pyramid, even though none of his published works included a visual representation of that hierarchy as a pyramid. People usually remember Maslow's considerations about *basic needs* and that only after those are satisfied should we seek increasingly higher needs. Nevertheless, what most do not readily remember are the five elements or levels of the hierarchy and their sequence. Would you like to try?

This is the kind of exercise I like to engage in when starting from scratch and when lecturing to practitioners. I ask them to take a blank sheet of paper and write down or draw any theory of human motivations they might remember. I want to know if they have any *map of motivations* in their mind that they use daily when managing people and making decisions. It is quite remarkable that most of them think first about Maslow's pyramid as a plausible map, and this is probably down to its intuitive graphical appearance. Nevertheless, only a few of them are able to write down the five human needs of the hierarchy and in the right order.

Moreover, for some strange reason, in my experience, teaching the theory of human motivations in organisations for more than twenty years, it seems that people almost always overlook the need for *self-esteem* described by Maslow or they confuse it with *social need*, or *self-actualisation*. This is remarkable; the most widespread and remembered theory and, most of the time, not even HR managers are capable of remembering Maslow's five levels.

The lower-level needs of Maslow's pyramid are the easiest to remember. They include *physiological needs*, understood as all the biological requirements for human survival (e.g. air, food, drink, shelter, clothing, warmth, sex, sleep). If these needs are not satisfied, the human body cannot function properly. He therefore considered them the most important needs, as all others become secondary until these are met.

Among the lower-level needs he also included the *safety needs*, comprising protection from the elements, security, order, law, stability and freedom from fear. Finally, he described the third lower-level needs as *social*, those that involve feelings of belongingness. Examples of such needs include friendship, intimacy, trust, acceptance, affection and love. They also imply affiliations, such as being part of a group (friends, family or work).

According to Maslow, when the lower-level needs are met, one would start developing sensibility for those from the upper level. From them he distinguished *esteem needs*, including esteem for oneself (dignity, achievement, mastery, independence), and the desire for esteem, reputation or respect from others (e.g. status, prestige). Finally, among the upper-level needs, he underlined the highest level of need, *self-actualisation*. This need refers to realising personal potential, seeking personal growth, self-fulfilment and greater experiences. A desire "to become everything one is capable of becoming" (Maslow, 1987, p. 64).

As I just did here, I like to be sure my students revisit Maslow's theory, including lower-order needs (physiological, safety and social) and higher-order needs (self-esteem and self-actualisation). The next stage is to ask them if they consider this a sound theory and why or why not. Again, the answers usually vary from group to group, but most agree that Maslow's theory does make sense.

They all feel that the needs Maslow described are universal. Furthermore, most people recognise that a higher number of basic physical needs must be met, to some extent, prior to addressing higher psychological and self-fulfilment needs. Nevertheless, they are not so sure that there are just five levels, or why these five levels and not others were chosen or formulated, and why they were arranged in that specific order.

What's more, students tend to agree that the theory's logic seems too rigid and reductionist. It is distinctive that we sometimes prefer to sacrifice lower-level needs (like food or drink) to attain other higher levels of needs (like another person's appreciation). Just think about the times spent nowadays working out in gyms; this requires us to sacrifice lower-level needs (e.g. time, effort, comfort, physical rest) to attain higher-level needs (e.g. appreciation and liking from others, based on looks or aligned interests in physical training).

Fortunately, Maslow himself later clarified that meeting a need is not an "all-or-none" phenomenon, admitting that his earlier statements may have given "the false impression that a need must be satisfied 100 per cent before the next need emerges" (Maslow, 1987).

Let's go back to the question concerning how much students really appreciate Maslow's theory. While they seem to be keen on the framework, they have a lesser appreciation for its added value, given that the hierarchy of needs idea seems to be just common sense. Nevertheless, from a historical point of view, Maslow's real contribution, as one of the fathers of "humanistic psychology", was presenting his novel perspective. He believed that people have an inborn desire to be self-actualised, that is, to be all they can be, to grow and be happy.

Moreover, this is something that relevant schools of psychology, such as *psychoanalysis* and *behaviourism*, were not interested in during the middle of the twentieth century. Before Maslow, most psychologists had been concerned with abnormal conducts and the mentally ill; they tended to focus on problematic behaviours. Maslow, on the other hand, with a new original vision, wanted to know what constituted positive mental health. He urged people to acknowledge their basic needs before addressing higher ones and, ultimately, self-actualisation. For him, that was a way of learning to become humanly mature and, hence, happier.

Even while acknowledging the popularity and important contribution of Maslow's early ideas, students still tend to be critical about its added value and usefulness. They do not see its practicality, nor how it may help them to make better decisions in the future. My impression is that students around the world mainly study this theory to pass their exams but, later on, they generally don't tend to use it as a *map of motivations*. If they do, it is in a very haphazard way, distinguishing lower needs from upper needs and ensuring they cover the former. Sometimes, it is because they just don't see value in its applicability, and it tends to fall into oblivion for them. Maslow's framework is popular but does not seem to have much impact on people's behaviours.

When it comes to managers and practitioners, they do not use much of the theory either. One suggestion would be to try to understand what is amiss with Maslow's early ideas and discussing such issues by comparing his approach with other more "practical" theories, like that proposed by Herzberg as discussed before. It would be useful if we were able to come up with some kind of *map of motivations* that could be used to understand, describe and diagnose our own motivations.

Building a map of motivations

It is at this point I propose something that probably never happened but that would have been interesting to see: a scenario in which Maslow and Herzberg are debating their own approaches with one another. With that in mind, it can be said that if both theories are correct, they should be compatible to some degree, or even complementary and harmonious to each other. Ultimately, this is what science is all about: understanding reality from its different angles, finding patterns and order in nature, in this case, in human nature.

As social scientists, we should be able to provide theories that explain human reality universally, so that we may understand it collectively and, if necessary, transform it. I am convinced that when this happens, when theories of human behaviour are accurate and closely related to human reality, they become truly useful. Similar to an accurate and faithful map of a territory, a good integrative theory of motivations may aid in effective decision making.

Nevertheless, such an integrative approach may require pushing back against the fragmentation and hyper-specialisation of modern science and be open to others' findings, building bridges and promoting dialogue, just like that proposed between Maslow and Herzberg.

The aforementioned exercise of an imaginary debate between both theorists was fun. In almost every class, someone would suggest that both theories are not so different after all. The proposal being that the *lower-level* needs described by Maslow (physiological, safety and social) are indeed *extrinsic motivations*, whereas those of the *upper level* (self-esteem and self-actualisation) are *intrinsic motivations*. This is precisely how some textbooks liked to compare both theories (Hitt et al., 2011). It makes sense to point out that the basic and social needs are external or extrinsic, given that they refer to our dependency from others, whereas, on the other hand, the psychological needs of self-fulfilment (esteem and self-actualisation) seem to belong more to the intrinsic realm (see Figure 1.1).

Unfortunately, things are never that simple. When Maslow focuses on esteem, as we have noted, he set apart mainly two categories. On one hand, *esteem* is understood as the desire for reputation or recognition from others (e.g. status, prestige), which would be *extrinsic motivations*. On the other, *self-esteem*, or *esteem* for oneself (including mastery, independence, achievement and dignity), would represent *intrinsic motivations*. So, where do we finally place *esteem*? Is it *intrinsic* or *extrinsic*? Could it not be in both?

Human motivation theories 11

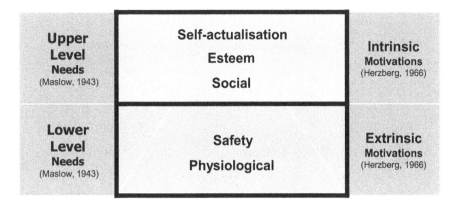

Figure 1.1 Comparing Maslow's and Herzberg's motivation theories

It is precisely because this comparison is not clear-cut that I suggest thinking outside the box or just thinking analytically and attempting a higher level of precision. The question is that, if we want to promote open and sincere dialogue between both established theories, we must first recognise that both classifications are using different criteria to categorise and differentiate human motivations.

Herzberg's distinction between *extrinsic* and *intrinsic factors* seems to refer to the origin of those aspects (either from the outside or from the inside), whereas Maslow's distinction of human needs refers to the type of needs people are motivated by and the reason, purpose or goal of those motivations, understood in a hierarchical higher or lower order, and given their particular contribution to human growth.

If both classifications are apparently right, then, to compare the two properly, I suggest not mixing the categories but first differentiating them and later comparing them. The easiest way to do this would be by building a *matrix structure* instead of a pyramid, leaving room for both criteria to play their role in the new categorisation or *map of motivations*. This would actually lead to a grid where the columns include Herzberg's *extrinsic* and *intrinsic motivations*, and the rows would embody Maslow's *upper* and *lower* levels of *human needs* (see Figure 1.2).

The appropriateness of comparing both theories by developing this grid or matrix is threefold. First, it makes it easier to understand the compatibility between both approaches. You may find motivations that even while being in the lower level of the pyramid are still *intrinsic*, such as our desire for achieving *competence* or *mastery*, even though Maslow did not explicitly mention them (see Figure 1.2).

You may also notice motivations that even if in the upper level of the pyramid are still *extrinsic*, as would be the case for esteem (from others).

12 *Mapping the territory of human motivations*

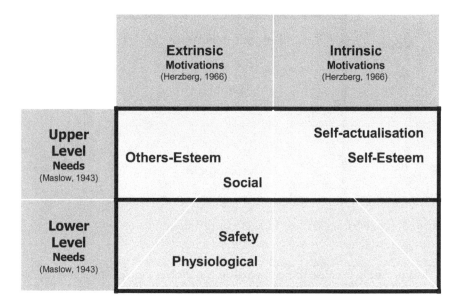

Figure 1.2 A different way of comparing Maslow's and Herzberg's motivation theories

In Figure 1.2, this *others-esteem* is distinguished from *self-esteem* precisely to make this differentiation more accurate. Likewise, as I mentioned earlier, many people tend to forget or confuse this level of the hierarchy (of esteem), maybe and precisely because they tend to erroneously mix theories and classifications in their minds.

Second, this matrix allows visualising how both theories are not only compatible but also complementary. For instance, the first conclusion people arrive at from analysing Figure 1.2 is that each of the levels of human needs described by Maslow can be satisfied in either an *extrinsic* or *intrinsic* manner, even though Maslow himself did not make this specific argument.

Finally, this framework offers a *map* where all possibilities of human motivations seem to be presented not just in a compatible and complementary manner but also in a way that is harmonious. The map represents an organisation of motivations template based on a logic that is simple and transcends its empirical origin, while ratifying it at the same time.

It additionally offers criteria to define and diagnose or interpret our own motivations as we will see throughout the book. In this sense, once we are able to describe our motivations, using the framework or *map*, we may also conclude if it is better to be motivated by *extrinsic* or *intrinsic motivations*, or by *lower-* or *upper-level needs*.

But, before we start reflecting on how to use the framework to diagnose our motivations, we should ensure that the tool is accurate enough to describe them. To do this, I always suggest my students compare and appreciate how compatible this classification is to other approaches and taxonomies of human motivations. If they do not contradict each other, then we will be able to define it at least as an acceptable *map of motivations*. With that purpose in mind, I ask them to check other descriptive or "content" theories of motivation[2] online and see how they fit the framework.

The result of this exercise is that students end up correctly assuming that the majority of popular taxonomies of motivation found in most textbooks today could fit within the proposed matrix framework quite well. In fact, as Figure 1.3 shows, there is strong correlation between most of Maslow's and Herzberg's findings and the discoveries of other renowned authors such as Alderfer (1969) or McClelland (1962). Furthermore, it is important to highlight that other later studies corroborate the conclusions of all these early theories.

In 2001, Ryan and Deci revisited the distinction between *extrinsic* and *intrinsic* motivations to better understand their development (Ryan & Deci, 2000). In addition to Maslow's basic *physiological needs*, they identified the existence of three basic innate *psychological needs*: *competence* (feeling self-efficacious, having the relevant skills to succeed); *autonomy* (an internal perceived locus of causality, of a self-determined behaviour); and *relatedness* (a sense of belongingness and connectedness).

As amazing as it sounds, these three motivations fit exactly into our grid (see Figure 1.3). The consistency of all these approaches, and the fact they all still appear in the majority of today's textbooks describing human

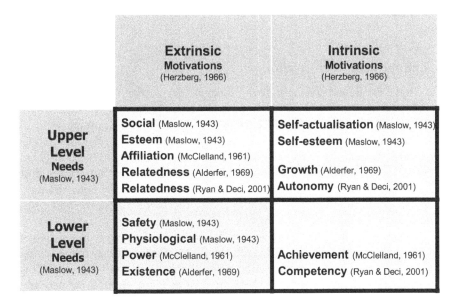

Figure 1.3 Comparing Maslow's, Herzberg's and other authors' motivation theories

motivations, validates that the way of organising them is accurate and constitutes a good synthesis and therefore a precise *map* of pre-existent classifications.

Using the terminology of authors other than Maslow and Herzberg, and revisiting the framework we suggest, Figure 1.3 shows that among the *extrinsic motivations* (left column) we can include, in a lower level, the *physiological* and *safety* aspects of human *existence* itself. The left column moves us to look for things like external *support*, *reward* and *power*.

Similarly, among the *extrinsic motivations* of an upper level, we find motivations like *relatedness*, *esteem*, *affiliation* or *social relationships*, all related to external recognition. Moving to the right column, the *intrinsic motivations* include, at a lower level, the universal desire for *achievement*, which in work environments would mean *mastery* and *competence*. At an upper level, we find the motivations of autonomy, growth, self-esteem and self-actualisation (see Figure 1.3).

According to the students, the advantages of this new framework converge on simplifying their work when preparing for exams. It becomes easier for them to effectively retain the ideas and the empirical findings from the specialised literature. The main aspect they have to remember now is essentially the criteria from both classifications that have been used to identify four kinds of motivations.

The first criteria referred to the *origin* of our motivations (columns of the *map*), which denotes that we engage in actions to *receive* an external good (extrinsic) or to *attain* an internal one (intrinsic). Furthermore, the second criteria indicate the kind of good we expect to obtain (rows of the *map*), specifically, being more practical (lower level), or more psychological (upper level).

Using the map of motivations

As I have explained throughout these pages, developing this simple *framework*, this *map of motivations*, has been the result of hours of meaningful discussions with students, and it represents a worthwhile summary of all the other traditional approaches. Nevertheless, and regarding our main purpose, the *framework* is also a source of reflection concerning the usefulness and accuracy of existing theories. Thus, in regard to its usefulness, the best way I have found to substantiate it has been by asking the students (and practitioners attending my seminars) to use the *map* to describe and diagnose their own personal motivations.

I suggest my students think about the reasons why they want to work as managers in the future and write down their motivations for studying a degree in Business Administration using the *map* we built together. This exercise has different purposes. First, it verifies if the *framework* actually helps them to better identify the *origin* or *source* of their motivations (*extrinsic* or *intrinsic*). Second, it helps them grasp how many of their motivations are related to more practical matters (*lower level*) or with other higher psychological reasons (*upper level*).

Finally, this exercise helps them to reflect not only on the quantity but also on the quality of their motivations, simply by weighting the score they give to each motivation. The entire exercise will serve them in testing the accuracy of the theories and how those theories could help them understand and transform their motivations so they ultimately make better personal and professional decisions.

In Figure 1.4, I present some of the most common responses from my students over the years. As part of the *lower-level extrinsic motivations* for studying management, they normally include aspirations such as getting a job, having a decent salary, ensuring stability and security, purchasing a home, being able to travel extensively and getting to a comfortable level of life whereby spending money is of no concern.

Among the *upper-level extrinsic motivations* for choosing to study business, they consider issues such as finding workplaces with suitable environments in which they may develop valuable social relationships with colleagues and superiors, feeling part of an important mission or project, being recognised with admiration and pride and being considered and treated as worthy and unique individuals (see Figure 1.4).

Regarding their *intrinsic motivations* to study business, they include, at the *lower level of the grid*, interests such as acquiring knowledge and skills or gaining experience. Finally, on their *intrinsic motivations* to study

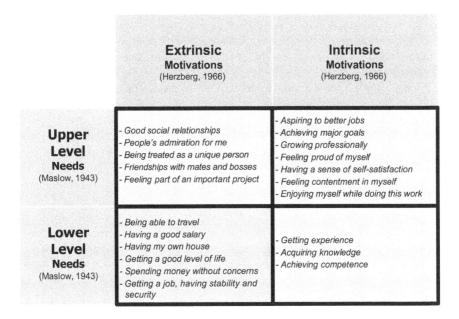

Figure 1.4 Using the 2x2 map: Diagnosis of students' motivations

business, students' answers at the *upper level* of the grid are feeling proud of themselves, achieving meaningful goals, professional growth, enjoying themselves by doing this work, aspiring to better work experiences and having a sense of self-satisfaction and feeling contentment within themselves (see Figure 1.4).

Looking back on the results of this exercise with my students, it seems clear to everyone involved that the higher the number of motivations present, the better. Earning a good salary and having an excellent work environment are almost universal aspirations, and, on top of this, having the kind of job they can enjoy and in which they can improve their abilities is very desirable. These results show that the four kinds of motivations summarised in this framework seem to have a universal value; they are different human goods that we all particularly aspire to in our jobs and our lives.

When it comes to reflecting on the quality of the motivations, things become less universal to some extent. For instance, once each student has written down their own motivations, I ask them to think about what motivation they would choose if they could choose only one. As you can imagine, they usually all choose one from the extrinsic lower level, such as having a job or getting a good salary. These results make sense; the first thing we all expect from our jobs is to be rewarded and to make sure it serves us in making a living.

This is where Maslow hit the nail on the head; we all have some *basic needs* that are necessary for our existence for practical reasons. In fact, most of the *extrinsic lower-level motivations* are indispensable. This is why the more we experience their scarcity, the higher the tension, fear or concern about not getting them. This idea is also consistent with the findings of Herzberg regarding *extrinsic motivations*. When we do not get the kind of human goods that belong to the realms of *extrinsic motivations*, we feel dissatisfaction.

Hence, the less we are motivated by fear or dissatisfaction, the more our aim can be focused on personal satisfaction, meaning placing more importance on the *intrinsic motivations* in this framework. Following the logic of this *map*, it seems to be better if you are motivated more by *intrinsic* than by *extrinsic motivations*. We will return to this issue, and the role of fear in motivation, in Chapter 9.

All these findings are consistent with the answers you get from students today. When you ask them which group of motivations they would leave out, if they had to sacrifice one of them, you may be surprised by their answers. On courses where students are more competitive, because our universities require better grades for admission or good standing, the motivations connected with relatedness usually pay the price. These students seem to be much more focused than others are on money, rewards, achievement and success.

It is interesting that this exercise helps them learn more about the relative importance they assign to each group of motivations and reflect on which of them they believe are of lesser importance. What also seems clear is that this *map* helps them identify their own motivations and assess the importance they give to each group of them in terms of intensity. In other words, this *map* helps them reflect on their "motivations at work". At this point, they might know where they are "located" on the *map*.

We must exercise extreme caution when it comes to the question of how we as scientists can help ourselves and others (students and practitioners) interpret and improve their motivations using these conclusions. As far as I understand, the normative power of a theory comes from its reliability, its conformity with reality. Therefore, if scientific studies in this field are considered reliable and trustworthy, there are a few conclusions and practical tips that we may offer at this point.

Some practical tips

Regarding *intrinsic motivations*, over recent decades, behavioural scientists have been figuring out the dynamics and decoding the power of such motivations. It seems that empirical studies keep proving the power of enjoyment-based *intrinsic motivations* rather than the *extrinsic*. In many organisations today, extrinsic motivations respond mostly to reward and punishment logic (like salaries, bonuses, holidays, etc.). Authors today suggest the importance of (1) *promoting a way of thinking and an approach to life built more around intrinsic, rather than extrinsic, motivators* (Pink, 2009).

Intrinsic motivations are powered by our innate need to direct our own lives, to learn and create new things. They are among the strongest and most omnipresent drivers of human behaviour because they relate to our creative capacity, the joy of discovery and the delight in mastering challenges. Their "reward" is the activity itself, performing to the best of one's ability, and not the external aspects of the work. Therefore, one thing we all should attempt to do is (2) *"fall in love" with our own work, or at least with those aspects of our work that are more attractive for us* (Pink, 2009).

We should (3) *look at every activity in our daily work (any kind of work) as an opportunity for growth and, whenever possible, the joy in learning.* We need to keep in mind that those people with higher *intrinsic motivations* of self-esteem and sense of autonomy also tend to have better interpersonal relationships and a greater general well-being than those who are just extrinsically motivated. This does not necessarily depend on the nature of the task performed, as we will discuss later in Chapter 8.

Furthermore, intrinsically motivated people usually achieve more than their reward-seeking counterparts because *extrinsic motivations* can give us less of what we actually desire. In fact, they can extinguish *intrinsic motivation*, diminish performance and crush creativity, fostering short-term thinking. Too little *intrinsic motivation* would mean a lack of passion and interest in our work and lives, whereas too much, at the expense of forgetting extrinsic needs, would probably also be a mistake. We all need to (4) *satisfy our basic and social external needs* (Pink, 2009).

However, it does not mean that *extrinsic motivations*, those related to rewards and punishments – or "carrots and sticks" as some authors call them – are entirely reasonable. According to Herzberg, they have to be fulfilled in order to avoid dissatisfaction. Recent empirical studies have proven that the traditional "if-then" rewards system can be effective for rule-based routine tasks in organisations because there is little *intrinsic motivation* to undermine and not much creativity to crush. Still, they can be more effective if those giving such rewards offer a rationale as to why the task is necessary, acknowledging that it may be boring and allowing people autonomy over how they complete it (Pink, 2009).

I do not want to seem naive; it is just a matter of common sense to think that we all need to satisfy *extrinsic motivations*. Because, indeed, we need them. We all need jobs and money to have a happy or just functional life. In fact, when I find students not interested in money, I feel the need to correct them. They cannot and should not be dependent on their parents or another third party their entire lives and without repayment or a sense of earning and contribution of some sort. (5) *A lack or defect in extrinsic lower motivations would mean a lack of common sense and practical reasoning.*

The same can be said about *upper-level extrinsic motivations*. (6) *We all need to have well-balanced family and social relationships*. Neglecting them as a result of giving too much importance to our professional or personal achievements (*intrinsic motivations*) would be another serious disorder or miscalculation, and not just for students, for all of us. The lack of – or meagre – interest in external drivers would show maturity issues, not having your feet on the ground. What is more, (7) *too much concern for external incentives (financial security, others' appreciation) would show excessive dependence on our environment*, probably another manifestation of maturity issues. We will get back to some of these ideas, on how to read our motivations, in the third part of the book, which deals with the ways we can interpret and use this *map of motivations*.

It seems that some practical consequences may be drawn from the *framework* we just reviewed in this chapter. These consequences can keep us thinking about our own motivations. That is why I love to finish this first session by engaging participants in some more personal questioning, having the simple *map* we just built together in mind and what they discovered regarding their own motivations (see Figures 1.3 and 1.4).

Here are some of those questions, and you are welcome to use them for your own purpose to understand the kind and intensity of motivations that drive you in your daily work and life.

Some questions for reflection

1 *How often am I driven by interest and enthusiasm for my work and my life in general?* (intrinsic higher)

2 *How often am I driven by the fear of failing or not being competent enough in my work and in my life in general?* (intrinsic lower)
3 *How often am I driven by an interest in getting rewards or support at work and in my life in general?* (extrinsic lower)
4 *How often do I complain internally or externally about issues at work and in my life in general?* (extrinsic higher)
5 *How often am I driven by the concern of what others say or think about me at work and in my life in general?* (extrinsic higher)
6 *How often do I see opportunities and challenges where there only seem to be difficulties?* (extrinsic higher)
7 *Would I be able to assess (from 0 to 10) what level of intensity I have in each type of motivation described in this framework?*
8 *Which would I say are my true sources of motivation at work, and in my life in general?*
9 *What group of motivations would I like to improve in terms of my work and my life?*
10 *Am I missing any motivation type(s) in this framework?*

A final critical thought on why the map is not yet accurate enough

The reason I tend to ask this last question about any missing motivations in this framework is that I am convinced there are other motivation sets absent from this structure and that may be present in the real world of organisations. Therefore, this framework might not be so accurate after all.

I recall a joke I once heard about student asking their teacher if they would punish them for something they hadn't done. The teacher replied that of course they wouldn't, and the student said great because they hadn't done their homework. Should we blame our students for not telling us about the other motivations they probably have?

At this point, I wonder if those of us who teach motivations have done our homework. It is just common sense to consider that some people might be motivated by the wrong motives, and by "wrong" I mean morally wrong. Not everything in life is about money, power and prestige (extrinsic motivation) or about competence or satisfaction (intrinsic motivation). Or is it?

In other words, I do not think that every motivation I teach my students is always a good one, but, unfortunately, in our framework based on the most widespread motivation theories, we did not mention any moral issue. Maybe you know this joke about an employee asking one of his colleagues, "I heard that the boss has called you into his office every day this week to reprimand you. What do you have to say for yourself?" He replied, "I'm glad it's Friday".

Of course, no one likes to be unfairly reprimanded. We cannot deny that in our organisations, as well as in our lives in general, we all want to be treated morally well, with a sense of justice and fairness. We all want reasonable salaries, and students want to get a fair assessment of their capabilities through their grades. These are all goods that belong to the moral realm of human life. Accordingly, if the moral dimension is missing from our *map of human motivations*, there is something wrong with it.

Therefore, we should try to understand why ethics, the question characterising human behaviour as good or evil, is absent. We should revisit the classification to right what was once wrong, to propose a more *humanistic* theory of "human" motivations. Otherwise, if ethics – or morality – one of the most fundamental elements of human nature, is lacking, then these theories of human motivation cannot be linked to the human experience after all. This will be explored further in the next chapter.

Notes

1 The talk took place at the Real Colegio Complutense at Harvard, (RCC-Harvard), a non-profit organisation, aimed at providing academic, scientific, and cultural cooperation between Harvard University and the Spanish Higher Education system. https://rcc.harvard.edu/
2 Some authors distinguish "content" theories of motivation from "process" theories. The content approaches study what motivates people in acting. Among them, the hierarchical description of needs proposed by Abraham Maslow in 1943 is paradigmatic. Process approaches attempt to explain the motivational mechanism by way of changes in the process of satisfying human needs and how individual behaviour is encouraged, directed, and maintained with respect to desired goals. Some examples of these approaches would be those of Skinner, Adams, Vroom or Latham and Locke (see Guillén et al., 2015).

References

Alderfer, C. (1969). An empirical test of a new theory of human needs. *Organizational Behavior and Human Performance*, 4, 142–175.
Guillén, M., Ferrero, I. & Hoffman, W. (2015). The neglected ethical and spiritual motivations in the workplace. *Journal of Business Ethics*, 128(4), 803–816.
Ghoshal, S. (2005). Bad management theories are destroying good management practices. *Academy of Management Learning & Education*, 4(1), 75–91.
Herzberg, F. (1968). One more time: How do you motivate employees? *Harvard Business Review*, January–February, 46(1), 53–62.
Hitt, M., Black, S. & Porter, L. (2011). *Management*. New York, NY: Prentice Hall.
Maslow, A. H. (1943). A theory of human motivation. *Psychological Review*, 50(4), 370–396.
Maslow, A. H. (1987). *Motivation and personality* (3rd ed.). New Delhi: Pearson Education.
McClelland, D. (1962). Business, drive and national achievement. *Harvard Business Review*, 40, 99–112.
Pink, D. (2009). *Drive: The Surprising Truth About What Motivates*. New York, NY: Riverhead Books.
Ryan, R. & Deci, E. (2000). Intrinsic and extrinsic motivations: Classic definitions and new directions. *Contemporary Educational Psychology*, 25, 54–67.

2 The *extrinsic moral motivations*
Human yearning for dignity

Human motivation theories neglecting the moral dimension

Every year, I like to start my first Fundamentals of Management class by telling undergraduate students about a very simple experiment that I frequently carry out when using the lift at the university and visiting companies; I pay close attention to the conversations of those around me. This regular practice helps me reflect upon other peoples' motivations in their business schools or their workplace interests. Surprisingly, the topics people mostly talk about are not related to economic, financial, marketing, strategic matters or business metrics, etc. The conversations are usually more related to personal moral issues, at least in ordinary circumstances whereby we talk about what interests, affects or worries us.

Talking about moral issues is one of the most common events for human beings. People, in every human organisation, discuss matters in terms of injustice, mistrust, misunderstanding, and lack of respect or sincerity from colleagues and those in authority. This is not exclusive to the world of universities or business organisations, where this can be easily observed just by paying attention to conversations in lifts.

In almost every organisation, people mostly complain, gossip or judge, and regularly on matters related to the everyday behaviours of others. Have you ever had the same experience? Have you noticed the conversation topics of others around you? The topics usually revolve around what others have done wrong, reasons why you can or cannot trust others, and many arguments ensue about the "ethical health" of the organisation's environment and, lamentably, on rare occasions, what has been done the right way.

My eavesdropping, coupled with substantial empirical evidence (Forsyth, 1992; Lan et al., 2008), shows that human beings tend to discuss their everyday life issues through the lens of morality, a morality that refers to human moral principles and qualities such as justice, equity, truthfulness, reliability, etc. Unfortunately, the theoretical framework introduced in the previous chapter did not include a moral dimension when describing human motivations.

The majority of current classifications of motivations have neglected the moral dimension (Guillén et al., 2015). I strongly believe that if social scientists do not make this dimension explicit when building theories, the result will be an incomplete and artificial explanation of human reality. Furthermore, when omitting morality, management theories stop being realistic and can even become destructive and harmful (Ghoshal, 2005).

Going back to my business school classes, when I ask my students if any motivations are missing the framework we started building together in Chapter 1, they normally fail to see any missing moral aspect, and these concerns do not arise until I start asking questions. For example, I ask them if they would prefer to have lecturers who are fair or unfair. I also ask if they would prefer lecturers who limit themselves to explaining theories and concepts that are true and real, based on rigorous intellectual reflection and proven experience or, conversely, who base their lectures on their own opinions. Paradoxically, being fair, truthful and objective when teaching is something morally good and not neutral at all.

Likewise, I ask them if they would rather have lecturers who care about their students' learning and development or ones who are more distant with a penchant for impersonal presentations. Their answers usually follow the same vein. As all students want to receive fair grades, they assume they are learning the truth in everything they study; they also want to know in advance how they are going to be assessed, and, of course, they prefer to have lecturers who care about them, their learning and growth. The same could be said of any of us when asked about how we expect our bosses to behave in organisations; we want them to truly care about us as human beings.

We all want bosses who are fair, truthful, trustworthy and caring towards us, as this is a type of motivation that holds a moral content, one that can only be explained if we use the language and logic of philosophy and moral science. For this reason, and at this point, I suggest that my students (and now readers of this book) use their imaginations and invite an expert in moral philosophy to our discussion. Someone who twenty-four centuries ago was also fascinated by human nature and human motivations. I propose letting Aristotle, the great Greek philosopher, accompany us for the rest of our conversation about human motivations.

Inviting Aristotle to join the conversation with Maslow and Herzberg

Now, we can continue our dialogue between psychologists from Chapter 1, this time including Aristotle. Before we start this discussion, and for the sake of honesty, I cannot be sure whether Aristotle would accept or even if he would approve of our considering Maslow's classification of human needs as a theory of motivations. Nonetheless, we know for certain that he did reflect on these issues during his lifetime.

The extrinsic moral motivations 23

Most probably, Aristotle would say that Maslow's hierarchy of needs is not exactly a theory of motivations but a theory of motives. In other words, Maslow is less concerned with the reasons *why* we do things, our "motivations" and their origins (i.e. internal or external, as in the case of Herzberg's theory), than with the reasons *for which* we do things, our "motives", goals, or purposes (regarding the satisfaction of our human *needs* for growth). This might sound too philosophical, but, as I like to tell my students, what would you expect from a philosopher?

Being the philosopher he was, Aristotle would probably argue that Maslow's theory of needs is more a theory of human motives or *goals* (the *for which*) because it focuses on the purpose of our behaviour (the satisfaction of needs). On the other hand, Herzberg's two-factor framework could be considered more a theory of motivations, given that it deals with the reasons *why* people act (the origin or the forces that move us to act, i.e. internal or external).

To explain this simply, I suggest that the students think about their motivations in class: the reasons *why* they attend my classes. Normally, they would provide answers as diverse as out of fear of their parents (negative *extrinsic motivations*) or out of fear of failing (negative *intrinsic motivations*). In both cases, the reason *why* they attend classes is a kind of fear that, in the first case, has an external origin and, in the second, an internal origin. Both cases focus on the cause that moves them to behave in one way or another. They give that kind of answer precisely because I ask them *why*, where is the cause or the source of their behaviour?

On the other hand, when I ask them what they want to obtain from attending management classes, what they are looking for or what the reasons are for them coming, they then talk about their motives. They include things like passing the course, having fun with their classmates or learning something new. When the question is about the "what for", their answer relates to some kind of interest or *need* they want to satisfy. In other words, they are now thinking in terms of Maslow's hierarchy of unsatisfied needs or desires that demand to be fulfilled, a hierarchy that is not so much a grading of motivations as a hierarchy of motives, of needs, purposes or *reasons for* them to act in one way or another.

This distinction between motivations (reasons why we do things, i.e. fear of punishment or failure) and motives (reasons for doing things, i.e. having fun or achieving mastery) may still sound too philosophical for the students, but I consider this to be a key point in properly understanding any explanation or taxonomy of human motivations. For those wanting to know more about this distinction, I recommend studying the research carried out by Professor Velaz in 1996 on this issue (Velaz, 1996). However, it is easy to understand the difference between motives and motivations simply by looking at the map of human motivations that we discussed in Chapter 1 (see Figure 1.3).

24 Mapping the territory of human motivations

The columns on the map refer to our motivations (either an *extrinsic* or *intrinsic* origin), and the rows refer to our motives (our *higher-* or *lower-*order goals). Therefore, the map constitutes a theory of motivations that also considers our motives. In other words, by presenting a dialogue between Herzberg's and Maslow's approaches, the map proposed in Chapter 1 constitutes both a theory of motivations – understood as psychological forces that move us to act – and a theory of motives – understood as the intellectual reasons explaining our behaviour. It maps our different motivations (columns) and also the motives for those motivations (rows) (see Figure 2.1).

At this point, I love to tell my students that Maslow was not only a humanist but probably the most Aristotelian psychologist of his time. I imagine that both Maslow and Aristotle would really enjoy themselves if they had a chance to have this conversation. The reason I say this is that both thinkers conceived human behaviour as always being directed towards some motive, end or purpose. Humans do practically everything they do with a goal in mind (a *telos*, in Greek). In that sense, their conception of human behaviour can be considered "teleological".

Both were interested in understanding the motives, ends or purposes behind our desires and not only the motivations, their origins. In other words, they both cared about the content of what we seek to do, the purpose

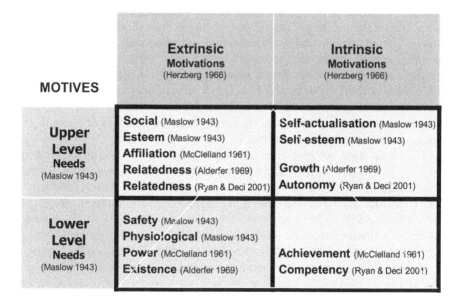

Figure 2.1 Philosophical distinction between motives and motivations

we pursue (i.e. passing the course) and, additionally, the source that moves us to pursue such a goal, its origin (i.e. fear of others' judgement).

To accurately compare Maslow's hierarchy of needs with Aristotle's view of human *motives for acting*, we should look more carefully at Aristotle's idea of what moves us to act. According to Aristotle, behind everything we do there is a reason for doing it, that every action, no matter how simple, is born from a purpose the action is meant to achieve, and what leads us to act is nothing more and nothing less than our desire for the "good".

We act because we want to gain some sort of good. Aristotle refers to the things that we desire, that we love, that appeal to us as human beings because we consider them worthy. In other words, human beings seek "good" in everything they do. That is why Aristotle sees happiness (eudaemonia) as the addition of all the possible human goods or, rather, as the highest human good, the one we all aim for (Aristotle, 2014).

It seems that Aristotle and Maslow agree on viewing happiness and the achievement of a "good life", a fulfilled one, as the main and final motive behind every human behaviour. Maslow was also interested in psychological health as an important part of that human fulfilment (or flourishing) (Daniels, 1982). Thus, unsurprisingly, when I ask students to tell me if they see any parallel between Maslow's pyramid and Aristotle's idea of the desire for good and happiness, they start seeing them as being the same thing.

If we think about it, lower-level motives or needs (such as food, sleep or shelter) can be understood as lower-level goods, those that are necessary for living. Upper motives or needs (such as relatedness or self-actualisation) coincide with the higher-level goods, those that we all aim for, which include social and psychological health and the "good" of our self-fulfilment. Therefore, to better compare Aristotle and Maslow, it is time to look at Aristotle's distinction of human goods and its hierarchy. Is there a parallel between Aristotelian kinds of good and Maslow's hierarchy of needs? Herein lies the key to understanding the absence of moral motivation in classical motivation theories.

Comparing Maslow's hierarchy with Aristotle's conceptions of good

Here is where I recommend one of Aristotle's most exciting works to my students: his *Nicomachean Ethics*, probably the first systematic treatise of moral philosophy in the history of humanity. This book includes his teachings to Nicomaco, his son, regarding human happiness. Aristotle explains to his son that the things we love, the motives for loving, can be directed towards three kinds of "good": the honest or moral, the pleasant and the useful. Based on this distinction, he talks about three kinds of friendship. "The kinds of friendship may perhaps be cleared up if we first come to know the object of love. For not everything seems to be loved but only the lovable, and this is good, pleasant, or useful" (Aristotle, 2014).

26 Mapping the territory of human motivations

Aristotle therefore distinguishes between three kinds of lovable things. First, the good itself, or what he later describes as the *honest good*, one that could be translated into today's modern language as the *ethical or moral good* (like fairness or justice). Second, the *pleasant good*, that which is attractive to us as it is nice (like enjoyment or pleasantness). Third, the *useful good*, which we also call good because it is useful or practical (like learning or mastering). Therefore, from an Aristotelian perspective, there are only three main *reasons* for doing anything: because it is morally virtuous, fun or practically necessary.

This simple distinction can be really useful to help us better understand the hierarchical order Maslow proposed when describing his two-level kinds of needs. If we go back to our initial framework of motivations (Figure 2.1) and look at the lower level of the grid, the needs Maslow described in 1949 included safety and physiological needs (Maslow, 1949). These two *basic needs* perfectly fit Aristotle's concept of *useful good* (see Figure 2.2). These are goods that human beings need for practical reasons. Alternatively, as Aristotle would say, we aim for them to attain other goods, for the sake of some other goods and not for their own sake (e.g. air, food, drink, warmth, shelter, sleep, money, working conditions, security, protection, law).

These kinds of lower-order goods cover practical needs or needs for *useful good*. Unsurprisingly, this can also be applied to the desire for *power* (McClelland, 1961) and the needs for *survival* and *existence* (Alderfer, 1969); the *extrinsic motivations for useful good*. Furthermore, the needs for *achievement* (McClelland, 1961) and *competency* (Ryan & Deci, 2000), can be considered as *intrinsic motivations for useful good* (see Figure 2.2).

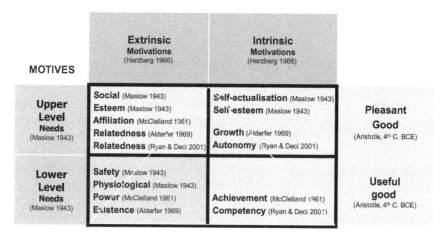

Figure 2.2 Comparing Maslow's hierarchy with Aristotle's types of human good

It is really gratifying to glance at the eyes of the students and participants in this session when they realise that the first level of Maslow's needs fits perfectly with Aristotle's concept of *useful good*. This "Aha!" moment then continues when they keep looking at Figures 2.1 and 2.2. They suddenly understand that the second kind of Aristotelian good, the *pleasant good*, also fits perfectly with Maslow's upper-level needs. These needs are attractive to us because they satisfy us without the brokerage of any other good and cause a sense of enjoyment or gratification when present. They are what Aristotle described as *pleasant goods*.

Pleasant goods are sought for their own sake because they are nice, enjoyable or just produce satisfaction. These goods include *esteem* and *social interpersonal relationships* (Maslow, 1949), *affiliation* (McClelland, 1961), *recognition* (Alderfer, 1969) or *relatedness* (Ryan & Deci, 2000). Correspondingly, they could all be labelled as *extrinsic motivations for pleasant good*, referring to a pleasant good received from the outside. On the other hand, the concepts of *self-actualisation* (Maslow, 1949), *growth* (Alderfer, 1969) and *autonomy* (Ryan & Deci, 2000) may also be considered *pleasant goods*. Since such concepts are attained or acquired personally, through our own self-satisfying actions, they could be labelled as *intrinsic motivations for pleasant good*.

Once we arrive at this point in the presentation, two things normally happen: the first is that everyone in the class realises that the Aristotelian view of human motives of conduct provides us with a very simple way of distinguishing between the upper and lower levels of Maslow's hierarchy, something that had not been too clear before. Similarly, this concept also allows motivations to be described in a very simple manner: as the human desire for the good. This understanding of the motivations of human conduct is thus also compatible with Herzberg's distinction of *extrinsic* and *intrinsic* factors (Herzberg, 1968).

It was not a surprise when I later found out that modern Aristotelian literature also makes a parallel distinction between external goods and internal goods, both contributing to a fulfilling and flourishing human life. The *external goods* are those coming from outside the person and include money and status, whereas *internal goods* derive from participation in specific practices, such as acquiring skills, knowledge or capabilities, but also refer to the enjoyment, sense of achievement, exhilaration and pride that we experience while doing these things (MacIntyre, 1981).

More recently, Aristotelian virtue ethics literature has drawn from MacIntyre's work to identify some practical steps that business managers should take to encourage achieving these external and internal goods in a balanced manner (Moore, 2005; Moore & Beadle, 2006). We will return to this idea later in this book to gain practical knowledge from these findings. Nevertheless, and regarding our purpose here, this Aristotelian distinction about human goods confirms the relevance of defining human motivation, understood as a rational desire for different types of goods (needs), and the

28 Mapping the territory of human motivations

convenience of suggesting a taxonomy or *map* of such needs (motives) based on the different kinds of human goods.

Therefore, as described in Figures 2.1 and 2.2, we could now present a *map* of four types of human motivation. The *extrinsic useful motivation* is the voluntary desire to receive an external and useful good; that which moves us to act is satisfying basic physiological and safety needs and those concerning existence and power. Meanwhile, *extrinsic pleasant motivation* can be defined as the voluntary desire to receive an external pleasant good, like satisfying social needs of esteem, relatedness and affiliation. The first two kinds of motivations, in the left-hand column, are both related to receiving goods from others.

On the other hand, the right-hand column presents two types of motivations related to personal achievement. The *intrinsic useful motivation* is the voluntary desire to achieve an internal useful good; what moves us to act is feeding the needs of achievement and competency. The *intrinsic pleasant motivation* is the voluntary desire to achieve an internal pleasant good; what moves us to act is filling the needs of self-actualisation, self-esteem, growth and autonomy (see Figure 2.3).

What students really like about this framework is that the definitions are quite simple and easy to remember. Now they are able to recognise human motivations by using two verbs: "receive" and "achieve" (left and right columns); and two predicates: pleasant and useful goods (upper and lower

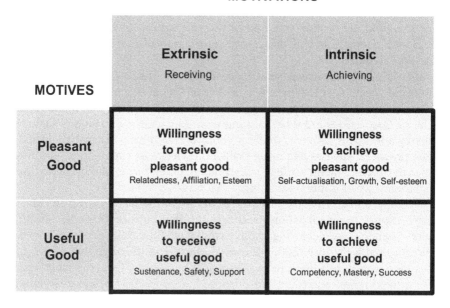

Figure 2.3 Definition of motivations based on Aristotle's types of human good

rows). *Extrinsic motivations* refer to the willingness to receive pleasant and useful goods and *intrinsic motivations* refer to the willingness to achieve pleasant and useful goods (see Figure 2.3).

However, after explaining the Aristotelian distinction of human goods, students are not oblivious to the fact that something is missing from Figure 2.3. This is the third "Aha!" moment of this presentation. Where is the moral good element in Herzberg's or Maslow's theories? What I tell my students is that, from a philosophical standpoint, we are not rigorous in incorporating the types of goods that, according to Aristotle, human beings pursue (pleasant, useful and moral). Where is the moral good element in McClelland's, Alderfer's or Ryan and Deci's approaches?

It seems that they did not explicitly consider this kind of good in their work. After all, that was precisely my point at the end of Chapter 1: human morality is absent from all these psychologists' work and conclusions. Thus, if Aristotle were here and having this conversation about motivations, he would most probably ask why we dismissed the moral dimension when describing human motivations.

Recovering the neglected moral dimension in human motivation theories

It seems evident that none of these early psychological taxonomies of motivation pays substantial attention to such moral goods as motives of human conduct. As a result, what I now argue, following Aristotelian tradition, is that to be considered really and entirely human, a taxonomy of motivations should include the *moral* good clearly and distinctly from *pleasant* and *useful*.

According to Aristotle, the *moral good*, as the *pleasant*, is chosen for its own sake and consists of everything that is right and worthy of cultivation, contributing to the flourishing of human beings (Guillén et al., 2015). Put simply, *moral good* is that which avidly contributes to making us better as human beings. Intuitively, we can all understand the difference between *pleasant* and *moral good*. This is what we have been taught since childhood. Our parents, families or caregivers would correct us every time we wanted to do something that we thought was fun, but that seemed wrong at the same time. For example, they would definitely tell us not to break our neighbours' windows by throwing stones at them, even though this might seem like fun to us.

Furthermore, our parents and educators would tell us to always tell the truth, even though it was not always pleasant and could lead to uncomfortable consequences for us. However, the consideration of *moral good* is not something just for children or exclusive to some negative aspect of our early education. It is a universal desire; we all believe that we deserve this kind of good, and we all aspire to what we consider is right for us. Imagine someone in your workplace found it funny and pleasant to hurt your feelings or constantly lie to you. What would you think if that person did not care for moral qualities such as integrity, honesty or truthfulness? Would you be able to trust this person?

We all want others to tell us the truth all the time, even if it may hurt. It is a universal desire to strive for the truth in all matters. We all consider it a right to be provided with the truth from others, precisely because it is a *moral good*; a universal one. When someone lies to us, or when we perceive we are being lied to, we inevitably feel bad and react by avoiding that person because they are treating us unjustly, as if we are not given the right or are not worthy of knowing the facts. We feel as if we are being treated like children or, even worse, as fools. The same happens with every single *moral good*: we want the ability to get a hold of them all. We all feel we deserve to be treated as human beings (because we are human beings and worthy of being treated as such) and be thought of with sincerity, justice, respect, care and the like.

While reading these paragraphs, you may think that everything I am proposing is just common sense, and I agree, even though you could also agree with me that this is not always common practice, especially in the world of organisations. I believe a good part of the problem resides in that we have been teaching theories for decades in which morality has not been accounted for in human motivations. This narrow assumption explains many of the limitations in our current management theories and even our current wrong management practices (Ghoshal, 2005).

For decades, the existence and need for *extrinsic* and *intrinsic motivations*, the human necessity to receive and achieve good, has been unquestionable. What is debatable, however, is the reduction of them to just the *useful* and *pleasant levels of human good* without also explicitly considering our universal desire for the *moral good*. This universal desire is a real *extrinsic moral motivation*. As Harvard expert in conflict resolution Dr Donna Hicks put it simply, "We all want to be treated as if we matter, and when we are not, we suffer" (Hicks, 2011).

We all have a universal yearning for dignity that drives our species and defines us as human beings. It is our highest common denominator. Dignity not only explains an aspect of what it means to be human but is also a hallmark of our shared humanity. We were all born worthy of dignity, and because of that, dignity is something we all deserve, no matter what we do or who we are. It is the building block for the way we treat one another. Therefore, it is imperative to respect each other's dignity as a measure of healthy and sensible relationships (Hicks, 2011).

As Dr Hicks argues, dignity is not the same as respect. While dignity is an attribute that we are born with – our inherent value and worth – the concept of respect is different. Respect, must be earned (Hicks, 2011). We do not always get respect, sometimes because we do not deserve it, other times because we do not even respect ourselves and sometimes because others do not see and recognise our dignity and worth so they do not respect us.

However, the truth is that we all are moved by the desire to be treated as human beings and not just as simple life forms or as part of a working

The extrinsic moral motivations 31

system or machine, which is something that might be occurring now in many of our modern organisations. This is what *extrinsic moral motivation* is about – the universal desire or willingness to receive the moral good that we deserve, founded on our human dignity and including respect and fairness but also interest, appreciation, care and even love.

How do you feel when someone cheats you or betrays you, especially when it is someone you have trusted? How do you feel when this person does not share information that they should share with you? How do you feel when someone does not keep their word or the commitments they made? Neuroscience is proving that when we suffer a moral pain (as a result of an argument, deception or humiliation), the same region of our brain is affected as if the pain suffered were physical (Hicks, 2018).

We all want moral good, and when others deny it to us, we suffer as we would suffer from physical pain. We all are affected to a greater or lesser extent by the quantity and quality of the moral good we receive. This constitutes a real human need and is an object of our desire and interest. Unfortunately, this *moral good* that we all lean towards, which Aristotle described more than twenty-four centuries ago, did not concern Maslow's early ideas in the 1940s. Neither was it relevant in Herzberg's theories nor to other scientists studying motivations in the second part of the twentieth century.

On the other hand, in the early 1960s, another well-known behavioural psychologist, John Stacey Adams, developed his theory on motivation in the workplace, but here he found the consideration of the moral dimension in human motivations highly significant. In his *equity theory*, he explains that the perception of equity or justice (a moral factor) affects an employee's assessment and perception of their relationship with their job and their employer. Moreover, when that is not the case, employees will be unhappy, which can manifest itself in different ways, including demotivation, reduced effort, becoming disgruntled or, in extreme cases, perhaps even becoming disruptive (Adams, 1963).

The idea behind Adams' theory is to strike a fair balance, with inputs on one side of the scale and outputs on the other – both weighted in a way that seems equal. If the balance lies too far in favour of the employer, some employees may work to bring this balance towards their own interests, for instance, by asking for more compensation or recognition. Some will be demotivated, and others will seek alternative employment (Adams, 1963).

Consequently, his theory argues that managers should attempt to find a fair balance between the inputs that an employee contributes and the outputs they collect. As a result of this, high levels of motivation and other positive outcomes in organisations can only be expected when employees perceive their treatment to be fair (Adams, 1963). In short, this is the point we have been discussing all along: we all want to be treated fairly, and we all desire the *moral good*.

As you can imagine, Adams' theory is compatible and complementary with Herzberg's works. When this moral extrinsic factor is missing, when we perceive that we are not receiving this *moral good*, we will be demotivated. Examples of this demotivation could be students who feel they don't get the grades they deserve from their lecturers, or employees who think their boss is keeping information from them that they need for their jobs.

Conversely, when we perceive that we are treated morally well, with fairness, then we believe that they are giving us what we deserve, that we are treated with the respect our dignity deserves, and therefore this factor being present will not increase motivation but neither will it decrease it. Simply, we consider that we are receiving what we deserve. If all this is true, *moral good* should be part of the *extrinsic factors* described by Herzberg in his two-factor theory. Hence, Adams' theory fits perfectly with Herzberg's findings and suggests that we should expand *extrinsic motivation* to include a new moral motivation. The proposal is therefore to expand the *extrinsic motivations* column to explicitly include the *moral good* in our framework and add *extrinsic moral motivation* (see Figure 2.4).

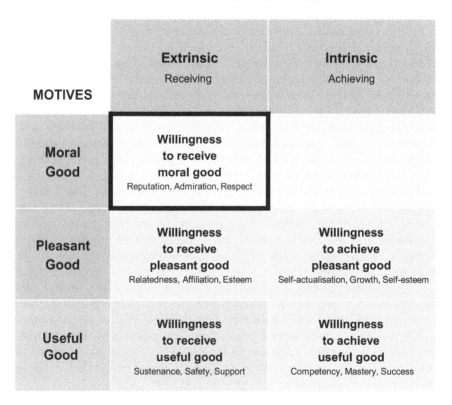

Figure 2.4 Definition of moral motivation based on Aristotle's types of human good

Furthermore, and in line with previous definitions, *extrinsic moral motivation* can be described as the voluntary desire to receive an external *moral good*. It is a universal human yearning and desire to receive external moral goods (e.g. the willingness to be treated morally well according to our human dignity). We all want to receive respect as human beings and appropriate moral recognition, reputation or legitimacy from others (Guillén et al., 2015).

Essentially, this is something that we all deserve and expect. Ultimately, I do not need any more arguments to convince my students of the need to include this *moral good* in our framework. It is evident that they all want to be treated with the respect that befits their human dignity, and if a lecturer (or anyone) treats them otherwise, their trust in those people would become non-existent.

Extrinsic moral motivation founded on human dignity and source of trust

For management students, it is crucial to understand the role of trust when dealing with others, and *extrinsic moral motivation* is key in understanding the ultimate reason for why we trust people. Trusting is nothing less than making yourself vulnerable to others. The main reason we do this is because we expect them to do the right thing by us. We trust someone mostly because we expect that person to be truthful and fair with us and because they will do right by us. In short, we know they care about us and consider us worthy of respect. Without this consciousness of dignity, it is more than likely that resentment and distrust will prevail at some point (Hicks, 2018).

At this point, in those courses I teach on management, we start discussing the importance of this universal desire to receive the moral good and its connection with trust in organisations. I love telling my students about research I carried out years ago with a colleague of mine at the University of Valencia, Professor Tomás González, an expert in Quality Management. Together, we published the study of a case comparing two companies and their Quality Managers. From our research, we found that one manager was a genuine leader, freely influencing the behaviour of those working for him; the other was not, and his subordinates did not trust him.

We observed that to maintain a good relationship with his colleagues, the former was not only technically proficient but also demonstrated a lasting commitment to do what was right for others. We found an ethical dimension of leadership related to treating others well consistently, to honouring their dignity, as Dr Donna Hicks would say. Moreover, this ethical dimension is the key, the quintessence, to understanding the relationship between leaders and those who follow them freely. Increased levels of moral behaviour from the leader resulted in higher levels of moral trust. Likewise, the trust is quickly lost when leaders stop doing what is right (Guillén & González, 2001).

Fortunately, other scientists are arriving at very similar conclusions nowadays. For instance, sociologist Randy Hodson's comprehensive study of dignity in the workplace concluded that real leaders were those who treat people with dignity, who give them a sense of autonomy and independence to work in the way that best suits them, who create an open and trusting environment where employees are acknowledged and recognised for their good work. Ultimately, they treat them in a way that enhances their self-worth and the worth of others. These are the managers who succeed as leaders (Hodson, 2001).

In more recent times, Stephen Covey and Douglas Conant rationalised that "trust between managers and employees is the primary defining characteristic of the very best workplaces" (Covey & Conant, 2016). This finding comes directly from The Great Place to Work Institute's report on the "100 Best Companies to Work For". In fact, they found this trait in companies that beat the average annualised returns of the S&P 500 by a factor of three. What these researchers concluded is that "trust is not a soft, social virtue – it is truly a hard, economic driver for every organization" (Covey & Conant, 2016).

The field of leadership seems to be proving once again that we all welcome *moral goods* in organisations and that *extrinsic moral motivation* is everywhere despite its absence in most classic theories on motivation. Researcher Sunnie Giles conducted another study in 2016 involving nearly two hundred leaders in more than thirty global organisations in fifteen countries. She wanted to ascertain what people felt were a leader's top skills. Not surprisingly, what she found at the top of the list was a demonstration of high ethical and moral standards (Giles, 2016).

She explained that leaders with higher ethical standards convey a commitment to fairness, safety, and inclusion – all elements of dignity and the *extrinsic moral motivation* that we have been discussing. She also described the importance of giving employees clear direction while allowing them to organise their own time and work, giving them a sense of autonomy and independence. Evidently, understanding the importance of *extrinsic moral motivation*, and the universal desire of people to honour their dignity, was one of the core skills expected and desired of those in leadership positions (Giles, 2016).

One of the examples I like using the most to explain the importance of this moral motivation is that presented by Donna Hicks in her latest book, *Leading with Dignity* (Hicks, 2018). Dr Hicks was invited by a company to address conflicts between management and employees. Everyone knew that the company was in a precarious position because five years earlier, the company was almost bankrupt. At that time, and in a desperate move, the management team asked its employees to help them avoid bankruptcy by taking pay cuts. They asked everyone to "pull together and win together", and so they did.

Five years later, the company's situation had improved, and it was clear that the strategy had worked out well, but that is when the problems started to appear. The employees fully expected their pay to be restored when the company started doing well again, but this did not happen. Worse still, the management team gave themselves big bonuses, arguing that it was a legitimate move as it was stated in their contracts (Hicks, 2018).

Of course, the employees felt betrayed. They had given the management team the benefit of the doubt that they would do the right thing if and when the company improved, and they felt exploited when that did not happen. The trust that the employees had for the management team during the time of the crisis vanished. They were not being recognised or acknowledged for the contribution they had made to help the company survive. They were treated unfairly, they felt a great injustice; they felt invisible and as if their identities did not matter. They no longer felt safe in their relationship with management.

Furthermore, what most bothered the employees was that management did not want to talk about the self-awarded bonuses, much less be held accountable for their actions. Unfortunately, the leadership team was not willing to take any responsibility for their decisions, making it impossible for the relationships to be repaired. The company never recovered from the rift with its employees. What were the chances that trust could ever be restored? (Hicks, 2018).

The crucial role of moral motivation to rebuild trust

Dr Hicks' graphic case shows that we all look for the moral good, and when we do not achieve it, we stop trusting others. I remember some years ago at a Harvard colloquium, in front of a group of lecturers and managers, Dr Hicks explained the importance of dignity awareness in fostering organisational cultures of trust.[1]

That same day, we discussed the difficulty of recovering trust in situations after it was broken. I recall telling the attendees an anecdote about a local politician from Spain – talking on TV a few days before this event – who did something wrong and never recovered the trust of her supporters. I reasoned that this politician had missed one of the three basic ingredients of recovering trust that I found essential in my years of people management: recognition, rectification, and reparation (what I like to call the three Rs for trust *recovery*). These three ingredients are the result of understanding our desire for *moral good*.

This politician *recognised* she had been using the government's money for personal purposes. She also said that she did it because everybody did the same in her party at that time. Nevertheless, she *recognised* that it was wrong, and she also promised that she would *rectify* her conduct in the future. At that point, I remember saying to the audience that this politician would never *recover* the trust of the public.

Due to our universal desire to receive *moral good*, and even though she had *recognised* the wrongdoing (a first necessary ingredient regarding the past) and was *rectifying* her conduct (a second ingredient, regarding the future), she was not *repairing* the wrongdoing (the third essential ingredient, regarding the present). My point was that unless she asked for forgiveness, repairing her misconduct by paying back the money she had misappropriated and offering her resignation, she would never recover people's trust. That was exactly what happened: she lost the election and, as far as I know, all but disappeared from the Spanish political map.

Undoubtedly, all human beings want to be treated with the dignity characteristic of being unique. Moreover, this *moral extrinsic motivation* is present in every human endeavour, in politics, in business, in families and any personal relationship. Denying this motivation, or not giving it its proper value, implies a vision of human motivations that is not very human.

For this reason, *moral extrinsic motivation* has been incorporated into our *map of motivations* (Figure 2.2). It is at this time that I encourage students and seminar participants to expand the answers they gave about their own motivations in the previous session (see Figure 1.3) and to think about some practical consequences that they can draw from the discussion we just had.

Some practical tips

After expanding our map to include *extrinsic moral motivations*, when asked for moral issues they would consider when looking for future jobs, students normally include their desire to receive fair salaries and to be recognised for the value they contribute. They all want to have bosses who are sincere, who help them grow personally and professionally and who can be trusted (Figure 2.5).

In fact, all these answers from the students are not dissimilar to those you get from professionals attending these seminars on motivations. Everyone wants to work in an organisation where they are supported by their colleagues and managers (*useful good*) and where they feel that the environment is friendly and safe (*pleasant good*) (Edmondson, 2018). However, most importantly, we all want to work in places where we gain respect and trust and where others treat us with fairness, truthfulness and have a sincere interest for our professional development and personal growth. This is what makes a workplace a humane one.

In addition to being able to explicitly identify the moral issues that are crucial in explaining our behaviour, the expanded *map of motivations* also brings the consideration of some practical insights that usually arise in classes and workshops on motivation, leadership and trust, such as the role trust plays in creating a productive work environment and the kind of management behaviours that nurture trust in organisations (Zak, 2012).

Given the relevance of *extrinsic moral motivations*, as Professor Zak suggests and is in line with this chapter's previous discussion, from a purely practical point of view, I recommend my students look for leaders (managers,

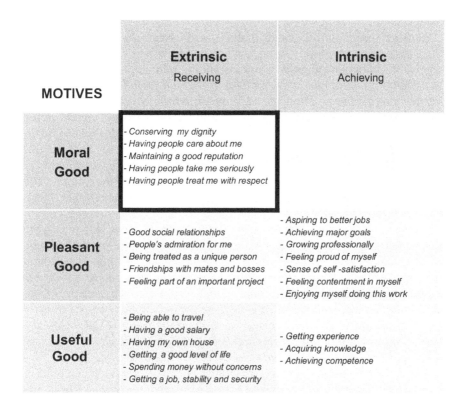

Figure 2.5 Examples of the extrinsic moral motivation

bosses, politicians, etc.) who understand and respect the *extrinsic moral motivations* described in these pages, who care about human dignity when managing others.

Namely, leaders who care about our *extrinsic moral motivations* are those who: (1) *recognise our excellence when we accomplish a goal at work*; (2) *give us autonomy and discretion in how we work when possible*; (3) *enable us to engage in job crafting, to choose the work we feel most passionate about when possible*; (4) *encourage hard work in us that produces a sense of challenge and a reasonable level of stress*; (5) *share information broadly so we know the direction in which the organisation is going*; (6) *intentionally build relationships at work*; (7) *facilitate whole-person growth*; and (8) *show vulnerability, recognise their limits and ask others for help when necessary* (Zak, 2017).

38 *Mapping the territory of human motivations*

These insights, from recent empirical research, offer clear evidence of the existence and importance of understanding and appreciating the *extrinsic moral motivations*, especially for those whose work is related to people management.

Another very practical insight that shows the relevance of understanding these *extrinsic moral motivations* is what Dr Hicks calls the ten elements of dignity. Leading with dignity is understanding that: (1) *we all want others to accept our identity and interact with us without prejudice or bias regarding our race, religion, ethnicity, class or disability*; (2) *we all desire to be treated with inclusion, feeling that we belong to our families, communities, organisations and nations*; (3) *we all yearn to feel safe, not only physically and psychologically but also morally, from being humiliated, without fear of retribution*; (4) *we all long for acknowledgment so that people give us their full attention, responding to our concerns*; (5) *we all deserve recognition, knowing the appreciation and gratitude that others give to our contributions, ideas, and work*.

Additionally, (6) *we all want to be treated with fairness, justly, without discrimination*; (7) *we all wish for people to give us the benefit of the doubt, judging that we have good intentions and motives and seeing us as trustworthy people*; (8) *we all expect the understanding of others and that they will listen to us, hoping that others believe that what we think matters*; (9) *we all need independence to act freely, on our own behalf, to be responsible for our actions*; and moreover, because we are morally free, (10) *we also want true accountability of our actions and behaviour, even though we make mistakes and need to apologise and start again* (Hicks, 2011).

These *ten elements of dignity*, as Donna Hicks describes them, could be viewed sceptically by some, maybe as too idealistic, in a world where others often do not appreciate our *extrinsic moral motivations*. However, these are the kind of behaviours that we all desire and deserve: to be treated with dignity.

It is also true that, at times, we are the ones who do not appreciate the *extrinsic moral motivations* and dignity of others. Sometimes, we violate other people's dignity as well as our own without even realising it. This is why the awareness of these moral ideals and the understanding of our own fragility becomes so essential. Both our capacity for ideas, and therefore ideals, and the ease with which we can violate them are aspects that belong to the realm of our free moral human nature. To deny or to forget this is a big mistake.

In our lives and our jobs, we hope others allow us to fully develop as moral persons, to flourish and be happy. The way others contribute to this aspiration is what I have called *extrinsic moral motivation*. We need to recognise that, as human beings, we all have a universal desire to receive *moral good*.

Likewise, if we decide to continue this exciting journey, trying to understand our motivations better, then we have to be aware of its implications.

We have to accept that an authentic theory of human motivations, a *humanistic* one, can never be a morally neutral theory. We need to recognise that moral motivations are real. As proof of this, I suggest you think about your own *extrinsic moral motivations* by answering the following questions.

Some questions for reflection

1. *How often do I wish people would give me the benefit of the doubt and trust me more in my work or my life in general?*
2. *How often do I feel not safe, with a fear of being humiliated or derided in my work or my life in general?*
3. *How often do I miss a sense of freedom and autonomy from others in my work or in my life in general?*
4. *How often do I not perceive how others understand my work or my life in general?*
5. *How often would I like to be given more information and for others to be more transparent with me at work or in my life in general?*
6. *How often do I think others treat me with prejudice or bias regarding my identity or my ideas at work or in life in general?*
7. *How often do I miss being treated with fairness at work and in my life in general?*
8. *How often do I think people do not recognise and acknowledge me or pay me full attention in my work or my life in general?*
9. *How often do I long for others to care about my personal growth at work or in my life in general?*
10. *How often do I think that I am not included as being part of a community in my work or in my life in general?*

A final critical thought on why the map is not yet accurate enough

Only if you answered "never" to every question could you say that you had never had *extrinsic moral motivations*. These are issues that we all consider in our lives because they are related to what it means for us to be human. Something that only we can consider because only humans care about their dignity. Obviously, other species do not even think about it because they do not possess the ability to think rationally. This is not a joke. This is it.

We are capable of reflecting on what it means to be treated properly as humans or just as beasts. In fact, this is what morality is. We are moral beings because we have the capacity to act freely, either as ideal human beings or as simple irrational creatures. We have the ability to pursue or not to pursue the ideals of what it means to be a good human being, a good professional, a good father, a good friend or a good citizen.

We have a permanent desire for these higher human goods or higher ideals that other species cannot even think of. We are moral beings precisely because we have the capacity to reflect on what is it that makes us better human beings and to demand it from others. Would it make sense to desire to be treated morally well by others and not treat ourselves in the same way? This sounds like a contradiction, like a beggar asking for money and then throwing it away, or a student asking for a grant and dropping out of university once they get it. Would that make sense?

It seems that our desire to receive moral good from others is the consequence of our interest to grow as human beings, to flourish, to be happy. In fact, this is what explains that, in addition to the *extrinsic moral motivation*, there exists an *intrinsic* one, a desire to "achieve" moral good, not just to "receive" it. This is another area of human motivation that has been neglected, forgotten, or at least misunderstood by social sciences but is also worthy of exploration. Now is the time to keep moving forward on this journey to another unexplored territory on this map of human motivations – the land of the *intrinsic moral motivation*. We will examine this in the next chapter.

Note

1 It was during the First IECO-RCC colloquium at Harvard University in 2013. The event can be viewed here: www.youtube.com/playlist?list=PL2SOU6wwxB0tC7m3-n-_BnBOOyv9QPjt9.

References

Adams, J. (1963). Toward an understanding of inequality. *Journal of Abnormal and Social Psychology*, 67, 422–436.
Alderfer, C. (1969). An empirical test of a new theory of human needs. *Organizational Behavior and Human Performance*, 4, 142–175.
Aristotle. (2014). *Complete Works of Aristotle: The Revised Oxford Translation*. Princeton, NJ: Princeton University Press.
Covey, S. & Conant, R. (2016). The connection between employee trust and financial performance. *Harvard Business Review*, July.
Daniels, M. (1982). The development of the concept of self-actualization in the writings of Abraham Maslow. *Current Psychological Reviews*, 2, 61–75.
Edmondson, A. (2018). *The Fearless Organization: Creating Psychological Safety in the Workplace for Learning, Innovation, and Growth*. Hoboken, NJ: John Wiley & Sons.
Forsyth, D. (1992). Judging the morality of business practices: The influence of personal moral philosophies. *Journal of Business Ethics*, 11, 461–470.
Ghoshal, S. (2005). Bad management theories are destroying good management practices. *Academy of Management Learning & Education*, 4(1), 75–91.
Giles, S. (2016). The most important leadership competencies, according to leaders around the world. *Harvard Business Review*, March 2016.
Guillén, M., Ferrero, I. & Hoffman, W. (2015). The neglected ethical and spiritual motivations in the workplace. *Journal of Business Ethics*, 128(4), 803–816.

Guillén, M. & González, T. (2001). The ethical dimension of managerial leadership two illustrative case studies in TQM. *Journal of Business Ethics*, 34, 175.

Herzberg, F. (1968). One more time: How do you motivate employees? *Harvard Business Review*, January–February, 46(1), 53–62.

Hicks, D. (2011). *Dignity: The Essential Role It Plays in Resolving Conflict*. New Haven and London: Yale University Press.

Hicks, D. (2018). *Leading with Dignity: How to Create a Culture That Brings Out the Best in People*. New Haven and London: Yale University Press.

Hodson, R. (2001). *Dignity at Work*. Cambridge, UK: Cambridge University Press.

Lan, G., Gowing, M., McMahon, S. et al. (2008). A study of the relationship between personal values and moral reasoning of undergraduate business students. *Journal of Business Ethics*, 78, 121–139.

MacIntyre, A. (1981). *After Virtue*. London: Duckworth.

Maslow, A. H. (1949). The expressive component of behavior. *Psychological Review*, 56(5), 261–272.

McClelland, D. (1961). *The Achieving Society*. Princeton, NJ: Van Nostrand.

Moore, G. (2005). Humanizing business: A modern virtue ethics approach. *Business Ethics Quarterly*, 15(2), 237–255.

Moore, G. & Beadle, R. (2006). In search of organizational virtue in business: Agents, goods, practices, institutions and environments. *Organization Studies*, 27(3), 369–389.

Ryan, R. & Deci, E. (2000). Intrinsic and extrinsic motivations: Classic definitions and new directions. *Contemporary Educational Psychology*, 25, 54–67.

Velaz, J. (1996). Motivos y motivación en la empresa. *Ediciones Díaz de Santos*, p. 312.

Zak, P. (2012). *The Moral Molecule: The Source of Love and Prosperity*. New York: Dutton, Published by Penguin Group.

Zak, P. (2017). The neuroscience of trust. *Harvard Business Review*, January–February.

3 The *intrinsic moral motivations*

Aiming to do the right thing

Revisiting Maslow's latest ideas on the moral dimension of motivations

Back in 2001, I published the results from a research project I undertook with Professor Tomás González, a colleague from the University of Valencia, whom I briefly mentioned in the previous chapter. We studied two companies that were implementing a Total Quality Management Programme (TQM).[1] In one company, employees acknowledged the person in charge to be a moral leader, whereas in the other, it was the opposite. What we observed was that, given all other intervening factors remaining constant (*ceteris paribus*), only in the presence of a moral leader was the ability to implement all the TQM principles of the programme guaranteed, coupled with the involvement of everyone in the company and a strong level of commitment (Guillén & González, 2001).

When we presented the results in Cambridge at the EBEN conference in 2000, one attendee asked if both companies were making any money at the end of the day. "Did it really matter that the moral leader was able to implement all the principles of TQM?" My answer was simple: yes. It was clear, from a managerial point of view, that in the first case and based on their higher level of trust towards their leadership, the group would more easily be able to confront any future difficulties in meeting their goals.

This actually proved correct when, some ten years later, the second company ended up being sold due to poor financial results. I then followed up this person's question with one of my own: "What type of company would you prefer to work for?" I still remember the look on her face. It was evident from her expression that she, and indeed anyone, would prefer to work in a more humanistic organisation.

Usually, we prefer to work in places surrounded by good people, those we can trust. Most would also prefer to work in places with people of honest intentions and behavioural traits based on moral virtues such as reliability, industriousness, sincerity, and honesty (i.e. working with integrity). If you were a student, you would probably like the same qualities in your class environment and in your teachers.

Years ago, one of my best students came to my office to complain about the excessive competitiveness in her class. She told me: "No one shares their class notes, nor helps the others. They all want to get the A+ to prove they are the best". Clearly, she felt bad that she could not find collaborative classmates she could trust.

This case is just another everyday example of why the *extrinsic moral motivations* described in Chapter 2, the willingness to receive moral good founded on our human dignity (Hicks, 2011), are not only important but also quite real. Who would oppose the fact that most of us would like to work in environments with individuals who have high ideals and superior human qualities? We have a desire for the good, a longing that, as we discussed in the previous chapter, was proposed centuries ago by Aristotle.

What I would like to consider now is that, if you ask people around you (who are trying to do good things) why they behave this way, they will usually answer: "Because it is the right thing to do". Indeed, every time I ask any of my colleagues why they are trying to work competently, or why they are always telling their students the truth, they will invariably reply that this is what they are supposed to do. Is this not, in fact, a kind of human motivation to do what one perceives to be the "right" thing to do? To put the "good" into practice?

Of course it is, but not everyone has the same good moral intentions. We are all free to decide if we want to behave well or not precisely because we are moral beings. Therefore, we do not always necessarily pursue this motivation of attaining the good, but, without a doubt, it is a human motivation that we would like to see in others and that we all try to engage in more often than we tend to think.

In this chapter, I will champion the premise that, in addition to the intrinsic human psychological drive of *self-actualisation*, there is another kind of motivation, an *intrinsic moral motivation*: a desire to behave well, a yearning for moral good and moral growth. A motivation that is and that has been neglected for decades by classical motivation theories (Guillén et al., 2015). This *intrinsic moral motivation* was glanced at in Figure 2.4 in the previous chapter.

This is one of those moments where a teacher must be honest with their students by telling them about their mistakes. For years, I believed that Maslow did not capture this moral dimension of motivations at all. I thought I was right, based on his early works, and the views of other relevant scholars. I believed that, for the psychologist in Maslow, the concept of *self-fulfilment* meant developing people's personal idiosyncrasy in a positive way (not focusing just on mental disorders). Therefore, it seemed that, in his work, Maslow was not paying much attention to the ethical side of this moral development, namely, the growth of the noblest potentials of each human being, their moral virtues (Melé, 2003).

The truth is that I was wrong about Maslow, and only after an observation from one of my students during one of our discussions did I decide to investigate further. This is when I discovered *The Farther Reaches of Human Nature* (Maslow, 1971), a book published posthumously. It was a text I had never heard of before and not one that, as far as I know, my colleagues had read. I do not think less of my colleagues here, I blame myself for having been part of an academic system that was teaching what everyone else was teaching, without a healthy dose of critical thinking. I hope acknowledging my own mistakes may contribute to changing this situation.

Maslow devoted quite a few pages in this book to talking about aspects that are directly engaged with morality. He explained that the object of human life is to fulfil all the motivations that he described in his early hierarchy – or at least as many of them as possible. He contends that those who do so are psychologically happier and healthier. Moreover, when talking about the need for self-actualisation, he says that *self-actualisers* are the most emotionally healthy and most fully developed people on the planet (White, 1988).

When referring to these more fully developed individuals, he describes them as being more objective and accurate in their judgements, having their perceptions less distorted by their hopes, fears or desires and being very understanding of others. This is when the moral dimension appears more explicitly, giving them a clearer notion of right and wrong in their moral judgements, he explained. "They listen to their own voices; they take responsibility; they are honest; and they work hard" (Maslow, 1971, pg. 49).

Maslow affirms that *self-actualisers* can recognise good and bad fairly easily and that they consistently side with the good. Therefore, it is not only about having sound judgement but also about behaving well. Self-actualisers are aware of their own limitations, without arrogance, and have a sincere willingness to listen to and learn from others. They are also comfortable resisting popular opinion or the ideas of their surrounding culture when either goes against their own point of view. Maslow came to say that these people represent the best that the human species can attain. He even called *self-actualisation* the "growing tip" of humanity (Maslow, 1971).

Likewise, this is what Aristotle would say about virtuousness and virtuous people. It seems that Maslow's later understanding of self-actualisers, and their moral character development – a concept that he does not use but would probably accept – could have been written centuries ago by any of the classical Greek philosophers.

Maslow's and Aristotle's common ideas on human nature and moral goodness

In 2019, I defended the position that Maslow was not too far from the findings of Aristotle, Plato or Socrates while giving a presentation at the Abigail Adams Institute (AAI)[2] in Cambridge, Massachusetts. I was insisting on the importance of revisiting classical philosophers if we truly want to understand human motivations and on the need for a higher-level dialogue between psychologists and philosophers.

I was surprised by a comment from an attendee who said that he totally agreed, and not only that, but that I should read a book he had written thirty years earlier in which he claimed the same premise. A few days later, I got to read the book by my now colleague – and good friend – the philosophy professor Thomas White (White, 1988).[3]

I could not believe that in the late 1980s, Professor White had already found reading of Maslow's posthumous book fascinating and, when describing Maslow's view of human personality, he asserted that Maslow's idea about morality and the healthy personality is virtually identical to Socrates' ideas stating, "Both men think that ethical behavior is consistent with the strong, healthy human personality. And both imply that unethical behavior is unhealthy" (White, 1988, p. 142).

He explains that, in Maslow's findings, everything we consider to be a part of someone with a strong moral character are characteristics of the healthy human personality. Consequently, the opposite is therefore true: people lacking virtues, who regularly manipulate others, cheat, or otherwise foster human harm and violate human dignity, are engaging in actions that are in some sense humanly unhealthy, or at least signs of a frail or less developed personality.

It seems then that, after all, the traditional conception of moral virtue is a conspicuous part of Maslow's later ideas. Furthermore, as Professor White explains, Maslow claimed that self-actualised individuals tend to agree about matters of right and wrong and suggested that, because of this agreement, their "value judgements" seem to be more objective than subjective. Maslow went on to say that "at least in the group I studied they tended to agree about what was right and wrong as if they were perceiving something real" (Maslow, 1971, p. 9). Actually, their sense of right and wrong results from how accurately they perceive reality, the objective truth.

It is surprising that, after more than twenty centuries, philosophers and psychologists are arriving at the same conclusions. Aristotle always thought that one lives a virtuous life when one is capable of knowing how to choose correctly, putting that decision into action and being emotionally engaged with good behaviour. Virtuous people, or mature people as we would say today, feel love for the good and aversion towards the evil (Abbà, 1989).

If we just think about an ideal boss (for those who have a boss), or an ideal teacher, the Aristotelian view is that they would be always judging the right thing to do in every circumstance and doing so with joy. I guess here is the reason why *intrinsic moral motivation* is contagious. We can all trust that someone who is in charge looks for the true objective good with joy and avoids the true objective evil with hate.

This is the model, the ideal, that I propose to my students. I encourage them to be excited about becoming great leaders in that sense. In fact, I normally ask them to think about examples of people they know and are as such. Many of them talk about their parents, but even more often about grandparents, and in this, I fully identify with my students. Does it happen to you? Do you feel motivated to do good things like you saw your grandparents do? We all need role models, good examples of morally mature people, those who do not get carried away by the current moral relativism. They call good, good, and evil, evil.

As a philosopher in dialogue with psychologists, Professor White states that, "one of the most important implications of Maslow's perspective is that ethical judgements are basically objective. He suggests that when self-actualized humans make ethical judgements, they use a standard of human good that is universal, not relative to either an individual or culture" (White, 1988, p. 143).

He continues saying that, when it comes down to it, "Maslow doesn't offer us ideas that we don't already find in Socrates. The two thinkers state things differently, but both assert an ultimate connection between moral goodness and a healthy and well-developed human personality. What Maslow does, that Socrates doesn't do, however, is to base his findings on research". To make his statement clear, Professor White says that, "there may be ways to question it. But you can't argue that he doesn't have a body of research that convinces him that there is an ethical dimension to the self-actualized human being" (White, 1988, p. 143).

The existence of such an ethical dimension is consistent with more recent findings in the area of *psychology* and the concept of *conscientiousness*, a personality trait of being careful, diligent, showing self-discipline and acting dutifully. This is one of the five traits of both the Five Factor Model and the HEXACO model of personality, which is intermingled with what has traditionally been referred to as having character. According to these models, conscientiousness is considered a continuous dimension of personality, rather than a categorical type of person (McCrae & John, 1992).

This consciousness personality trait reveals the existence of a universal yearning for moral goodness that I included in our map of human motivations labelled as *intrinsic* and *moral* (Figure 3.1). However, unlike Maslow's contention, I maintain that this kind of motivation, this yearning for moral good, is not only characteristic of a privileged group of self-actualisers but of every single human being.

This desire of doing the right thing is a lot more common than it seems. Most of our ordinary daily lives involve doing things in a righteous manner. The majority of us pursue these kinds of motivations when trying to do things well, *doing well what needs to be done*. This is what I mean by *intrinsic moral motivation*, something that a good father and mother, a good friend or a good worker tries to accomplish every single day in every single action.

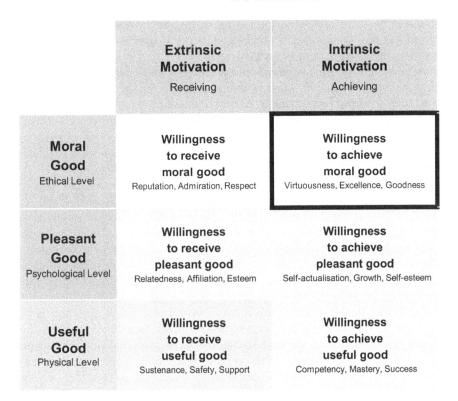

Figure 3.1 Defining intrinsic moral motivation

Intrinsic moral motivations: The human desire to do good, honouring our own dignity

In the realm of work, this *intrinsic moral motivation* means trying to do a good job, to perform well, not only technically but also humanly. In other words, to bring about good workmanship, and therefore attain the moral good while doing what has to be done. The motive behind achieving good conduct here refers not only to technical mastery (acquiring useful good), or to the achievement of a personal satisfaction (attaining pleasant good), but to achieving moral good (accomplishing moral perfection or quality) (Figure 3.1).

Likewise, this is what Socrates, Plato or Aristotle would call a moral virtue (*arête* in Greek, or moral excellence), achieving a state of excellence in how you act, like working with method or the virtue of order, with constancy, and intensity. Correspondingly, the view of classical philosophers was that these moral qualities become traits of our character, traits that enable a person to be better as a human being and to achieve human blossoming or flourishing. As I said, this is not far removed from what Maslow found in his later intellectual period regarding the most self-actualised and happy people. Of course, if you ask students if they would like to have teachers like that, the answer is invariably yes.

At this point in our conversation, my students and I arrive to the conclusion that, most probably, Maslow would agree on the necessity of including the *intrinsic moral motivation* as part of a sound hierarchy of human needs (Figure 3.1). If we want to build an accurate *map* of truly human motivations, the assumption made by the early psychological theories of motivation regarding the amorality of human behaviour does not seem to make sense.

As we noted in Chapter 2, it is clear that we all expect others to care about our dignity and moral good (*extrinsic moral motivation*). In addition, we also aim for our own dignity to be honoured. We all have or might have this *intrinsic moral motivation*, meaning that what moves us to act is to achieve the moral good or to reach an integral human growth, honouring our own dignity. As Dr Hicks would say, it is a moral motivation to treat others with dignity because it is the right thing to do: to demonstrate value for human life (Hicks, 2011).

Of course, the existence of this *intrinsic moral motivation* does not mean that every human being always pursues actions trying to accomplish the moral good but that we do have that potential. In the same way that we do not always necessarily aim for the useful good, utility is one potential reason for us to act. Regarding the moral good, as we discussed before, we are moral beings precisely because we have the capacity to act, either aspiring to the moral good or not.

This means that we have the ability to behave freely as human beings, according to our dignity, but also as savages, or as beasts and irrational beings. We have this capacity to pursue ideals, to seek purposes in life and motives in our behaviour beyond useful and pleasant goods, but the opposite is also true. This is why we are morally free; we are free to act well and not so well. Only human beings are capable of freely choosing and wanting their good, of being moved by higher goods or ideals.

This reminds me of another student I had several years ago. I asked the whole class about which heights they would like to reach as professionals in their lives. Everyone laughed when one said, "In the future, I want to become Spain's Economy Minister". This is a great example of what it means to be an idealist. Someone who thought that he could change the world by studying economics and then becoming a true influencer in the country's economic decisions. I remember telling him that I expected to receive some special favour or treatment once he got the position. I was kidding, of course; I am still waiting to see if he gets the job, though.

Each of us has ideals; at some point, we all dream about doing great things in our lives, and it does not necessarily mean getting an important job or role. We dream about being good at sports, good as parents, good friends with our friends and good at our jobs. We all wish we could do great in our lives. This is not just a desire for psychological self-actualisation or the psychological trait of *conscientiousness*; it is also about being or becoming the kind of person we dream of becoming.

It means having the qualities of a good sportsperson, of a good mother or father, of a good friend or a good professional. Having ideals means having not just the right practical skills (useful goods) or the passion for the things we do in our professions (pleasant goods) but also desiring to achieve the personal qualities of a good professional (moral goods), as Figure 3.1 shows.

Why is it important to make the distinction between these *useful*, *pleasant* and *moral* realms? First, it is because they are different domains of human nature, as classical philosophers found centuries ago. It would be a mistake to confuse the *physical*, *psychological* and *ethical orders* or realms and to not be able to distinguish between them properly. Second, it is because these different *realms* or dimensions of human nature allow us to better understand the hierarchical order that Maslow discerned decades ago, a kind of order that now we can explain more precisely by using the Aristotelian classification of human goods. Finally, it is because the explicit consideration of the *ethical* or *moral order* allows us to better understand and to explicitly consider the importance of freedom when describing human motivations. Let us now reflect on these three different realms and their hierarchical order.

Moral motivations are higher than *useful* and *pleasant* motivations

When teaching motivations, I find that now is about the right time to reflect on the hierarchical order of Maslow's classification of human needs. As we saw in Chapter 1, Maslow's theory has been criticised for not giving a theoretical reason justifying its hierarchical order. At least, he never explained this from a philosophical point of view, mostly because he was not a philosopher. However, if his hierarchy is correct, there should be a logical explanation. Right?

It seems common sense that the practical or *useful goods* belong to the material or *physical realm*, the one that is proper for the physical creatures we are. This is why we all need to satisfy physiological and safety needs, those that Maslow named basic at the lowest level of his hierarchy. We are physical beings and we are also living beings, rational animals, and therefore we have a physical but also a psychological constitution whereby we can appreciate everything that contributes to our pleasantness, and we call that *pleasant good*.

In addition to our condition as physical and psychological animals, and at an even higher level, we are free *rational* beings. There is an *ethical realm*. We are capable of finding rational meaning in our actions and lives, something that other animals cannot do, which explains why this order or level is higher than in other animals. More so, our behaviour is not explained exclusively by the sensitive reaction to external or internal stimuli or incentives. We are *free rational* animals, capable of willingly deciding the purpose of our actions, our voluntary motives and the kind of lives we want to live.

This capacity to think and freely choose is precisely because of the human *ethical* or *moral realm*,[4] that which makes humans different from other animals. In this sense, we call anything contributing to betterment in this realm, contributing to our humanness, a *moral good*. To put it simply, a lion cannot be a better or worse lion; lions behave as lions, as wild animals, but human beings have the capacity to freely act in a manner that is better or worse, more or less in accordance with their human condition, their human nature. This is what ethics and morality is all about.

As Maslow sensed, the hierarchy of our needs or the good we pursue is founded on our human nature, one that, as we just described, has several dimensions pertaining to different orders or realms: the practical or *physical*, the pleasant, sensitive or *psychological* and the moral or *ethical* one. This is why Aristotle distinguished *useful*, *pleasant* and *moral* goods when referring to the kind of goods that friends could desire in each other. They belong to the three realms or dimensions of what constitute human nature, which is why I decided to include the *physical*, *psychological* and *ethical* levels in our map of human motivations, following this hierarchical order (see Figure 3.1).

What I just wrote might sound too philosophical for some people or even a matter of common sense for others. This is frequently the case with philosophical arguments and is one of the reasons why I love teaching business ethics. At the end of the day, moral philosophy or ethics should never be absent in our teaching because human reality is moral by nature. With each of our actions, we can hurt others or contribute to their betterment, and, of course, with each one of our actions we become better or worse human beings. This is something that seems obvious but has been absent for decades from the theories of motivation and the hierarchical order of goods they offer.

It is at this point that I tell my students it took me several years to truly understand the hierarchical order of goods in human nature. In fact, it was with help from a business management professor, Juan Antonio Pérez-López,[5] that I understood it. I recall a class in which he gave a very illustrative explanation of this hierarchical order of nature in general and of human nature in particular. Being the engineer he was, he liked to offer visually descriptive examples.

I remember him saying, "Imagine there is a big box on the teacher's table. A box that is about 1.8 metres tall and weighs 80 kilos". He then added,

"If we wanted to predict the behaviour of the box regarding the moment at which it might fall off the desk, what do we need to know? What kind of knowledge do we need?" The answer he gave was quite simple, "We need to know physics and some physical laws (i.e. the law of gravity). Only if we know about the laws that belong to the *physical* level can we say how much force is necessary to push the box off the desk. We are facing a physical phenomenon in the *physical* level of nature". This is the order or dimension of reality in which physical and mechanical sciences operate.

Following this visual example, he then added, "Imagine that instead of a box, what we now have on the table is a brown bear with the same height and weight. The question now is, what do we need to know to predict the behaviour of the brown bear regarding the moment at which it might fall off the desk. Is the knowledge of the physical laws enough? We still need to know the laws of the *physical* level, but this knowledge is not enough to predict the bear's behaviour. We also need to know the laws of the *sensitive* order (i.e. social norms of brown bears, etc.).

By knowing the laws of both the *physical* and *sensitive* levels, we can predict how much force is necessary to push the bear off the desk". Clearly, if the bear were hungry, or just violent by nature, it would be best to leave it alone. We are facing a phenomenon that belongs to the scope of the *physical* and *sensitive* orders at the same time. We just need to know the laws that govern over both orders, the ones in which physical and natural sciences operate.

The professor then asked a curious question, "In which case would the physical laws be enough to explain the bear's behaviour?" The answer seems clear: when the bear is dead. In that case, it will behave like the box, as an inanimate object. The lower laws of physical order apply to every physical object. However, if the physical object were a living creature, we would also need to consider the higher-level laws of living nature to understand its behaviour.

What if, instead of a brown bear, we had a person standing on the table? Would having the knowledge of *physical* and *sensitive* biological laws be enough to predict human behaviour? The answer is obviously no. Using only *physical* and *sensitive* biological laws, we cannot predict human behaviour. This knowledge is certainly necessary but not sufficient.

We would also need to know something more about the laws of human nature, including what *sensitive* level is specific to human minds (like temperament traits), which explains why we call this the *psychological* realm in the case of human beings, but we also need to know about the laws of *ethical* or *moral* nature (what is good or evil, human and inhuman behaviours, moral and immoral habits, etc.).

Moreover, these laws of moral nature belong to what classical philosophers call the *ethical order*, one that in modern sciences has been neglected and reduced to its *psychological* dimension. In fact, many of today's social scientists would include the *psychological* dimension as just part of the second-order sensitive biological realm. That would explain why classic taxonomies of human motivations did not include ethics.

To predict the behaviour of someone standing on the professor's table, we would need to know, among other things, if that person was violent or not, if they are there because they want to be or for other reasons. Would they get down if we asked amicably, or would we need to force them down? The questions are limitless given the free nature of human beings.

In other words, to predict human behaviour, it is not enough to only know the laws of *physical* and *psychological* orders but also those laws of the human *ethical* order. What this example allows us to understand is that human reality is affected by *physical*, *psychological* and *ethical* dimensions, where each one belongs to a different hierarchical level of reality.

The lower-order dimensions support the higher ones. We would not be able not make the right moral judgements (*ethical level*) without having a healthy living brain (*psychological level*). Moreover, this would not be possible without having daily access to the necessary natural resources for survival, such as food, water, clean air, etc. (*physical level*). Furthermore, in normal life, these different realms or dimensions can be theoretically distinguished but not separated because we are just one and the same person, with a living *physical*, *psychological* and *ethical* nature. Moreover, as we will discuss in Chapter 5, there is actually a fourth human *higher spiritual realm*.

These different realms each have their own laws, and we can only explain the way these realms work if we first get to know these laws. Besides, what Professor Pérez-López wanted to make clear with his example was that to become good managers when dealing with people, we should properly understand the different orders of human nature. For example, if one employee is feeling ill, a manager should first care about that. However, the logic also applies to the manager themselves. If they are not feeling well in the lower level (*physical*), they may not be able to make good decisions in the higher ones (technical, economical, *psychological*, and also *ethical*). Thus, to understand our own behaviour and that of others, we have to recognise the complexity of human nature, including the hierarchical order of its needs.

After using the example of the brown bear, I like to explain that Aristotle studied this hierarchical order of human life, and it was later revisited by other philosophers. It was the case, for instance, of St Thomas Aquinas, in whose view these goods are ordered in a hierarchy corresponding to the hierarchy of living things described by Aristotle several centuries earlier (i.e. those with *vegetative*, *sensory*, and *rational* souls, respectively). Aquinas also defended that the higher goods presuppose the lower ones; for example, one cannot pursue *moral* truth if their brain does not function properly from a biological or *psychological* standpoint, and this will not happen unless one preserves oneself in existence in the *physical* level.

In addition to the hierarchical order of these realms of human nature, Aquinas indicates that the lower goods are subordinate to the higher ones

The intrinsic moral motivations 53

in the sense that they exist for the sake of higher ones (see Figure 3.2). The point of fulfilling the *vegetative* and *sensory* aspects of our nature is, ultimately, to allow us to fulfil the higher defining *rational* and *spiritual* dimensions (Feser, 2009).

We cannot deny the importance of understanding each different dimension of human nature and its hierarchical order (see Figure 3.2). There is a universal need or desire to receive and achieve higher *moral* goods (*extrinsic* and *intrinsic moral motivations*). They are different from the desires to also receive and achieve *useful* or *pleasant* goods, so, at this point, once again I do not need any more arguments to convince my students of the need to include this *moral good* in our *map of human motivations*.

We all want to be treated with the respect befitting our human dignity, and we all have the capacity to behave or not according to this dignity. This capacity is precisely what we call moral or *ethical* freedom, something exclusive to humans, to moral beings, that belongs to this higher order of goods and distinguishes us from other living beings. In fact, we can distinguish at

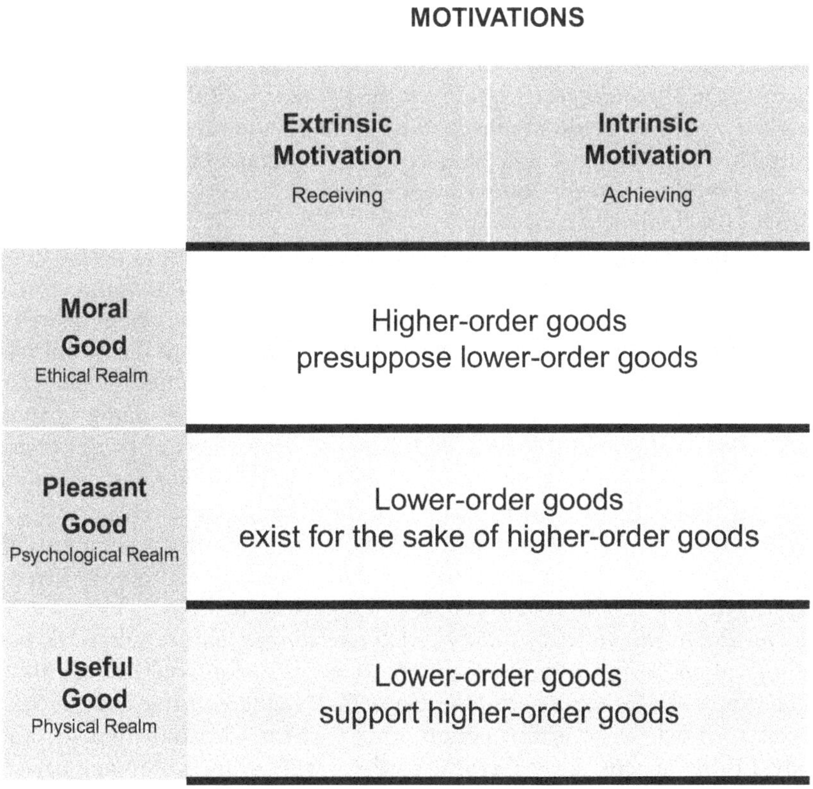

MOTIVATIONS

	Extrinsic Motivation Receiving	Intrinsic Motivation Achieving
Moral Good Ethical Realm	Higher-order goods presuppose lower-order goods	
Pleasant Good Psychological Realm	Lower-order goods exist for the sake of higher-order goods	
Useful Good Physical Realm	Lower-order goods support higher-order goods	

Figure 3.2 The hierarchical order of human nature and human goods

least three different kinds of freedom, each one belonging to one of the three realms of human nature included in the three levels of our map of motivations: *physical*, *psychological* and *ethical*.

The first two are the *freedom from* physical or psychological constraints, and the third is the *freedom to* attain some purpose. This third kind, the moral freedom, is the one characteristic of human beings. We are not necessarily moved by every external or internal stimulus, craving, urge or pressure we feel, as that would mean reducing the concept of freedom exclusively to its psychological aspect. Instead, and in addition to the feeling of freedom, we are quite capable of freely deciding to follow such feelings, impulses or tendencies, or to act in a radically different way for other reasons, purposes or intentions.

We human beings can follow our tendencies and impulses or not after having rationally evaluated and, consequently, accepted or rejected them. Freedom refers to the willingness, the voluntary decision, to follow or not to follow some tendency. In this sense, human motivation consists of the energy or drive that impels a person to make choices and to seek goals actively (Cloninger, 2004).

Of course, for the people who are not concerned about morality, human freedom is then artificially reduced to *psychological freedom*, meaning the ability to do whatever you want. Therefore, there are those who falsely separate the *psychological* realm from the *ethical* one, but these two realms or levels, while different, are inseparable in human nature. When you artificially separate them, you will go as far as saying that a behaviour is right as long as you do whatever you wish with a sense or feeling of autonomy and with no psychological constraint.

You could then simply lie, show injustice, harm others and do whatever you want. Given that, from this perspective, freedom has nothing to do with morality, then the question of moral good or what is morally right or wrong would not matter, a perspective that, unfortunately, leads to the moral relativism that reigns in Western society today. It seems common sense that, because of the laws of *physical nature*, we are not able to fly, and we cannot think about a hundred things at once because of the laws of *psychological nature*. For the same reason, we cannot constantly lie without becoming liars and being untrustworthy because of the laws of *moral nature*.

The more you understand the truth of the laws of science, the more scientific you become. In the same way, the more you know about the laws of a sport, the more skilful you become in that sport. Moreover, for the same reason, the more we understand the laws of human nature (physical, psychological and ethical), the freer we are to live and enjoy our human life.

That is why the expression "the truth shall make you free" (John 8:32) makes so much sense in this context, not just for Christians but for anybody. From the denial of reality (the truth) that there are *moral laws* derived from human nature (just as there are *physical* and *psychological* laws), the relativist position follows. Disregarding the existence of moral principles and intrinsic moral motivations leads to moral relativism. This is why the map of human motivations proposed in this book presupposes the existence of these three realms considered as different but, again, inseparable levels of one and the same reality (see Figure 3.2).

Intrinsic moral motivations shape our moral virtues and our moral conscience

In a thought-provoking way, I like to tell to my students that sometimes we are less free than we think, and they ask me why. It's clear that they want to feel free, but they also want to make sure that they are really free, as nobody likes a kind of "fake freedom". Instead of giving a direct answer, I keep asking them if we are really free when we are incapable of saying no to something urgent, and we can't stop doing it.

For instance, when we are incapable of not looking at our smartphones if a message suddenly pops up, or when we can't help but distract ourselves by surfing the internet when we should be studying or paying attention to someone in class, we are not really free. More precisely, we are not using our freedom well – we are lacking the necessary willpower to say no. Thus, we become "slaves" to our urges.

We may feel that we are free because we have the apparent ability to do whatever we like (*psychological freedom*). Indeed, if we cannot stop doing that which distracts us from our tasks, then we are not putting our *moral freedom* into practice. In these cases, we are less free than we thought, as we are letting our urges and instincts make our decisions for us; like non-rational creatures (machines or animals), we just respond to external impulses, without using our willpower to make our final decisions freely.

When we are incapable of governing our own impulses with self-mastery, ensuring we put them at the service of higher goods and human ideals, then we are slaves to our own cravings. We may feel that we are doing what we want, but we are powerless to do anything other than just what our comfort-seeking, lower, pleasant goods motivations are suggesting. This same thing happens on the *physical* level, for example, when we do any sport. If we want to do well in any sport and master it, we have to practice to acquire a full skillset.

This is exactly the same as in the three levels of our map (see Figure 3.2), including the *psychological* and *ethical levels*. To not be driven solely by feelings and impulses, we all need to practice the skills and engage in habits that will allow us to do the right things. This is something that requires willpower to say yes to some cravings and impulses and no to others, depending on how they contribute to our own good. This is what moral life and the traditional concept of moral virtue are about.

Here, it is relevant to mention *The Power of Habit* by Charles Duhigg, which I recommend to my students every year. It is a research work that describes the scientific discoveries that explain why habits exist and how they can be changed. He brings the findings of neuroscientists to life exploring how habits work and where, exactly, they reside in our brains (Duhigg, 2012).

This work brings new insights to an old understanding of human nature and character development that philosophers, such as Plato and Aristotle, explained centuries ago. This is another work that shows how the findings of scientific research in modern social sciences are consistent with the conclusions of the moral philosophy more than twenty-four centuries ago.

Imagine a father who is incapable of returning home early enough every day to take care of his children. If this becomes a habit because of work pressures or the fear of looking irresponsible in front of his colleagues, then he is probably trapped by a lower-order kind of motivation in our map (*useful* or *pleasant*). In cases like this, one lacks the necessary moral virtue or habit to aim for higher-level motives (*moral*) (see Figure 3.1).

If this person is incapable of choosing a different higher good, if he is unable to leave his workplace earlier at the risk of losing his job to spend more time with his children, then they are morally free but lacking the strength of moral character to use that freedom properly. By not choosing the higher moral good in this case and not using his free will well, he is actually doing morally wrong, even though he might be doing well from a purely economic point of view (getting *useful* good), or even from a psychological perspective (getting some *pleasant* good).

Of course, you may argue, however, that being a good employee is not always compatible with being a good parent. Sometimes, sacrifices have to be made, like working overtime to better support your family. In this, I agree. If that is the case, though, then you are just facing a decision that includes a *moral* good, in opposition to other kinds of lower-order goods. This is the real world. Our daily lives are crowded with this kind of tension about goods (*useful*, *pleasant* and *moral*) and, therefore, about different motivations.

This is why I subtitled this book: *Searching for a meaningful work-life balance*. We will further discuss this in the last part of the book, but for now, let us say that it is one thing to understand the *map of motivations* and the place where we are right now, but moving to a better place in the map is much more complicated.

In practical life, things are not so simple. It is not enough to just know the theory. Any theory of motivation, in order to be accurate, has to explicitly consider this tension between motivations and the role our freedom plays in making such decisions because this is what happens every single day in our personal lives.

Being morally free implies the necessity of engaging in moral judgement all the time regarding the purpose or good that is at stake in every moment and situation as well as in deciding the necessary means to attain our purposes. Judgement about the good we are trying to pursue, our purpose or intention, in addition to the effort we make to accomplish such a goal, is precisely what makes us responsible for our own human actions.

This kind of verdict or rational judgement about our motives of conduct is what has traditionally been described as *moral conscience*: the judgement of our reason whereby we recognise the moral quality of a specific action. This may be applied to the action we have already completed, the one we are going to take or, more frequently, the one we are doing.

By choosing the appropriate good here and now, our reasoning approves the good and censures the evil we do or might want to do in every specific situation. This is precisely what makes us essentially different from irrational beings. This is what it means to be human, to be capable of moral judgements and moral decisions. A theory of human motivations should not therefore dismiss the role of moral conscience if it wants to be described as human. It is essential to distinguish *good* from *evil* (a privation of the good).

This reminds me of what happened to me at the end of one of my MBA classes. One student came to me and said, "Today was the first time in my life that I heard someone say that we always have to follow a moral criterion to make good management decisions. No one talks about this in our other management classes", followed by, "in my personal life, I have always done what I pleased. I never thought about any other criteria than my personal satisfaction. That is what I was planning to do in my future job as a manager, until today".

This student was grateful for the ethical decision-making lecture that day. I was even more grateful to see the sincerity of this student, who had made me aware of the importance of this topic. I became even more mindful of the importance of our moral training as management lecturers and the necessity of writing this book.

I also realised the direct influence that we may have on others when teaching (in this case when I teach classes on decision-making). If we lecture future managers on how to make good decisions without explicitly mentioning the moral dimension and the role of the moral conscience in distinguishing good and evil, then something must be wrong. Simply put, as already anticipated by the late prestigious management professor Sumantra Ghoshal, "Bad management theories are destroying good management practices" (Ghoshal, 2005).

Intrinsic moral motivations demand free moral character

We all have to make decisions at the end of the day, not just managers. When we are considering which motivation we want to follow, we are judging our own purpose, the good we want to choose. If the goods at stake are just those that are *useful* and *pleasant*, then we will reduce our analysis to things like efficiency and effectiveness, in terms of profit, results or satisfaction. However, if we expand the realm of goods at stake in our judgement to include the *moral* good, as well as the *useful* and the *pleasant*, then we will also think about the right thing to do when making that decision (see Figure 3.1).

As I like to tell my students, to make a good decision you must always consider at least three E's; *effectiveness, efficiency*, and *ethics*. The first two belong to the *useful* and *pleasant* realms, the third to the *moral*. If we do not implicitly or explicitly consider the third E (the ethical dimension), we will most likely make a bad decision and destroy the trust around us. This is not the place to explain how to make ethical decisions or how they affect trust building in organisations, something I did elsewhere in the context of teaching business ethics (Guillén, 2006).

When there is tension among the three kinds of motivations (*useful, pleasant*, and *moral*), it is time to stop and judge what the right thing to do is – to use our moral conscience, to be conscious of the situation. This is why I consider it important to offer "maps of good" to students so that they may distinguish the hierarchical order of the different kinds of goods. In this sense, I usually distrust public speakers who talk about *business ethics* and start their talks by saying that being ethical is profitable, when I think that, in the short term at least, it is usually the opposite. Likewise, in the long term, it is quite probable but not always necessarily true that putting the *moral good* first will lead you to reach financial success, a *useful good*.

The *useful good* has its own logic, one that should always be subordinate to the higher *moral good*. There are quite a lot of profitable businesses that will always be immoral and that should be avoided as being inhuman, like pornography, drug dealing, human or organ trafficking, etc. We management lecturers should not be afraid to make this clear because we are supposed to teach how to make good decisions (good in its three levels or meanings).

Regarding the distinction of the *useful, pleasant* and *moral* domains, there are a good number of moral businesses that may still not be profitable, as is the case with many social endeavours that require the help of external donors. I insist to my students that *useful, pleasant*, and *moral* goods belong to different realms, and to make the right decisions, given that *moral goods* are of a higher order, they should be the ones that we never give up.

Therefore, any business harming human beings is wrong by its own nature, because it is inhumane, and any decision that goes against *moral good* is wrong, even if it is quite profitable. As the traditional moral principle goes: a good end (making money) does not justify a wrong mean (any unethical decision) (Guillén, 2006).

I like to tell my students that learning ethics is quite exciting. Nevertheless, strictly speaking, ethics cannot be taught, but it may be learned. In fact, ethics may be presented but not imposed, precisely because moral motivation demands moral freedom, the capacity to choose and want the good.

Indeed, because we are morally free, we have to decide if we want to shape our consciences to make better decisions. Only we can make such decisions. Ethics is connected with judging the good but, most importantly, with the practice of the good, and that means engaging in the habit of always doing, or at least trying to do, the right thing and achieve moral virtues. Hence, the more we study and practice ethics, the higher our *intrinsic moral motivation* will be and, therefore, our desire and capability to do good (Guillén, 2006).

We do not always make good decisions, not because we lack the moral criterion, but because, at times we lack the strength of character, the necessary moral virtue or habit. At times, we lack the moral *temperance* to say "no" to pleasant goods in order to attain higher moral goods (e.g. from the earlier example, when we cannot move away from any distraction on a smartphone to listen to and pay attention to another person).

Other times, we lack the moral *fortitude* to say "yes" to higher moral goods despite having to sacrifice some lower useful or pleasant goods, for instance, going to visit a friend who is sick while giving up other personal interests, such as going to the gym. When that happens, when we lack the necessary moral strength to make the correct decision and choose higher goods when possible due to its difficulty, then we gradually lose the habit; we become inept at making other good moral decisions in the future. As on the *physical* plane, when you stop going to the gym for a while, you lose your *physical* strength, your habit, and then it becomes harder to lift weights or compete with the same speed and agility as before.

Temperance, or self-mastery, and *fortitude*, or strength of character, are two of the four cardinal classic virtues that govern moral life and are key in making good decisions. The other two cardinal virtues are *justice* and *practical wisdom*. This distinction was proposed twenty-four centuries ago by Plato. The more we practice these moral virtues, the better people we become. The opposite is also true. If we do not keep practicing all these moral virtues, then our moral character deteriorates (Plato, 1997); we become worse persons and, therefore, worse professionals, as both things are inseparable.

It is like any athlete who stops doing a sport they are competent at; they lose physical form and stop being proficient at that sport. Conversely, if they keep practicing, they could then become a better athlete. The same happens with the "moral muscle". As Aristotle would say, the more we practice the good, the easier it becomes and the more we enjoy it. In fact, mature people are those who enjoy practicing the good and suffer when they face evil and wrongdoing. Maslow found exactly the same evidence in his most recent studies, as noted earlier (Maslow, 1971).

Intrinsic moral motivations are a manifestation of our human ideals

Ideals and higher purposes in our lives constitute powerful engines for our behaviour, and this is what *intrinsic moral motivation* is about (see Figure 3.1). We all have ideals, so when people do not know what they are living for, or they just do whatever they please, they get bored with the use of their freedom. They feel as if they have surrendered responsibility and may develop anxiety. We all need ideals, *intrinsic moral motivations*, which give meaning to our daily decisions. Many times, our ideals are the main reason we do what we do, even if we do not feel like it. That is why we try to be good members of our families, honest members of our professional organisations and upright citizens of our communities and societies.

Don't get me wrong, though, as I do not want to sound naive here: you can only be virtuous in a society where you can also be vicious. In the same way, you can only be a saint in a world where you can also be a sinner. Having high ideals, and struggling to pursue higher moral good, is compatible with frequently feeling the lowest desires for just the lower goods and even the greatest vileness. This is simultaneously the greatness and wickedness of human nature, something we all experience on a daily basis.

You would be surprised by the responses from young undergraduate students regarding these ideas. This is one of the most exciting ingredients of the teaching profession: we are always surrounded by young idealists, and they recognise the truth of these ideals to achieve the good. We do not have to convince any of our students of the existence of the *intrinsic moral motivation*. I would dare to say that only those who do not have them, or do not know how to put ideals into practice, get into trouble with drugs, alcohol, stress, etc.

The majority of young people have noble ideals and dreams. In fact, at times, the problem is that they are too *idealistic*. Normally, they have dreams but do not have clear plans on how to achieve them. This is a different issue, however, and one that I will discuss at the end of this book, in Chapter 9. For now, let us just say that *intrinsic moral motivations*, moral high ideals, such as attaining justice or peace in the world, are, in fact, one of the most common drivers among young people. This is my experience from more than twenty-five years of teaching at the university level.

All these young people detest poverty and aim for higher levels of progress and justice. They all aim for peace and aspire to see a better world and a society that thrives, but not only students long for moral good. This is common to all of us. In fact, every attendee in professional seminars I give all over the world agrees on the importance of a life driven by moral ideals. Furthermore, their *intrinsic moral motivations* are not so different from those of the eighteen-year-old, first-year students I also teach.

Mature professionals, as well as young students, all have purposes and ideals that include things like growing and becoming a better person, caring and giving the best of themselves, earning morality and respect for themselves, learning moral and good practices, achieving their main goals ethically or knowing that they are doing the right thing and not being corrupt (see Figure 3.3).

For most young students, the question of moral ideals and personal excellence or virtue do not sound so familiar at the beginning of the sessions. However, once you describe the concepts, they understand that these moral questions and their awareness are part of their process of personal growth and the unfolding of the full potential of our human dignity. Depending on

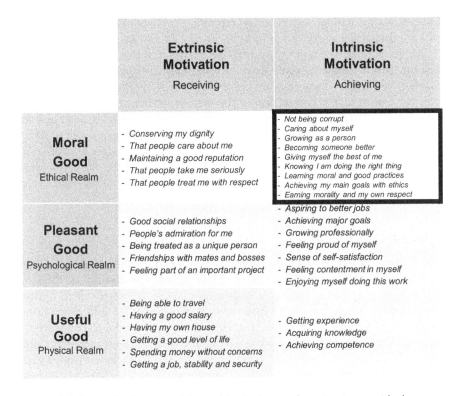

Figure 3.3 Examples from participants' intrinsic moral motivations or ideals

how mature their minds are, they see these ideas as powerful tools to help them grow and make better decisions in the future.

Of course, you also find students that do not care at all about this "stuff". They just look at you with indifference. It also makes sense because, as I said before, ethics cannot be taught, it has to be learned, and learning requires time and personal experience. We all learn from our own mistakes, and no one likes to be pressured or urged. No one likes to be reminded that we are not doing well. Moral learning takes time for everyone, and what normally drives us to improve are great ideals and good models.

My research and years of teaching experience have taught me that while the majority of young people dream with virtues and with models of conduct that are related to making a better world in the future, older participants and practitioners in seminars find this *intrinsic moral motivation* important because of their previous personal experiences; they look to the past. They see other colleagues not always doing the right thing, or even if they work in ethical organisations, they know of many institutions that end up being corrupt precisely because this *intrinsic moral motivation* was absent. Therefore, most of the older professionals attending my seminars love the idea of making this dimension explicit in a theory of motivations.

Moreover, many of them want to delve deeper into this topic when I suggest that it is through our daily work, through our daily professional activity that we find higher meaning and achieve personal excellence or the opposite. Nevertheless, the connection of the *map of motivations* and the *meaning* we give to our work will be the subject of the final part of this book in Chapters 8 and 9. This idea of achieving personal excellence through daily work is not new and, in fact, has become an area of increasing interest among scholars in the field of education (Gardner et al., 2001). As before, let us finish this chapter by considering some practical insights from some of these researchers.

Some practical tips

The well-known Harvard professor Howard Gardner, honoured for his theory of multiple intelligences, carried out an empirical study in the late 1990s with his team at Harvard, known as The GoodWork Project. In this study, they conducted in-depth interviews with more than 1,200 professionals in nine different spheres of work. Their findings led them to conceptualise good work as exhibiting three components: excellence, engagement, and ethics. To finish this chapter, let us now consider some practical insights that emerged from this research and that strongly support the ideas I have just presented (Gardner et al., 2001).

As Professor Gardner maintains, to achieve our higher potential in our work, we need to always keep in mind what makes work excellent. Likewise, work is good when it meets the technical standards of our profession or craft. This is indeed an essential part of what it means to do the right thing, to work well. Therefore, (1) *we all should stop and reflect on how good we are in the way we work and how this workmanship affects our motivation to work better, recognising that we can always improve and keep learning.*

We should examine the means we employ to keep up with our training, including all the skills and knowledge befitting a good professional in our area. It is also important to ask for help and corrections from our colleagues, students, clients, patients, etc. Here, *intrinsic* practical or *useful motivation* intermingles with the intrinsic moral one. To be a good professional requires humility (a *moral* virtue) to recognise that we can and should always keep learning.

In addition to this attitude of continuous improvement, "good work" is that which is personally meaningful or engaging. This is the essence of *intrinsic moral motivation*; as Professor Gardner would suggest, (2) *we should keep asking ourselves how our work is helping us to attain our higher purposes in life*. We need to bear in mind that we spend most of our day working, and the more we see our daily tasks as opportunities to attain our higher ideals, the more motivating and engaging our work will be. A good way to start every working hour, therefore, is to ask ourselves how this specific task is contributing to our ideals.

Finally, what Professor Gardner found is that good work is one that is ethical, one that is carried out responsibly. Therefore, if we really aim to be good workers (3) *we should constantly cross-examine ourselves about what it means to be responsible, to be a good professional, seeking to behave in that way and admitting our shortcomings before correcting them*. Once again, humility, the ability to recognise our frailty and limitations as well as our virtues and strengths, becomes a key moral virtue that we all should aim for in our work if we want them to help us thrive as human beings.

It is fascinating to see increased academic interest in the area of professional work. Another Harvard lecturer, Dr Kevin Majeres, is also interested in this area of well-done work. He studies how working at our best affects our motivations and behaviours, but especially our habits. This renowned psychiatrist, who teaches at Harvard Medical School, has recently developed a project called Optimal Work,[6] a mentoring tool aimed at helping young students and professionals work at their best.

We all experience optimal work from time to time; it is a way of working that seems to happen effortlessly at times, in a state of flow. What Dr Majeres supports is that this way of working is also something we can learn to do intentionally. His programme is based on the theory of classical virtue, physiology, the latest neurosciences and the cognitive-behavioural therapy approach, a methodology that, as noted before, focuses less on the pathology and more on human flourishing.

According to this approach, to have the most meaningful life, in which you meet all your potential, you must incorporate your highest ideals in your work. Based on Dr Majeres' findings, (4) *our motivation increases exponentially every time we reframe the purpose of our work*. Then, we stop looking at every task solely through the lens of pressure, stress and seeking goals and start looking at them as opportunities for growth. Moreover, *we see every hour of work as an opportunity to attain our higher ideals but also specific moral virtues, such as humility, patience, consistency, order, intensity, and many others*.

At work, (5) *we have repeated opportunities to engage in challenges every day. They give us the chance to grow in every virtue*. It is at work that we may change our approach to challenges in life from a reactive and negative view to a most proactive, stable and positive one. Rather than being passive – seeking to reduce challenge – we can actively stretch ourselves according to our ideals.

Thus, following virtues in our work, by facing challenges, is how we best develop the habit of living according to our highest ideals. Ironically, challenges are the path to a richer and more satisfying life. Happiness comes from living out our ideals to the fullest, and challenges are the way we do

64 *Mapping the territory of human motivations*

that. In fact, because work is a hinge upon which life turns, the growth that we attain while working well, following virtues, applies not just to work but also to every area of our lives.

Paradoxically, by facing daily challenges, seen as opportunities that help us to grow, we attain virtues; we become better persons. The workplace then becomes the natural situation for personal growth. When going to work, (6) *in every activity we can aim to grow in specific moral virtues, such as honesty, patience, strength, wisdom or justice, but also in other less celebrated virtues, such as flexibility, creativity or cheerfulness, among many others.*

In recent years, I have reflected with my students on how the knowledge of our own motivations can help us not only to put our higher ideals into practice but also how to work at our optimum level by finding a meaningful work-life balance. For now, I will end this chapter by suggesting some practical questions related to this *intrinsic moral motivation*, the inner desire to do the right thing, practicing the good and attaining moral virtues in our lives.

Some questions for reflection

1 *How often do I get anxious and rush about at work? Does it affect my motivations?*
2 *How often do I complain about the new challenges at work? Does it affect my motivations?*
3 *How often do I lose patience and get angry at work? Does it affect my motivations?*
4 *How often do I have arguments and conflicts at work? Does it affect my motivations?*
5 *How often do I criticise, slander or gossip at work? Does it affect my motivations?*
6 *How often do I dream of attaining my higher ideals in my profession? Does it inspire me daily?*
7 *How often do I seek to behave responsibly, doing the right thing at work? Does it encourage me to perform better?*
8 *How often do I try to work at my best level, to be good in my chosen profession? Does it challenge me?*
9 *How often do I perceive the challenges in my work as opportunities to grow in virtue, to become a better human being?*
10 *How often do I reframe the purpose of my work, from stress and pressure to personal growth?*

A final critical thought on why the map is not yet accurate enough

These questions, among other similar ones, may help us to better understand the realm of *intrinsic moral motivation*. The answers can tell us something about our ideals and how the practice of virtue, or its absence, may affect our motivations. We have been able to reflect on these issues because we expanded our Map of Motivations to a new territory that was practically unexplored by the early theories. As we noted, for decades, psychologists did not pay much attention to this kind of *intrinsic moral motivation*, a universal desire to do something because it is the right thing to do.

Unfortunately, the moral dimension of human behaviour was taken for granted, and, consequently, integral personal development was reduced in most cases, if considered at all, to its psychological realm. Furthermore, as we will see in the next chapter, for decades, this amoral view of human nature has led to another erroneous assumption: a conception of human behaviour understood as exclusively self-centred and egotistic. For this reason, it will be necessary to review the limitations of our *map of human motivations* to discover a new and little-explored territory – that of motivations to give selflessly.

Notes

1 Total Quality Management (TQM) describes a management approach to long-term success through customer satisfaction. In TQM, all members of an organisation participate in improving processes, products, services, and the culture in which they work. The TQM Programme involves implementing a number of principles.
2 Founded in 2014, AAI is a scholarly institute dedicated to providing supplementary humanistic education to the Harvard intellectual community. They foster shared intellectual life by exploring questions of deep human concern that cut across the boundaries of academic disciplines. www.abigailadamsinstitute.org/
3 On 10 July 2018, I gave this presentation as part of the Scholars' Workshops of the Abigail Adams Institute, in Cambridge, Massachusetts. Professor Thomas White was one of the attendees.
4 Although some ethicists want to make a distinction between the terms ethical and moral, in this book I am using them interchangeably, as moral is the translation into Latin (*mōris*) from the Greek (*ethos*).
5 Juan Antonio Pérez López (1934–1996) was a Spanish business theorist. He was a professor of Organisational Behaviour at the IESE Business School (Spain). In 1970, he received his PhD in Business Administration from Harvard Business School. His research and publications focus on action theory and its implications for organisational behaviour. He delved into issues like motivation, learning, rationality, etc.
6 For more information, see www.optimalwork.com/

References

Abbà, G. (1989). *Felicità, Vita buona e virtù. Saggio di filosofia morale*. Ed. LAS. Rome: Biblioteca di Scienze Religiose.
Cloninger, C. R. (2004). *Feeling Good: The Science of Well-being*. New York: Oxford University Press.
Duhigg, C. (2012). *The Power of Habit: Why We Do What We Do in Life and Business*. New York: Random House Trade Paperback Edition.
Feser, E. (2009). *Aquinas. A Beginner's Guide*. Oxford, UK: Oneworld Publications.
Gardner, H., Csikszentmihalyi, M. & Damon, W. (2001). *Good Work: When Excellence and Ethics Meet*. New York, NY: Basic Books, Perseus Books Group.

Ghoshal, S. (2005). Bad management theories are destroying good management practices. *Academy of Management Learning & Education*, 4(1), 75–91.

Guillén, M. (2006). Ethics in Organizations. Building Trust. Madrid: Prentice-Hall, Pearson. (Spanish Edition). There is a forthcoming English version.

Guillén, M., Ferrero, I. & Hoffman, W. (2015). The neglected ethical and spiritual motivations in the workplace. *Journal of Business Ethics*, 128(4), 803–816.

Guillén, M. & González, T. (2001). The ethical dimension of managerial leadership two illustrative case studies in TQM. *Journal of Business Ethics*, 34, 175.

Hicks, D. (2011). *Dignity: The Essential Role It Plays in Resolving Conflict.* New Haven and London: Yale University Press.

Maslow, A. H. (1971). *The Farther Reaches of Human Nature*, Ed. Arkana. New York: Penguin Books.

McCrae, R. & John, O. (1992). An introduction to the five-factor model and its applications. *Journal of Personality*, 60(2), 175–215.

Melé, D. (2003). The challenge of the humanistic management. *Journal of Business Ethics*, 44(1), 77–88.

Plato. (1997). *Plato Complete Works.* Cambridge: Hackett Publishing Company.

White, T. I. (1988). *Right and Wrong. A Practical Introduction to Ethics.* New York: Pearson. (There is a 2nd edition published by John Wiley & Son, Oxford, UK, in 2017 with the same title).

Part II
Exploring the region of higher human motivations

4 The *transcendent motivations*
Human readiness to give

Overcoming a self-centred vision of human motivations

A year ago, I learnt that Andrew Fastow, former CFO of Enron and the man responsible for one of the most egregious corporate frauds in the history of the US, is nowadays being invited to give presentations in several prestigious institutions all over the world. Fastow, who was indicted and imprisoned for six years for his part in the infamous Enron investor fraud,[1] is now publicly acknowledging his part in the scheme and attempting to explain the mindset that led him to participate in such a deception. Unfortunately, this has become one of the paradigmatic cases showing the lack of ethics in the world of business, and I have been using this in my classes for years. These events show the consequences of having an exclusively materialistic and selfish worldview of business.

Since being released from prison in December 2011, Fastow has been on the lecture circuit giving dozens of speeches a year, acknowledging that what he did was wrong. He was not alone, though, as former chairman Kenneth Lay was also convicted in the 2006 trial. He died before he could be sentenced. Another Fastow collaborator, Jeff Skilling, actually Fastow's boss as CEO of Enron, also ended up in prison. He ultimately served twelve years before his release in February 2019. Skilling has steadfastly maintained his innocence to this day.

However, what – if anything – caused Fastow to adopt such a bleak perspective on humanity? He was convinced that we human beings are, at our core, egotistical and self-centred. It seems that the book *The Selfish Gene* by Richard Dawkins was one of the sources for these views for him. Underpinning all his criminal activity while at Enron was this materialist, amoral and self-interested logic, a logic that is as disheartening as it is wrong.

Unfortunately, this logical framework of human behaviour portrayed as exclusively self-interested, continues to be taught explicitly or implicitly in many business schools and universities all over the world. Similar to the majority of my colleagues, I also taught human motivations under that same assumption for years, at least implicitly (i.e. that we humans are always egocentric and driven by that trait).

If you look at the framework of human motivations discussed in the previous chapter, this is precisely what it says, at least implicitly, that human nature is always self-centred (see Figure 3.1). Normally, one does not realise this until someone else clarifies it, asking you to look more closely at the described framework. The unveiled supposition under these approaches to human motivation that we have been teaching for decades is that we human beings are always and basically selfish beings. What drives us is reduced to the good we are expecting to receive from the outside (*extrinsic motivations* in the left column of our map) and the one we could achieve from our own actions (*intrinsic motivations* in the right column of our map).

In other words, if we agree uncritically with the distinction between *extrinsic* and *intrinsic* motivations, then there are only two main drives for human conduct: receiving and achieving. Therefore, by admitting this framework, we are assuming that the only end result of human conduct, whether extrinsically or intrinsically motivated, is self-regarding. A perspective that seems to be wrong in its basic assumptions about human nature, as simply self-centred. Do you agree? Do you think that all our motivations are always and only self-centred?

In this chapter, we will reflect on what empirical studies are furthering – that the purpose of giving, and not just receiving or achieving, is a common and universal driver and part of our humanity, a kind of motivation that considers the impact our actions have on other people and not just on ourselves. Luckily, more and more empirical studies are proving that, in addition to the so-called Selfish Gene, or innate interest for receiving and achieving, there is also an Unselfish Gene (Benkler, 2011) related to a universal desire for giving (Grant, 2013).

Moreover, the decision to follow such a selfish or unselfish impulse is precisely what was defined in Chapter 3 as moral freedom, or the "freedom to". We human beings have the freedom to receive, to achieve and to give. Thus, as we noted, this moral freedom is what makes us responsible for our decisions and what makes us humans capable of giving and taking.

In practical terms, this might sound like common sense. Whenever I ask any student, they agree – they prefer lecturers who care about them. They are convinced that some really care about them and consider the impact of their actions on the students, whereas others do not. If you look from the perspective of us lecturers, or professionals in general, when we go to work every day, our normal purpose for going to work is to be helpful to others, do useful things for our students, to serve our customers, etc.

Most work consists of providing something of value to others. This means that we are putting a "giving" desire or interest into practice, what some scholars would describe as a "transcendent" or "transitive motivation" (Melé, 2003). Can you imagine a teacher who was unable to teach? A car mechanic incapable of fixing cars? A manager who does not produce results? Being useful to others is the main justification or reason for being – *raison d'être* – of practically every professional job, and I maintain that it is therefore a kind of human motivation.

Knowing that our actions are useful to others is something that virtually everyone values. Of course, there are people who are mainly, or exclusively, motivated by their salary (receiving, *extrinsic motivation*), but others are moved by just a desire for personal development and success (achieving, *intrinsic motivation*). However, this does not mean that helping or serving others (giving, *transcendent motivation*) should not also be considered as a universal motivation, a third in addition to the *extrinsic* and *intrinsic*.

These three types of motivations are not exclusive, they are compatible, and in daily reality, they intermingle. The usefulness of our actions, its contribution in aiding others, is a powerful human drive, a "transcendent" one, which drives us to work better and that could provide a deeper meaning to our work, especially when we perceive our work as an inner call to do something for others, as we will discuss in depth in Chapter 8.

I love telling my students about my personal discoveries in this area as a researcher. In this sense, I explain to them that I was shocked when, as mentioned in Chapter 3, I discovered that Maslow was mistaken and had admitted his mistake. In his posthumous book, he admitted that he had not recognised the importance of transcendent motivations in his early studies.

He then described, as some of the latest findings of his research, what he called the "transcenders", meaning those people who are moved by the motivation of giving (Maslow, 1971). Unfortunately, as I mentioned before, even today, many professors who teach Maslow's theory are not aware of the existence of his latest ideas, as I myself was not aware for decades.

Maslow would probably agree with the suggestion that our map of motivations should be expanded (see Figure 3.1) to include a third column for the *transcendent motivations* of giving. Maslow also states that these transcenders are among the happiest people in the world. In fact, in an attempt to better explain the importance of this motivation, he expanded his popular hierarchy of needs to include transcendence, a personal self-giving, as the highest human endeavour.

Transcendent motivations: Human willingness to give

To be specific, and more precise, Maslow was neither the first nor the only scholar to admit to the existence of this third kind of *transcendent motivation*. Decades before Maslow's later findings, there were other academics aware of the importance of this *giving motivation*. Therefore, and aiming to promote positive critical thinking in my students, I suggest they do some new online research about other authors in the field of psychology who also wrote about this kind of *transcendent motivation*. I then propose inviting the other less-celebrated researchers to our conversation on human motivations.

In their quest, students come up with authors, such as Lersch from the late 1930s or Allport and Frankl in the 1960s, who recognised the existence of a universal driver for *giving*. Lersch was one of the first scholars who described *self-transcending drives* as one of the groups of motives that

72 Exploring the region of higher human motivations

characterise human development from infancy to adulthood, striving for cooperative, creative or loving behaviours (Lersch, 1938).

On the other hand, Allport viewed the human being as *proactive* and *purposeful*, whose personality is less a finished product and more a transitive process that requires this transcendent driver (Allport, 1961). Some years later, Frankl held a similar position, arguing that there are two specifically human phenomena by which human existence is characterised: the capacity of *self-detachment* and that of *self-transcendence* (Frankl, 1966).

This self-transcending of the individual domain means that we human beings can be moved by the impact that our actions have on others and not just in ourselves. Therefore, in order to grow as individuals, we are capable of moving from a self-perspective to an others' perspective.

This idea was put forward and boldly defended years later by IESE Business School professor Juan Antonio Pérez-López, who maintained that human beings have three kinds of motivations: two belonging to the realm of self-interest, *extrinsic* and *intrinsic* motivations, and a third in the realm of others-interest, the *transcendent* motivation (Pérez-López, 1974). As we will see, this means that our *map of motivations* should be expanded to now include a third column for the transcendent giving motivations (see Figure 4.1).

The literature review by students always pays off: they themselves verify that the desire to give is a human (transcendent) motivation that is not new. Although not all the researchers fully agree on their approaches and ideas,

	Extrinsic Motivation Receiving	Intrinsic Motivation Achieving	Transcendent Motivation Giving
Moral Good Ethical Realm	Willingness to receive moral good Reputation, Admiration, Respect	Willingness to achieve moral good Virtuousness, Excellence, Goodness	
Pleasant Good Psychological Realm	Willingness to receive pleasant good Relatedness, Affiliation, Esteem	Willingness to achieve pleasant good Self-actualisation, Growth, Self-esteem	Willingness to give Serve, Care, Goodwill
Useful Good Physical Realm	Willingness to receive useful good Sustenance, Safety, Support	Willingness to achieve useful good Competency, Mastery, Success	

Figure 4.1 Defining transcendent motivations

they all recognise the existence of this universal type of giving motivation (see Figure 4.1).

As Faldetta explains, when describing what he calls *the logic of gift-giving* in business relationships, "giving comes from the awareness of having received something (from another person, from a social group, from society as a whole or even from God), and the inevitable responsibility of answering this gift" (Faldetta, 2011, p. 71). Other authors, such as Frémeaux and Michelson, contend that "giving for its own sake with 'no strings attached' presents an opportunity to provide deeper and more enduring meaning to a wide range of social and business relations" (Frémeaux & Michelson, 2011, p. 73).

Regarding this motivation of giving, among the first sources that students find online in the task I set them is Daniel Pink's 2009 TED Talk "The puzzle of motivation", which has been viewed more than 25 million times. In this talk, Pink asserts that a "new operating system for our businesses revolves around three elements: autonomy, mastery and purpose. Autonomy: the urge to direct our own lives. Mastery: the desire to get better and better at something that matters. Purpose: the yearning to do what we do in the service of something larger than ourselves. These are the building blocks of an entirely new operating system for our businesses".[2]

In the same sense, in his bestselling book, Pink explains that many entrepreneurs, executives and investors are realising that the best-performing companies stand for something that contributes to the world. He claims that the old "Motivation 2.0" approaches were centred on maximising profits, while the new "Motivation 3.0 does not reject profits, but it places equal emphasis on purpose maximization" (Pink, 2009, p. 133).

He insists on the importance of this "purpose" motivation when he says, "we know that the richest experiences in our lives aren't when we're clamouring for validation from others, but when we're listening to our own voice – doing something that matters, doing it well, and doing it in the service of a cause larger than ourselves" (Pink, 2009, p. 146).

Unfortunately, Pink does not differentiate *transcendent motivations* from *intrinsic* ones, most probably due to the influence of traditional thought in this area (as presented in Chapter 1). As I noted before, this distinction is still not commonplace at all. Paradoxically, Pink has become popular because he talks about the *transcendent motivation* – one that was already described not so popularly a century ago – but he still includes the transcendent purpose among the *intrinsic motivations* category.

Pink insists on calling *intrinsic motivation* the *purpose* motive, but I will maintain here that *purpose* can be either *extrinsic*, *intrinsic* or *transcendent*. The three kinds of purposes corresponding to three types of motivations are distinct and compatible. Of course, they can be present in a simultaneous and interconnected manner, however, they are entirely different.

As I explain to students, while the *extrinsic* and *intrinsic* purposes look for the person's own interests (i.e. getting rich or famous), the *transcendent purpose* looks for others' interests (i.e. shaping a better world). They respond to three different kinds of motivations: our willingness to give in addition to receive and achieve.

To make this distinction clearer, I suggest looking again at Figure 4.1, which offers a graphic illustration of the distinction between *extrinsic*, *intrinsic* and *transcendent* motivations. The figure shows an expanded version of the *map of human motivations* as we move forward in our investigation. This expanded map includes now a third column for the *transcendent* motivations, those that point outside the person. This third column graphically reflects the new category of the motivation for *giving*, distinct from *receiving* and *achieving*.

I have to confess that defending the existence of this third kind of human motivation has become a challenge for me among some of my colleagues, especially the economics professors, as some of them are totally convinced that there is no such a thing as a *transcendent motivation*. They would argue that there are behaviours of external giving, but behaviours that are all self-driven nonetheless.

They maintain that, when people give, it is always because they are expecting to receive something in exchange. Therefore, from their point of view, we would always be driven by the *extrinsic motivation*, perhaps the *intrinsic*, but there would be no such a thing as a *transcendent motivation*. Would you agree with this position? Have you never given anything in your life just for the sake of giving? Without expecting anything in return? The presence of *extrinsic motivations* in human behaviour is a debate that I have with my students every year at some point, one that is still taking place today among academics. Are *transcendent* giving motivations a reality or not?

Transcendent motivations or human generosity in debate among academics

The self-centred and transactional view of human nature has been immortalised in economics by Adam Smith (1976a [1776]). For him, *exchange* is the most basic, operative logic in business transactions. As he famously noted: "It is not from the benevolence of the butcher, the brewer, or the baker that we expect our dinner, but from their regard to their own interest" (1976a [1776], Bk. 1, Ch. 2).

However, Smith also famously attributed a great deal of importance to benevolence in his *Theory of Moral Sentiments* that same year, going so far as to assert, "The wise and virtuous man is at all times willing that his own private interest should be sacrificed to the public interest of his own particular order or society" (1976b [1759], VI.II.46). Scholars have long debated how to reconcile Smith's account of sympathy and benevolence in his *Theory of Moral Sentiments* with the necessities of self-interest explored in *The Wealth of Nations*, the so-called Adam Smith problem (Montes, 2003; Baviera et al., 2016).

This Adam Smith problem is indicative of a tension that has long existed. Do we always give in order to receive? Are we capable of sacrificing our own good for the good of others? When discussing this with my economist colleagues, I tell them that I understand that we are definitely prone to receive. Nevertheless, not every time we give is in order to receive. Many times, we give just for the sake of giving.

When I take this position, some of my colleagues concede that sometimes we give without expecting to receive. However, they argue that in those cases, people give because it makes them happy or because they like it, so they feel satisfied with themselves, which, of course, makes it an *intrinsic motivation*. So, if at the end of the day, it is all about personal satisfaction, why do we need to talk about such a thing as *transcendent motivation*?

If *transcendent motivation* does not exist, then it seems that it is all about ourselves. We human beings would either give to receive (an *extrinsic* reward) or to attain something (a personal *intrinsic* satisfaction) but really not care about others' good. Others' good would just be the result of all our selfish conducts. Does that sound right? According to this position, people with transcendent purposes in their lives would be moved exclusively by their personal satisfaction, the desire of fulfilling their own purposes, but not by the good that those purposes would promote in others.

There are examples of people like St Teresa of Calcutta, who gave her entire life for the good of others, that seem to disprove this position. Of course, you will always hear critical voices asserting that Mother Teresa served her own religious beliefs and reputation (Hitchens, 1995). If true, this would not deny the existence of disinterested motivations in Mother Teresa. What I mean is that our generous and selfish motivations intermingle, but they are not all selfish. Just think about soldiers who risk their lives for their country. An even simpler example would be the millions of mothers who care about the good of their children.

Therefore, I maintain that, in addition to the *extrinsic* and *intrinsic motivations*, there may be a third reason why we give, a *transcendent* one, a new third column on our map (see Figure 4.1). Of course, if there is no such thing as a *transcendent motivation*, then the *transcendent purpose* of human beings would most probably fall under the category of the *intrinsic motivations*, and this could be why Daniel Pink included the motivation of purpose among the *intrinsic* motivations – because he did not distinguish the *transcendent* purpose from *extrinsic* or *intrinsic* purposes (Pink, 2009).

As I noted before, I have to disagree with Pink's position despite the great work he has done on promoting the concept of purpose as a kind of human motivation in the workplace (Pink, 2009). If we reduce motivations to just the desire to receive or achieve things and deny the existence of the *transcendent motivation*, then any generous, altruistic or disinterested behaviour would always be implied selfishly.

Undoubtedly, this position reflects a pessimistic view of human nature as always being based on ego. This view is not real, at least in the world in which the majority of us live. This is the position I defend with my colleagues and students. If we do not expand our map to have a third column (see Figure 4.1), to include *transcendent* motivation, we are implicitly assuming quite a negative view of human beings and one that is not so human after all.

It could be that we give part of our time to others to receive something in exchange later, like a salary or a favour we might need in the future (*extrinsic motivations*). Alternatively, maybe we give our time to feel personal satisfaction for giving (*intrinsic motivations*). However, we could also say that there are times in which we give our time just for the good that it will produce in others, neither necessarily expecting anything in exchange nor without feeling any special satisfaction (*transcendent motivations*).

Who can deny that our motivations are often a mix of *extrinsic*, *intrinsic* and *transcendent* reasons? Many times, we give partly to receive something in exchange, partly for our personal satisfaction and also partly for the sake of others' good. Denying the possibility of this *transcendent* motivation would be rejecting the possibility of giving, at least in part, for the sake of giving, for the good it produces in others.

To prove this point to my colleagues, I like to engage them with a puzzle and ask them a personal question regarding their children. If in the middle of the night, one of their children starts crying, why should they wake up and check on them? Why should they help their child who is feeling bad? Do they get up because it is rewarding and nice? If they are consistent with their ideas, as rational beings, they should probably answer that they wake up in the middle of the night exclusively to stop the children from bothering them (a negative *intrinsic motivation*). It is hard to believe that they will get up expecting to receive some type of repayment from their children later in life (*extrinsic motivations*). Reducing the explanation of their behaviour to these two kinds of motivations would be foolish, silly or proof that they are not good parents.

Keeping with the puzzle, I suggest that denying the motivation of giving is either unrealistic or inhumane. Can we absolutely deny the fact that we human beings might freely choose to give just for the sake of giving? That we care about others' good? By the way, this is not just a human kind of conduct; you can also find this transcendent behaviour in the family life of many non-rational animals. This logic does not apply to just family relationships as, even in the workplace, we tend to try and help others. We spend hours working together and serving each other, collaboratively.

Thus, if we deny this *transcendent motivation*, the only explanation for helping others would be to eventually receive something in exchange, or for fun. However, again, this does not fit with ordinary common experience. This is precisely what Maslow found in his later research; that there are people involved in transcendent causes outside themselves, which they consider central to their lives (Maslow, 1971).

Maslow avows that "because it will be so difficult for so many to believe, I must state explicitly that I have found approximately as many *transcenders* among businessmen, industrialists, managers, educators, political people as I have among the professionally 'religious', the poets, intellectuals, musicians, and others who are supposed to be transcenders and are officially labelled so" (Maslow, 1971, p. 285).[3]

Surely, what this evidence proves is what common sense suggests, that transcendent motivation is not exclusive to a profession or a particular group of people; rather, it is a behaviour that every human being can engage in. Fortunately, a large and growing number of scholars are now offering empirical evidence of the existence of this *transcendent motivation*. For example, according to Cloninger's general model of temperament based on genetic, neurobiological, and neuropharmacological data, self-transcendence refers to the interest people have in searching for something elevated or beyond their individual existence (Cloninger, 2004).

As suggested by other well-known psychologists and psychiatrists, such as Carl Jung and Viktor Frankl, Cloninger has emphasised that self-transcendence is an essential component in the processes of integration and maturation of personality; it underlies the human capacities for self-awareness, creativity, and freedom of will (Cloninger, 2004).

It is comforting to confirm that social scientists are proving this again under different nomenclatures. For example, the phenomenon has been captured by evolutionary sociologists under the empirical construct of strong reciprocity (Fehr et al., 2002). By "strong reciprocity", these researchers mean "a propensity, in the context of a shared social task, to cooperate with others similarly disposed, even at personal cost, and a willingness to punish those who violate cooperative norms, even when punishing is personally costly" (Gintis et al., 2008).

They deem this "reciprocity" because it embraces an ethic of treating others as they treat us, granting favours to those who cooperate with us and punishing those who take advantage of it. A good example of this is the British concept of buying a round of drinks, where people who don't buy their rounds become extremely unpopular (Fox, 2004).

Among other good examples of empirical evidence proving the existence of the giving *transcendent motivations*, I am especially partial to the studies of management professor Adam Grant from the Wharton Business School. In his now popular book *Give and Take: A Revolutionary Approach to Success*, he illustrates how vital this behaviour of giving is for organisations (Grant, 2013). Grant explains that "When [employees] act like givers, they contribute to others without seeking anything in return. They might offer assistance, share knowledge, or make valuable introductions. When they act like takers, they try to get other people to serve their ends while carefully guarding their own expertise and time" (Grant, 2013).

Ultimately, what Grant and many others have recognised is that successful organisations require uncalculated contributions and a spirit of service and collaborative generosity from everyone. In other words, he proves that the *transcendent motivation* of disinterested giving is not so irrational after all. Maslow called people showing these behaviours *transcenders*, and Professor Grant called them *givers* (Grant, 2013).

I am aware that giving without the expectation of a reward is sometimes difficult to understand in organisational contexts. This issue sometimes causes confrontational debates among some of my colleagues at the Business School, in particular, and among academics in general. In fact, as a way of bringing this discussion into the academic realm, I co-authored an article titled "The 'Logic of Gift': Inspiring Behavior in Organizations Beyond the Limits of Duty and Exchange" (Baviera et al., 2016) on this subject a few years ago with two colleagues.

In the article, we explained that contrary to a logic based on *self-interest* or a *sense of duty*, a *logic of gift* is also possible. In fact, this logic explains the phenomenon of free, unconditional giving. We endorsed the balanced integration of all three logics, promising to enhance organisational life and outcomes. Moreover, this logic fosters more humane relationships within organisations, enabling individuals to be generous in ways that inspire trust and promote creativity in the workplace (Baviera et al., 2016).

All these corroborations are some of the many examples that can be found in the social science literature. They just show what common sense also dictates regarding the human motivation for giving. Most of us can recall a time when we were touched by another person's generosity toward, affection for or real interest in us. Perhaps they helped us with a difficult task or project, showed us the warmth of their sincere smile in a difficult moment or gave us a good piece of advice to help with a personal decision, all without expecting anything in return.

In Chapter 8, we will return to the outcomes and practicality of this *transcendent motivation* when talking about the meaning of work as a *calling*. However, now is the time to explain in depth what it means to be moved by this new category of motivations, which are reflected in the new third column on our map.

Transcendent useful motivations: Human willingness to give useful good, to serve

Let's return and look carefully at the expanded map of human motivations (see Figure 4.1). Once we include the category of giving, three new kinds of motivation arise. These new types of motivations are the result of linking the logic of giving with the three kinds of Aristotelian goods we described before: the *useful*, the *pleasant* and the *moral*. Therefore, and starting from the bottom of the third column, the first new type of motivation emerges: the *transcendent useful motivation* (see Figure 4.2).

This *transcendent useful motivation* is a kind of human driver that can be defined as the voluntary desire or willingness to give useful good to others. It refers to being eager to be useful to others that we discussed at the beginning of the chapter or, likewise, the wish to assist and serve others. It is defined

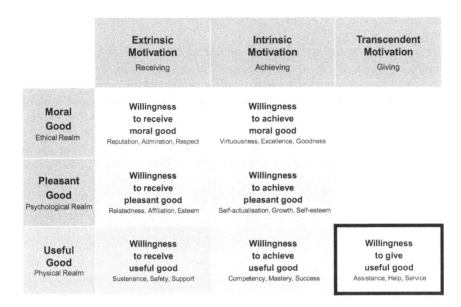

Figure 4.2 Mapping the territory: The transcendent useful motivation

as providing help, aid or any kind of support, including all different ways of providing practical good. These are the motivations of many people in many everyday circumstances (i.e. parents, teachers, doctors, nurses, civil servants and others) (see Figure 4.2).

No one can deny that firefighters, police officers or judges should all aspire to assist others, to provide them with some kind of service. This type of interest in others' practical good is present in every profession. It is widespread and common to the majority of human jobs and endeavours. Moreover, meaningful interpersonal relationships are indeed characterised by continuous acts of receiving and, therefore, of giving.

People in organisations give their time and resources beyond legal and formal requests, in ways that are not restricted by their work contracts or role definition and do not necessarily benefit them directly. Furthermore, it is safe to assume that such attitudes towards service are crucial to the success of most human institutions. Effective organisations often depend on this "logic of gift", a form of generosity and of giving freely without expectation of return (Baviera et al., 2016).

This human phenomenon of giving without expecting anything in return has been underappreciated by modern social scientists for decades, especially in the world of business management, as I noted earlier. Unfortunately, we have lacked and still lack adequate language and a set of concepts to understand unconditional, interpersonal giving. In the absence of these, such giving can easily appear as something irrational or having a hidden self-interest, and the importance of this phenomenon remains neglected (Baviera et al., 2016).

As proven by general experience and dictated by common sense, the first purpose of the majority of our professions is service, a *transcendent motivation*. As it happens, university management professors are supposed to serve students by teaching them how to be good business managers and how to serve better, and serving is nothing except providing useful good to others, helping them in a useful or practical way.

This kind of reasoning may be applied to any daily task, as long as we engage in it as an opportunity to serve others. Professionals who are often more aware of their co-workers' needs, will in turn get higher levels of motivation in their own work. The same would happen with any service provider in the professional realm. The more we understand the needs behind the services we provide, the higher our motivation will be.

Something similar can be said about our students; the more they dream of becoming professionals at the service of society, the more they will benefit from their classes and their professors' knowledge. Curiously enough, it is not rare that the more you feel useful to others, the more you want to keep serving them. In addition to being paradoxical, is this not a meaningful and powerful human motivation?

We will return to this idea of finding more meaningful work through this type of motivation in Chapter 9. Moving further with this idea, the *pleasant good* can also accompany this motivation of service when providing a *useful good*. In other words, you can serve others with or without affection. The practical interest to help others might go hand in hand with warm-heartedness, kindness, compassion and authentic caring or just the opposite, by bitterness and contempt (Brooks, 2019).

Transcendent pleasant motivations: Human willingness to give pleasant good, to please

Of course, you may provide a *useful good* without providing a *pleasant good*; for example, you can be teaching a quite practical class in a really boring manner. However, the opposite is also true; you can provide pleasant good with no utility to it at all. Your class could be quite funny but also totally pointless. As we discussed in Chapter 2, *useful*, *pleasant*, and *moral* goods belong to different realms.

To illustrate this, I remember that when I was a boy, my mother used to tell me that it was not enough just to help my siblings at home and that I should try to do it cheerfully. She would say that because sometimes I did not like to help at all (especially with some of the more unpleasant tasks); I used to do it with a sad expression on my face. That was a clear display that I was not doing my chores with much or any interest. In fact, I was not motivated at all, and you could tell that just by looking at my face.

My mother knew quite well that trying to make life more pleasant for my siblings was a different kind of motivation (*transcendent pleasant*) from that of just helping them (*transcendent useful*) (see Figure 4.3). In fact, teachers may be interested in helping students and transmitting their knowledge (*transcendent useful*), but at the same time, they may not transmit passion nor sensation of enjoyment when teaching (*transcendent pleasant*). Someone that teaches without passion for what they are communicating is normally not a good teacher.

In similar fashion, a nurse taking care of a patient without compassion and affection is not usually perceived as a good nurse. They might be quite proficient technically, but if they serve with rudeness and without care, that service might be considered less human, and it may also show a lack of motivation. Therefore, the need for warmth and affection (*transcendent pleasant motivation*) is not an exception in any act of service (*transcendent useful motivation*) to be described as more human and more highly motivated.

This interest in making life more pleasant for others (*transcendent pleasant motivation*), for instance, constitutes another driver for millions of mothers and fathers towards the care of their children, and so it is with other members of the family and friends as well. However, once again, this desire to satisfy others does not happen exclusively in family-type environments; this may be also applied to every human environment.

I remember when, many years ago, I arrived in South Bend, Indiana, as a visiting scholar at Notre Dame University. It was the first week of September, and the academic year had just started. I was walking through campus

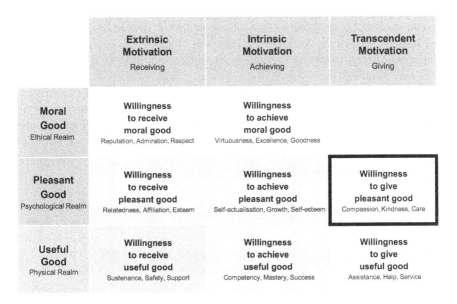

Figure 4.3 Mapping the territory: The transcendent pleasant motivation

to my office, and, surprisingly, every person I came across on campus was smiling at me and greeting me. At some point, I had the silly thought that, somehow, they all knew about me.

Maybe because I was from Spain, coming from the exotic city of Valencia, they all wanted to greet me. Surely, this did not make sense. Nonetheless, everyone continued saying "hi" to me every day of that week and the following one, too. It took me several weeks to learn that being so amiable is part of the culture at this institution and part of the culture in the Midwestern United States and many other places as well.

After that experience, I spent time on other campuses all around the world, and I decided to keep practicing what I had learnt at Notre Dame, smiling at every person I passed on campus. It is fair to say, however, that many times I forgot, or I just got distracted. Have you ever tried smiling at everyone you meet on the street? It is an interesting exercise, and if you do it, you will find that most people will instinctively smile back. Of course, others who might not be used to this kind of experience may only respond with a half-smile, but a smile nonetheless. Even if they are strangers, almost everybody, given the time, will smile back and/or greet you. I later learnt that this was a clear example of the functioning of our *mirror neurons* (Association for Psychological Science, 2007).

It seems that a good spirit or joyfulness is contagious, but sincerity is a pivotal factor here. Being false may be awkward and off-putting, such as an overly excited waiter who seems to be trying too hard to be liked. Nevertheless, normally, no matter the type of work environment, most people prefer to be surrounded by others who show their joy naturally, with authenticity and simplicity, and seem genuinely happy to be there. Contributing to a positive/pleasant environment for others is also a personal powerful driver of human behaviour. Making life nicer for others is, therefore, a kind of universal driver, a *transcendent pleasant motivation*, distinct from the useful one (see Figure 4.3).

This *transcendent pleasant motivation* can be defined as *the voluntary desire to give pleasant good to others*. It refers to the eagerness to being nice to others, to please them, to connect with their feelings and not just with their minds. This is something that is totally consistent with some of the human strengths described by positive psychology, such as forgiveness, compassion, empathy and altruism (Snyder & Lopez, 2002).

In this matter, both humanists and positive psychologists coincide in encouraging human flourishing not only through high levels of emotional and psychological well-being but also of social and relational well-being. Therefore, continuous self-development grows out of a purposive and meaningful life but also out of close and high-quality relationships (Keyes, 2007).

Within a humanistic framework, the quality of an interpersonal relationship reflects at least five characteristics: warmth, genuineness, empathy, interpersonal acceptance and confirmation of the other person's capacity for self-determination (Kramer, 1995; Reeve, 1996; Rogers, 1973, 1995).

These five characteristics are but manifestations of the *transcendent pleasant motivation*.

Unsurprisingly, all these self-transcendent emotional qualities of human relationships, described recently by humanist and positive psychology, were already witnessed by Maslow's later studies. He stressed the important role of intimate and fulfilling relationships – rather than the all-too-common superficial ones – as the soil for cultivating peak experiences (Hardeman, 1979).

Such relationships require transcendent human qualities belonging to the sphere of emotions and affectivity. Moreover, these qualities, as well as those of kindness, consideration, sympathy and assertiveness, among others, are not only positive psychological traits but also moral virtues, belonging to the realm of the *moral goods* as well, which leads us to distinguish *transcendent moral motivation* from those that are *useful* and *pleasant*.

Transcendent moral motivations: Human willingness to give moral good, to do good

When we learn to empathise and be assertive, we become better human beings while also contributing to the pleasant good of others. Sympathy and assertiveness are moral habits of behaviour that contribute to our own personal flourishing while also contributing to the joy of others. In fact, these habits are not always innate or part of our temperament or genetic constitution, and we need to put in the effort to attain them.

Some people may engage in them more naturally, others not so naturally. However, for everyone, these habits require a process of learning through continuous and laborious practice until, little by little, they become part of our moral character (Havard, 2019). They imply a transcendent voluntary intention to connect with others' emotions and feelings, to search for others' pleasant good.

As we discussed in Chapter 3, from an Aristotelian perspective, the realms of the *useful*, *pleasant* and *moral* good are different. Moreover, it is important to distinguish between them properly but at the same time not separate them. In fact, in real life, the pleasant and moral spheres are permanently intertwined. Strictly speaking, attitudes and motivations of empathy, assertiveness or compassion belong to the realm of the pleasant good, but they cannot be separated from the moral. In many cases, the pleasant conveniently coincides with the moral, but not always, hence the importance of distinguishing between these two dimensions of human reality.

Let me use an example to explain this. Imagine that one of your colleagues tells you that they want to have some fun after a really hard day at work. They ask to borrow some money from you. You know that the money they are asking for is to consume hard drugs that will surely harm them. You may decide to lend them the money just to be helpful, a *transcendent useful motivation*. Alternatively, you might lend them the money just because you

84 Exploring the region of higher human motivations

like them and you want them to have fun, a *transcendent pleasant motivation*. In any case, whatever the motivation is in these two realms (*useful* or *pleasant*) you also must consider the third dimension, the *moral*. As we saw in Chapter 3, as far as this is a human and free decision, it always has moral implications. We human beings are moral beings by nature.

If you decide to lend money to your colleague, irrespective of the level of *useful* or *pleasant motivation*, the *moral* must also be considered because we are all moral beings. This is what traditional views of motivation have been taking for granted. The three realms of motivation can be differentiated, but they cannot be separated if we want to really understand what is going on in the human action. We need to distinguish between, but not separate, the three kinds of transcendent motivations that are at stake (see Figure 4.4).

In this example, you might find that contributing to this person's future neural damage (through drug use) is morally wrong, so you don't lend them the money. Although you want to help and please this person (transcendent positive, useful and pleasant motivations), you do not want to cause them moral harm (positive transcendent moral motivation). In other words, not every transcendent motivation is always morally good. You could be moved by the desire to help or please someone and still cause that person moral damage.

What this simple example shows is that the three realms of human behaviour (*physical*, *psychological*, and *ethical*) are different but inseparable,

	Extrinsic Motivation Receiving	**Intrinsic Motivation** Achieving	**Transcendent Motivation** Giving
Moral Good Ethical Realm	Willingness to receive moral good Reputation, Admiration, Respect	Willingness to achieve moral good Virtuousness, Excellence, Goodness	**Willingness to give moral good** Gentleness, Understanding, Good
Pleasant Good Psychological Realm	Willingness to receive pleasant good Relatedness, Affiliation, Esteem	Willingness to achieve pleasant good Self-actualisation, Growth, Self-esteem	Willingness to give pleasant good Compassion, Kindness, Care
Useful Good Physical Realm	Willingness to receive useful good Sustenance, Safety, Support	Willingness to achieve useful good Competency, Mastery, Success	Willingness to give useful good Assistance, Help, Service

Figure 4.4 Mapping the territory: The transcendent moral motivation

as we saw in Chapter 3 when discussing the example of the bear on the teacher's desk. Moreover, in our relationship with others, that *transcendent moral motivation* can be positive, negative or apparently neutral, but, like it or not, it will always affect our actions.

It also means that, as we noted, not every *transcendent motivation* is always morally good. We can be moved to give a *useful* or *pleasant* good to someone but still hurt them from a moral point of view. We can lend our car to our friend who is drunk, thinking that will help them get back home or contribute to their personal satisfaction at that moment, but if we are putting their life – and potentially the lives of others – at risk, we are in the wrong, as our *transcendent moral motivation* has not been considered in our train of thought (see Figure 4.4).

Again, being moved by a *transcendent motivation* is not necessarily synonymous with actually doing the right thing. In other words, not every transcendent motivation is morally good. This is why making the distinction between the three realms of human good is relevant. To understand the full range of transcendent human motivations, we need to pay careful attention to the *useful* and *pleasant* dimensions but also the *moral* dimension.

In that sense, the *transcendent moral motivation* may be described as the voluntary desire or the willingness to give moral good to others, to be benevolent (from the Latin *bene-volere*, or well wishing) or simply to be moved by goodwill, by the desire of honouring others' dignity as human beings (see Figure 4.4).

Transcendent motivations' presence in ordinary and professional life

To review the logic of our *map of motivations*, we can reconsider the motivations at stake in the example of the parent waking up in the middle of the night to care for their child. Most probably, getting up late at night is not motivated by some kind of later support, esteem or respect the parents expect in the future from their child (the three motives from the first column of *extrinsic motivations* in Figure 4.4). Neither do the attainment of personal mastery, satisfaction or virtue seem to be the motivations at stake (the three motives from the second column of *intrinsic motivations* in Figure 4.4).

It therefore seems clear that the main motivation for parents to care for their children, day or night, is *transcendent*. They will wake up at any time to help, give affection to and care for their children (the three motives in the third column of *transcendent motivations* in Figure 4.4). This simple example, or any other example of cooperation among people, even in the workplace and any professional setting, shows that human beings have the capacity to transcend their own personal interests, to be *transcenders* (Maslow, 1971).

The most graphic examples of transcendent motivations probably come from public service professions, as in the case of public health, even though Maslow found them in every professional setting. I recall one day, at dawn, while on my way to Valencia Airport in Spain, I ran into a friend who is a doctor. I asked him where he was going so early in the morning. In a teasing tone, he replied, "I'm off to make a lot of money", and a smile broke across his face. I smiled back and said, "But you're a doctor, not a businessman, right? Did you choose to become a doctor just to make a lot of money?" "Well", he said, "I am just doing some extra work early in the morning. Most of my colleagues prefer to start work later, so I just wake up earlier and take care of the first surgeries at the hospital and, you know, it translates into extra cash".

It was clear that my friend's motive here was the *extrinsic useful motivation*. Nevertheless, and because I am an optimist when it comes to human motivation, I was curious if there were any other drivers at play, so I kept insisting. "Is money the only reason why you do this kind of work so early in the morning?" I asked. "Well", he said, "I do love getting up early", but, of course, he was joking. Knowing about my perspective on human motivations, my friend was enjoying a prime opportunity to tease me – an opportunity he rarely misses. Smiling, I called his bluff. "No way! I know you quite well, and it's just the opposite, you wouldn't get up earlier unless there was some other reason, and I don't think it is the money".

At this point, we both made the time to grab a coffee before heading off to our destinations, and he told me more. "The extra money doesn't hurt, you know. However, in addition to the money, I really love a new technique I'm using in this surgery. I have a lot of fun working on this and becoming proficient at the same time, which is why they keep calling me for this particular surgery at the hospital, and I keep accepting such requests".

Eureka! I thought. It isn't just about making money but is also enjoyment and mastery; the *extrinsic* and *intrinsic motivations* were in play simultaneously. My friend's motivations were to receive some external good (*useful*) and to achieve some internal good (*mastery*), and both reasons played their part in his behaviour that morning. Nevertheless, he did not allude to any *transcendent* good at all, which, knowing him well, I found suspicious.

It was early, and not the best time for a deep conversation, but taking advantage of our close friendship and the fact that we still had some time, I asked him, "Don't you care about the patients? Is it all just about you, your mastery and financial needs?" He looked at me with a surprised look on his face, and replied, "Of course I care. I don't talk about it much, but I care".

My friend noted that talking about how much he cares for the patients does not make his job any easier. In fact, he told me that he was on his way to amputate a woman's leg and, though it would save her life, caring about her medically would not necessarily make the experience more pleasant. Some surgeries were fun, some others not so much – either for him or the patient – but he definitely seemed to care about his patients as people.

The final part of the conversation took on a more serious tone, and given that we were both now in a hurry, we decided to have another coffee at a later date to continue the conversation. When we had our chance to talk again, we discussed this *transcendent motivation*, the one related to taking care of others.

We both agreed that every time you help someone else it is not necessarily pleasant for either party. Pleasing others in our relationships is sometimes at stake, but not always. There are other kinds of goods that we desire for those we care about that are not essentially useful or enjoyable and still are considered "goods": moral goods, those related to the person as a whole. Saving the life of a patient, even if it means amputating their leg, is a higher good that a doctor will carry out over the immediate comfort of the patient.

Moral goods are higher than the useful and *pleasant* as we discussed in Chapters 2 and 3, and they are essential to a proper understanding and flourishing of human growth. Life itself is a fundamental human good, and appreciation of life over pleasantness is a manifestation of the value instilled in each person, their uniqueness and dignity. As Maslow recognised, this *self-transcendent motivation* of helping others to have a dignifying life is indeed the highest natural human motivation (Maslow, 1971).

Contributing to others' good is not just a motivation for naive or weak people but the opposite. Many times, aiming to do the right thing for others demands a strong character, and, undoubtedly, an unselfish one. Something that, of course, you would expect from good parents, for example. The same could be said of a good teacher, courageous enough to correct their students, as well as a good manager properly assessing their staff. All the motivations described in Figure 4.4 may be present in every single profession and human activity. It seems that the higher the level of the transcendent, the more humane the motivations.

By now, it seems irrefutable that all these motivations are universal. However, this does not necessarily mean that we have them all and in every action. It just means that, in every decision we make, any one of these motivations may be at stake, if not all, and that each of them may present a different level of intensity.

When I ask the students to think about their own *transcendent motivations* in working as managers in the future, they have no difficulty filling in the third column of the *map of motivations*, including their own. Once we all accept the existence of *transcendent motivations* in theory, everyone is able to identify them effectively in practice.

Within their *transcendent useful motivations*, students, but also professionals attending these presentations, include an interest in helping their customers with their products/services, as well as helping their co-workers better do their work. Secondly, in regard to their *transcendent pleasant motivations*, they include a desire to contribute to others' satisfaction, putting all their energy into making them feel good, being kind to them and being grateful with customers, co-workers and even managers.

Finally, among their *transcendent moral motivations*, they include trying to give the best of themselves to others and being honest with their

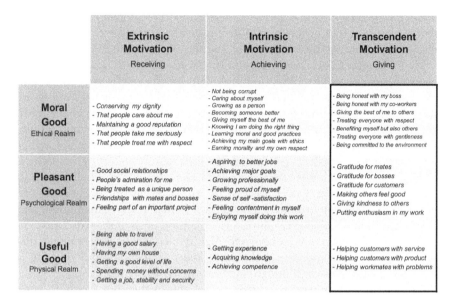

Figure 4.5 Examples from participants' transcendent motivations

co-workers and bosses, while also being committed to the more transcendent purposes of the organisation and of society in general, to something greater than themselves (see Figure 4.5).

Some practical tips

As we will discuss in Chapter 7, there must be some kind of balance and order among all our motivations (see Figure 4.4). It is clear that (1) *it would be wrong to be moved exclusively by extrinsic motivations*, always aspiring just to *receive* (first column), or just by *intrinsic motivations*, always aspiring just to *achieve* (second column), without really caring about others. Likewise, (2) *it would also be wrong to be driven exclusively by transcendent motivation*, always trying to do good to others (third column) without caring about oneself.

As Professor Adam Grant discovered in his research, in order to grow, (3) *we must find the right balance between other people's good and our own*. As we will have the chance to reflect upon later, being generous, for instance, in giving your time to others, is also compatible with a reasonable and balanced or well-ordered self-esteem. How can you really care about others if you do not care about yourself? If we completely neglect our own needs and interests, this would be misunderstanding our own needs, a disorder; we would not really be happy. Oddly enough, becoming generous is one of the smartest things we can do for ourselves.

Paradoxically, and this is the great news, when our motivation moves from the realm of self-interest towards a wider view, aiming at others' good, our humanity starts to really flourish. We grow morally when we look for the good in others; we become better human beings. Nevertheless, and to be consistent with the ideas we just discussed, if our motivation is really to contribute to the good of others, then attaining such a good for others will be our true reward (Baviera et al., 2016).

In other words, (4) *when transcendent motivation prevails in us, it becomes a habit, and then we start seeing potential for human growth in everyone we meet*, so we will be able to find and nurture talent around us. Besides, (5) *the more we put the transcendent motivation into practice, the more we'll see its benefits and the higher it will become in our set of motivations* (Grant, 2013).

Additionally, it seems that, (6) *people who engage in the habit of being generous end up achieving top positions in society*, and not because they are aiming for them or have a desire to excel but because they focus on the greater good. Unfortunately, we tend to criticise most of our leaders as self-interested and power seekers (Brooks, 2019).

Nevertheless, the truth is that real leaders are influential because they care about others; they are driven by the desire to help others, for their organisations and communities to be successful. Successful leaders have a sense of a *transcendent purpose*; they cultivate and use their vast networks to benefit others as well as themselves (Grant, 2013).

Creating relationships only with people who can give us something in return is not the smartest decision, and it usually takes its toll. Instead, (7) *when someone's joy is in helping others, the natural consequence will be to "activate" lots of relationships*, building networks without even realising it. Most people value reciprocity and fairness but value generosity even more. Being genuinely interested in others' needs leads us to build trust and goodwill in them. This helps us serve others in a reciprocal fashion (Grant, 2013).

On the other hand, and regarding group work in organisations, (8) *transcendent motivation makes everyone better off (including ourselves) by making the group better as a whole*. This happens through simple actions in which we put the group's common good ahead of our own, for example, by gathering many contributions, helping colleagues or just taking on tasks that others will not do (Grant, 2013).

Remarkably, (9) *the more we are driven by the motivation of giving, the less we lose in the process*. In other words, the more we give, the higher our personal growth. This logic of giving produces a virtuous cycle as noted before: (10) *the more we give, the more we want to keep giving*, and therefore the higher the *transcendent motivations become* (Grant, 2013).

After reviewing all these benefits of giving with my students, I wonder if they will start giving more often in the future. This is something I will never know. However, I keep reminding them that we choose how we appear in

90 *Exploring the region of higher human motivations*

the world. We can choose to act through solely self-driven motives or by *transcendent motivations*, helping others without worrying about receiving anything in return.

Many of them thank me at the end of the course for having studied this theory. Gratitude is one more manifestation of the logic of the *transcendent motivation* of giving. Again, as paradoxical as it seems, giving more makes us happier. However, unless we stop to reflect personally on this, we might not be conscious of our way of doing it. Let us think about it and, from time to time, examine our own conscience. The following questions may help.

Some questions for reflection

1. *How often do I give my full and undivided attention to others, being truly present for them?*
2. *How often do I really care about others, actually being interested in what they have to say?*
3. *How often do I try to serve and do my best to help others, to help in solving their problems?*
4. *How often do I acknowledge people's existence around me by just smiling at them?*
5. *How often do I sincerely give thanks for services provided to me by others?*
6. *How often do I try to make people around me feel good?*
7. *How often do I try to leave people around me feeling better than when I found them?*
8. *How often do I interrupt others when speaking?*
9. *How often do I genuinely care for others' well-being?*
10. *How often do I give others the chance to help me?*

A final critical thought on why the map is not yet accurate enough

Question 10 may seem contradictory. Are we helping others if we ask them for help? Certainly, helping others to be led by generosity seems to be a way to contribute to their human betterment, too. As we discussed, putting *transcendent motivation* into practice makes us better human beings, which is yet another paradox of human motivations. However, this is not a simple matter; we still need to decide how much of this transcendent motivation we could demand from others freely.

We want to be led by *transcendent motivations*, but we don't want others taking advantage of us. It is always a personal choice to decide how much you want to be moved freely by these motivations, especially how much you want to overcome the narrow, amoral and self-interested vision of human behaviour that has been taught in universities and business schools for decades. Therefore, how do we get a balance between all these kinds of motivations? Is it possible to have them all in our working environments?

As we move forward in our study, the apparent contradictions and paradoxes of human nature begin to appear, and we will need to stop and reflect on all these findings in our workplaces, in an organisational context, and this is something we will do in the third part of the book. However, before getting there, is the map of human motivations that we have built accurate enough? Is it all-inclusive?

As we will see in the next chapter, the map we have presented (see Figure 4.4) is not yet complete. As a Spanish MBA student at Harvard showed me, in this conceptual framework, we are missing the explicit consideration of *spiritual motivations*. There is objective evidence that spiritual drivers have been present in every civilisation and every human experience since the beginning of humanity. Should these also be included in our *map of human motivations*?

Notes

1 There is an Enron Fraud documentary titled *Enron: The Smartest Guys in the Room*, written by Bethany McLean (2005).
2 www.ted.com/talks/dan_pink_the_puzzle_of_motivation (12 minutes, 30 seconds).
3 Maslow's quote continues saying, "And most industrialists will carefully conceal their idealism, their metamotivations, and their transcendent experiences under a mask of 'toughness', 'realism', 'selfishness', and all short of other words which would have to be marked off by quotes to indicate that they are only superficial and defensive".

References

Allport, G. W. (1961). *Pattern and Growth in Personality*. New York: Holt, Rinehart & Winston.
Association for Psychological Science. (2007). Mirror neurons: How we reflect on behavior. *ScienceDaily*. www.sciencedaily.com/releases/2007/05/070504114259. htm, May 21, 2020.
Baviera, T., English, W. & Guillén, M. (2016). The logic of gift: Inspiring behavior in organizations beyond the limits of duty and exchange. *Business Ethics Quarterly*, 26(2), 159–180.
Benkler, Y. (2011). The unselfish gene. *Harvard Business Review*, July–August. https://hbr.org/2011/07/the-unselfish-gene.
Brooks, A. (2019). *Love Your Enemies. How Decent People Can Save America from the Culture of Contempt*. New York: Broadside Books. HarperCollins Publishers.
Cloninger, C. R. (2004). *Feeling Good: The Science of Well-Being*. New York: Oxford University Press.
Faldetta, G. (2011). The logic of gift and gratuitousness in business relationships. *Journal of Business Ethics*, 100(Suppl.), 67–77.
Fehr, E., Fischbacher, U. & Gachter, S. (2002). Strong reciprocity, human cooperation, and the enforcement of social norms. *Human Nature*, 13, 1–25.

Fox, K. (2004). *Watching the English: The Hidden Rules of English Behaviour*. London: Hodder & Stoughton.
Frankl, V. E. (1966). Self-transcendence as a human phenomenon. *Journal of Humanistic Psychology* (6), pp. 97–106.
Frémeaux, S. & Michelson, G. (2011). No strings attached: Welcoming the existential gift in business. *Journal of Business Ethics*, 99(1), 63–75.
Gintis, H., Henrich, J., Bowles, S., Boyd, R. & Fehr, E. (2008). Strong reciprocity and the roots of human morality. *Social Justice Research Ed.*, 21(2), 241–253.
Grant, A. (2013). *Give and Take: A Revolutionary Approach to Success*. New York: Viking.
Hardeman, M. (1979). A dialogue with Abraham Maslow. *Journal of Humanistic Psychology*, 19(1), 23–28.
Havard, A. (2019). *From Temperament to Character: On Becoming A Virtuous Leader*. New York: Scepter Publishers, Incorporated.
Hitchens, C. (1995). *The Missionary Position: Mother Teresa in Theory and Practice*. London and New York: Verso Books.
Keyes, C. L. M. (2007). Promoting and protecting mental health as flourishing: A complementary strategy for improving national mental health. *American Psychologist*, 62, 95–108.
Kramer, R. (1995). The birth of client-centered therapy: Carl Rogers, Otto Rank, and "the beyond". *Journal of Humanistic Psychology*, 35, 54–110.
Lersch, Ph. (1938). *Aufbau der person*. München: Barth. (in German).
Maslow, A. H. (1971). *The Farther Reaches of Human Nature*, Ed. Arkana. New York: Penguin Books.
Melé, D. (2003). The challenge of the humanistic management. *Journal of Business Ethics*, 44(1), 77–88.
Montes, L. (2003). Das Adam Smith problem: Its origins, the stages of the current debate, and one implication for our understanding of sympathy. *Journal of the History of Economic Thought*, 25(1), 63–90.
Pérez-López, J. A. (1974). Organizational theory: A cybernetic approach. *IESE Research Paper*, July 1974, WP n° 5.
Pink, D. H. (2009). *Drive: The Surprising Truth About What Motivates*. New York, NY: Riverhead Books.
Reeve, J. (1996). *Motivating Others: Nurturing Inner Motivational Resources*. Needham Heights, MA: Allyn & Bacon.
Rogers, C. R. (1973). My philosophy of interpersonal relationships and how it grew. *Journal of Humanistic Psychology*, 13, 3–15.
Rogers, C. R. (1995). What understanding and acceptance mean to me. *Journal of Humanistic Psychology*, 35, 7–22.
Smith, A. (1976a). *An Inquiry into the Nature and Causes of the Wealth of Nations*. Chicago: University of Chicago Press.
Smith, A. (1976b). *The Theory of Moral Sentiments*. Oxford: Oxford University Press.
Snyder, C. R. & Lopez, S. J. (Eds.). (2002). *Handbook of Positive Psychology*. New York: Oxford University Press.

5 The *spiritual motivations*
Human aspiration for the highest goods

The neglected spiritual motivations

In the first chapter, I described how, years ago, while giving my first presentation at the RCC building at Harvard, an MBA student approached me and said, "I think your ideas are right and quite new for me, but I think you are still missing something". He continued, "There is a kind of motivation that you did not mention that I still think needs to be addressed: the spiritual one".

His remarks left me completely stunned. Spiritual life is something I had always personally cared about but never considered within a speculative theory of human motivation. This student made me realise that the *map of motivations* that I had just presented was missing a part of the reality. As he had noted, many human beings are influenced in their daily behaviours by spiritual motives. So then, why are these motives of behaviour not explicitly included within current theories of motivation?

I remember telling some of my colleagues that I believed that these spiritual motivations are real and that they influence the lives of many people. I told them that a good theory of human motivations should make them explicit. Many of their responses were similar. They were something like, "I'd never thought about it, but now that you say it, I guess you're right". That simple yet insightful comment that day changed my research interest for the following years. I decided to further investigate this issue, and this is what led me to finding Maslow's final posthumously published book.

In this work, he not only described the *transcendent motivations*, he also explicitly mentioned *spiritual motivations*. In particular, he defined the concept of human "meta-motivations" as those giving the highest meaning to human life and the spiritual motivations being a part of them. For him, "the spiritual life (the contemplative, religious, philosophical, or value-life) is within the jurisdiction of human thought and is attainable in principle by man's own efforts" (Maslow, 1971, p. 312).

The spiritual life and *spiritual motivations* belong to aspects of human reality that are intangible and immaterial, related to the mysteries of human life and death, with those realities that the empirical sciences can only glimpse. Although now taboo topics in most modern university settings, they are crucial in understanding human motivation. As Maslow noted, they are universal and reasonable (Maslow, 1971), even though they go beyond rationality. To deny their existence in the ordinary lives of millions of people would be to deny the obvious.

As I mentioned in Chapter 1, this MBA student's observation led me to study the concept of spiritual motivations in more depth and to write a paper on the topic titled "The Neglected Ethical and Spiritual Motivations in the Workplace" (Guillén et al., 2015) with my two colleagues Ignacio Ferrero and W. Michael Hoffman. While working on that paper, I also decided to organise a colloquium at Harvard-RCC under the same title.[1] To my surprise, a good number of attendees commended the audacity of choosing the theme of spirituality at work as one of the premises of the discussion. This was no surprise for me as, again, this has been a taboo topic in universities for decades.

After that colloquium in 2014, I was invited by the Harvard Kennedy School's New England Alumni Association to lead several leadership seminars in which this topic was a key part of the discussion. At each of these seminars, I was often introduced as "the guy who talks about spiritual motivations in the workplace with no shame or concern for criticism".

Even though attendees vary each year, all those seminars have been well received and complimented. Why is that? I believe it is because we all need an in-depth understanding of what is going on in our lives, which includes reflecting upon our deepest motivations. Even if we have diverging views on what our spiritual or religious motivations are, most of us still wish to delve into the substance of these metaphysical belief systems. This is something that Maslow – as well as other well-known scholars – saw as early as 1971 (Cloninger, 2004).

Moreover, a growing body of scientific literature suggests strong evidence of a spiritual reality at play in people's lives, affecting our behaviour in various conscious and subconscious ways (Pargament, 2013). Therefore, if we recognise spirituality as a legitimate category of human needs and desires, we should then expand the taxonomy of motivations in our map with the addition of a new category, that of "spiritual goods", on the top row of the motivational grid (see Figure 5.1).

As you can imagine, when I mention spirituality in a class or seminar about business management and motivation in organisations, the first reaction is usually amazement, then curiosity. What do I mean by spirituality? How can it be a human motivation? How is spirituality related to work in organisations?

Well, spirituality at work has been defined in many different ways, and, in fact, there is little consensus on it. Nevertheless, some scholars state that while the definitions vary according to different traditions, five themes are common to the realm of spirituality: connection, mindfulness, compassion, meaningful work and transcendence (Petchsawang & Duchon, 2012).

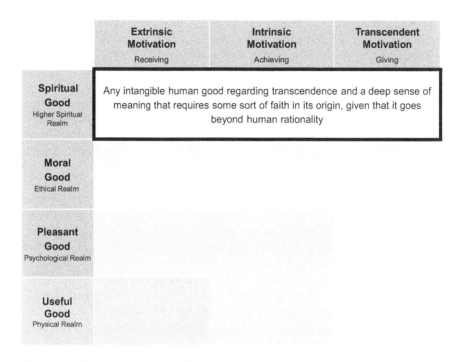

Figure 5.1 The spiritual good defined

When I mention these words in class or in my seminars, I see from the faces of participants that they all accept some part of this definition. Once I have their acceptance, I try to explain what I mean by "spiritual goods".

Spiritual motivations in pursuing the highest human goods

In the article I co-authored years ago with Ferrero and Hoffman, we wrote that, "one could say that the spiritual good refers to any intangible human good regarding transcendence and a deep sense of meaning that requires some sort of faith in its origin, given that it goes beyond human rationality. Some may call it supernatural good, given that it goes beyond nature" (Guillén et al., 2015, p. 810). In other words, we could say that a *spiritual good* refers to any intangible human good that possesses a deep sense of meaning, transcendence and mindfulness and that leads to a connection and compassion with nature and among human beings.

When I ask students what a "spiritual good" is for them, the first answers are often things like happiness, inner peace or love. As you keep asking, the answers include goods like true wisdom, being able to find yourself, self-awareness or self-control. It is striking that a type of good that is mentioned so little when motivations are studied can generate so many examples.

Among spiritual goods, students often also mention issues such as karma or positive energy flows, reincarnation or the possibility of eternal destiny. Normally, they do not see these matters as something exoteric but as something that many of them believe in and pursue in their lives.

Furthermore, in the case of students with a religious background, spiritual goods include all kinds of religious practices, a life of personal relationship with God, and, in most cases, they mention the desire to achieve endless happiness or eternal life in Heaven with God. We humans beings are aware of having an inner life that surpasses matter and somehow also transcends time. Who doesn't have a childhood memory? Who does not dream of what they would do if they had more free time or won the lottery?

We can recall our personal history, reflect on our identity and imagine our future during our lifetime and also afterwards. For that reason, every *spiritual good* involves some sort of faith in its origin and at its end because of its immaterial and intangible nature. We are not only capable of self-consciousness and self-development but also of communicating our intangible interiority to others in a compassionate, meaningful and transcendent way.

Just think about how people in love talk nonstop about their loves, or how friends share personal issues and have confidence when there is trust among them, or how a good work of art (a poem, a piece of music, a painting, etc.) is capable of conveying beauty and, many times, a deep meaning.

Only human beings have access to this spiritual dimension in their intimacy and are able to communicate it, a dimension that is higher in meaning than the other three natural realms of human life (the *physical*, the *psychological* and the *ethical*) that we described in Chapter 3. Therefore, *spiritual goods* are the highest level of the human goods because they relate to our conscientiousness of being unique creatures, with a nature that includes tangible and intangible aspects, material and immaterial dimensions, with body and soul, as the classic philosophers would say (see Figure 5.1).

It could be said that one of the main spiritual human goods at this highest level is life itself. By life, I mean its *physical, psychological, ethical* and mainly its *higher spiritual* nature, with an origin and a meaning or purpose. We are capable of thinking about the meaning of life, to find meaning in life. We may dream about visiting an inhospitable place or country in our lifetime. We may want to do something special to change the world. We may decide that we want to have as much fun as possible, but we also may decide to give our lives in the service of others. The human spirit is made to search for meaning (Frankl, 1959).

The mystery of the human spiritual life constitutes the epicentre of this nonphysical, metaphysical or supernatural domain. Neither physics nor biology, medicine, psychology or any other branch of natural sciences can explain the nature of life, its spiritual dimension, its origin, the reason why we exist and the purpose of such existence.

Furthermore, the meaning and purpose of life, together with its origin, are all transcendental realities. That is why we can call them the utmost human goods. Those that only human beings can think of. No other species grasps or cares about the meaning of life or is trying to find meaning in life, but who can deny that we humans certainly do?

As I said before, Maslow understood that these highest spiritual goods and aspirations belong to the kind that transcend human rationality but are still reasonable themselves. Moreover, in his view, they are crucial in explaining the way we live and the way we pass away. They are the highest ideals and motives of the human conduct. Let's stop for a moment to reflect on Maslow's findings regarding these highest spiritual human goods, needs or "meta-needs".

Spiritual motivations in Maslow's latest enquiries

To be precise, Maslow does not talk of spiritual goods but of values of the spirit, the being values or B-Values ("B" for short). He calls them being values because they are the ultimate values which cannot be "reduced to anything more ultimate". For example, he says that, "it is certainly demonstrable that we need the truth and love it and seek it" (Maslow, 1971, p. 38).

Maslow lists around fourteen highest needs or B-Values, including the truth, beauty and goodness of the ancients, as well as justice, order, law, unity, perfection, simplicity, comprehensiveness, etc. He says, "I would go so far as to claim that these B-Values are the meaning of life for most people, but many people do not even recognise that they have these meta-needs" (Maslow, 1971, p. 43).

Maslow sees this realm as an integral part of his hierarchy of needs. He affirms that "basic needs and meta-needs are in the same hierarchical-integration, i.e., in the same continuum, in the same realm of discourse. They have the same basic characteristic of being 'needed' (necessary, good for the person) in the sense that their deprivation produces 'illness'" (Maslow, 1971, p. 312). In this case, it would be a spiritual illness.

In relation to the dynamism of this spiritual realm, he continues, saying that "the spiritual life (the contemplative, religious, philosophical, or value-life) is within the jurisdiction of human thought and is attainable in principle by man's own efforts. Even though it has been cast out of the realm of reality by the classical, value-free science that models itself upon physics, it can be reclaimed as an object of study and technology by humanistic science" (Maslow, 1971, p. 312).

In Maslow's view, these final values, or what I call here *spiritual goods*, are real and universal, in the sense that all human beings yearn for them. As he explains, "Can we, therefore, say that everyone yearns for the higher life, the spiritual, the B-Values, etc.? Here we run full-tilt into inadequacies in our language. Certainly, we can say in principle that such a yearning must be considered to be as a potential in every newborn baby until proven otherwise" (Maslow, 1971, p. 315, 316).

When reviewing Maslow's latest enquiries regarding the further reaches of human nature, one can see that he does not distinguish between the *ethical* and *spiritual* realms (see Figure 5.1). As I like to tell my students, I must admit that his position is somehow accurate because, strictly speaking, all moral good is spiritual.

Nevertheless, as I will try to explain later, it makes sense to make the distinction between the *ethical* or moral dimension (philosophical and value-life in Maslow's terminology) from a *higher spiritual* one (contemplative), which would refer to those motivations giving the highest meaning and purpose to human life. Such a distinction is totally compatible with Maslow's findings.

Being the psychologist he was, and not a philosopher, he did not make philosophical distinctions that would probably have been beyond his interest and his field of expertise. Nevertheless, it seems that he was able to intuitively distinguish the *ethical* realm from the *higher spiritual* one when describing what he called human meta-needs.

As he himself claimed, "as we go on up the hierarchy of basic needs, words like desiring, wishing, or preferring, choosing, wanting, become more appropriate. However, at the highest levels, i.e., of meta-motivation, all these words become subjectively inadequate, and such words as yearning for, devoted to, aspiring to, loving, adoring, admiring, worshiping, being drawn to or fascinated by, describe the meta-motivated feelings more accurately" (Maslow, 1971, p. 324).

Although Maslow has been quoted extensively here, the reason for doing so is to prove how explicit he was regarding this spiritual dimension. It seems clear that, even in the early 1970s, Maslow was years ahead of his academic colleagues in his understanding of human nature and human motivations. In his later work, he found that there is a *higher spiritual* realm that constitutes an essential element of the highest human motivations, what he called meta-motivations.

At that time, he was also able to envisage the negative social consequences of neglecting and even denying the existence of these highest ideals of the human spirit. He envisioned the frustration of so many young people due precisely to the dominant materialist conception of the world. At this point, I really like to provoke critical thinking in my students. Was Maslow right? Is it so bad that we have forgotten the *spiritual goods*, the higher human motivations? This is what he wrote:

> I believe that much of the social pathology of the affluent (already lower-need-gratified) is a consequence of intrinsic-value-starvation. To say it in another way: Much of the bad behavior of affluent, privileged, and basic-need-gratified high school and college students is due to the frustration of the "idealism" so often found in young people. My hypothesis is that this behavior can be a fusion of continued search for something to believe in, combined with anger at being disappointed. ...
> A total cultural determinism is still the official, orthodox doctrine of many of most of the sociologists and anthropologists. This doctrine

not only denies intrinsic higher motivations, but comes periously close sometimes to denying "human nature" itself.

(Maslow, 1971, p. 310)

. . . How could young people not be disappointed and disillusioned? What else could be the result of getting all the material and animal gratifications and then not being happy as they were led to expect, not only by the theorists, but also by the conventional wisdom of parents and teachers, and the insistent gray lies of the advertisers? . . . The end product of such surfeit conditions is that material values have come more and more to dominate the scene. In the result, man's thirst for values of the spirit has remained un-quenched. Thus, the civilization has reached a stage which virtually verges on disaster.

(Maslow, 1971, p. 311)

You can find these words a bit catastrophist, as some of my students do. Most of them acknowledge that the question of the absence of spiritual motivations had never been an issue for them until I raised the subject. A few of them also recognise that these statements left them quite thoughtful since for them, and in their personal experience, these forgotten *spiritual motivations* are very relevant in their lives. What do we mean by *spiritual motivations*? Does everybody understand the same thing when we refer to these issues?

Spiritual motivations' different conceptions

If in the middle of a seminar on human motivations you ask how many participants consider spirituality to be something that motivates people in their lives, many will raise their hand and answer yes. On the other hand, if the question is whether everyone understands the same thing when we talk about spirituality, this time the majority will answer no.

Can we find consensus on what spiritual motivations are? It is obvious that there are different interpretations of what we mean by spiritual issues and *spiritual motivations*, depending on the cultural origin of those answering the questions, among other things.

When we consider how this is interpreted in an academic setting, at an organisational level, some authors describe the idea of spirituality characterised as a private, inclusive, non-denominational and universal human feeling. They distinguish it from the adherence to the beliefs, rituals or practices of a specific organised religion (Karakas, 2010). Other researchers, however, include the existence of the divine, of a spiritual being or God as an integral part of spirituality, overlapping between spirituality and religion (Mitroff & Denton, 1999).

Currently, there is no academic consensus on what constitutes a religion (Nongbri, 2013). Therefore, and in order to offer a systematic explanation of this issue, I propose three different conceptions of spirituality, which I understand could be accepted by anyone. First, *non-religious spiritualities*; second, *religious spiritualities in a broad sense* and finally, *religious spiritualities in its narrowest sense*, referring to the three main monotheist religions in the world.

In particular, *non-religious spiritualities* would include every human experience centred on the search for a higher meaning in life, in a mindful way, but with no religious affiliation; no formal attachment to institutional structures, creeds, cults, sacred texts, etc. (Saucier & Skrzypińska, 2006). Therefore, this spirituality is the one for those who describe themselves as *atheists*, *agnostics* or just people who do not identify with any particular religion.

Moreover, the content of this *non-religious spirituality*, the search for meaning in life, is a universal spiritual good shared by all the other spiritualities. What is common to the spiritualities included in this group is their religious non-affiliation, an estimated 16% of world's population (Pew Research Center, 2017).

What distinguishes one from another within this group is that *atheists* do not believe in God; *agnostics* are neither atheists nor theists, but the existence of a deity is unknowable for them and non-religious people could be *atheists*, *agnostics* or *theists*. In each of the three cases, there is no affiliation with any religion.

In a theoretical sense, it is possible to distinguish this *non-religious spirituality* from others considered *religious*, but empirical evidence shows that the distinction is not always crystal clear. Daily life shows that there are cases where religion and spirituality intermingle, and it is difficult to separate them.

In fact, there are studies reflecting that even among the religiously unaffiliated groups, some people still hold some kind of religious beliefs. For example, various surveys have found that a belief in God or a higher power is shared by 7% of unaffiliated religious Chinese adults, 30% of unaffiliated religious French adults and 68% of unaffiliated religious Americans (Pew Research Center, 2012).

Nevertheless, this first *non-religious* concept, including *atheists*, *agnostics* and *non-affiliated* religious people conceive spirituality as a personal search for an inner path enabling the essence of our natural being to be discovered. This view is quite common today in many young students, spirituality referring to the search for a pathway towards a higher state of awareness, wisdom or perfection of one's own being and contributing to the development of the individual's inner life to achieve happiness, peace and joy.

These spiritual goods of non-religious concepts of spirituality are universal, in the sense that they are desired by all human beings, including religious people of all kinds. In other words, most human beings seek to achieve some kind of knowledge or practical wisdom capable of providing bliss, inner peace and joy.

Mindfulness, transcendental meditation and the search for positive mental health are practices contributing to this inner growth and peace without demanding a belief in God or any religious affiliation (Gotsis & Kortezi, 2008). This *spiritual good* normally comes from personal experience, but it might also come from the teachings of "wise" people where it has been passed on from generation to generation.

A good example of this non-religious view is the shaman tradition of some cultures. The shaman is the healer, the connector, and the spiritual leader or sensemaker. Intellectual shamans help people identify their own gifts and find pathways to using those gifts in the world, no matter what their occupation, civic activity, or interests (Waddock, 2014, 2017).

The second group of spiritualities, which I have named here as *religious spiritualities in a broad sense*, would include traditional religions such as Hinduism (15% of the world's population) or Buddhism (7% of the world's population). It would also include folk religions (5.9%), which are those closely tied to a particular people, ethnicity or tribe, including African traditional religions, Chinese folk religions, Native American religions, Australian aboriginal religions and East Asian Confucianism (Pew Research Center, 2017).

This group would also comprise followers of other religions that are often not measured separately in censuses and surveys, such as Shintoism, Sikhism, Taoism[2] and many others. Believe it or not, there are an estimated 10,000 distinct religions worldwide (Pew Research Center, 2017).

All these *religious spiritualities in a broad sense* reflect the universal human openness to an external reality that is greater than us, to the mysteries of the cosmos and to the unknown and enigmatic of the afterlife reality. Some of these religious traditions have faith in the existence of a divinity or divinities, others do not.

For example, a survey found that approximately 60% of Chinese people express a personal belief in the possible existence of one or more supernatural phenomena, religious figures or supernatural beings that are often associated with Confucianism and popular forms of Chinese folk religion (Pew Research Center, 2008).

All these *religious spiritualities in a broad sense* demand different degrees of faith that are normally higher than those of *non-religious spiritualities*. In fact, spirituality itself could be named as the realm of faith, precisely because it refers to the highest aspirations of the human spirit that belong to the mystery of the unknown, common to *religious* and *non-religious spiritualities*.

These universal spiritual aspirations are related to the origin and purpose of life and with issues like the existence of good and evil, the meaning of joy and suffering and of life and death in the world. These are questions that always remain a mystery and to which the different spiritualities and religions try to give an answer. It is in this sense in which I said that the degree of faith demanded by each spirituality is undoubtedly different, but they are also different in their origins.

In many cases, the origin of the religious faith can go back millennia, for example, mystic experiences from wise people, revelations of spirits, of deities, fables and myths or just ancient traditions that have been handed down from generation to generation. This handing down of ancient customs is the case for the Buddhist tradition, as well as for many Hinduists, Taoists, most Chinese traditional religions, Japanese Shinto, Serer religions in Africa and many polytheist religions all over the world (Pew Research Center, 2017).

Finally, the group of *religious spiritualities in its narrowest sense* would include the three main monotheist religions of Abrahamic origin: Christianity, Islam and Judaism. What these religions have in common with many of the previous religious traditions is that they conceive spirituality as a human dimension open to the sacred, to a divine realm (Pargament & Mahoney, 2002). Nevertheless, at the same time, what distinguishes them from previous religious spiritualities is their belief in one personal God, the Creator.

According to these traditions, God took the initiative to reach into humanity and revealed Himself to different prophets. With the prophet Abraham, He established a covenant, calling mankind into a personal relationship with Him. Actually, one of the classical meanings of the word religion (from the Latin *religare*) means precisely a relation, link or connection with someone, with a personal deity (Guillén et al., 2015).

Jews, Muslims and Christians all believe in one and the same "personal" God, who reveals Himself to mankind and who expects a relationship, a religion, a personal response from each one of His creatures. This is the reason why I labelled *religious spiritualities in its narrowest sense* to include the three Abrahamic monotheist religions.

The demographic study carried out in 2015 – based on an analysis of more than 2,500 censuses, surveys and population registers – found there were 14 million Jews (0.2% of the world's population), 1.8 billion Muslims (24%) and 2.3 billion Christians (31%) (Pew Research Center, 2017). Therefore, this group of *religious spiritualities in its narrowest sense*, believing in one personal God, comprises more than 55% of the world's population.

Within this concept, God is the answer to the spiritual goods universally desired by human beings and present in every spirituality, including happiness, peace and joy. In this tradition, they are conceived as gifts from God. Moreover, the highest spiritual good would be the capacity to be united to God Himself, to share His supernatural life, His goodness or holiness for the duration of human life on Earth and, ultimately, one day in Heaven.

As we will see in Chapter 6, the desire to correspond to God's gifts will give rise to a specific type of *spiritual motivation*, the *religious motivations*, for those having a personal relationship with God. In this chapter, we will focus on the *higher spiritual* realm and the *spiritual goods* and motivations that are common to every tradition.

After this review of the different *non-religious* and *religious spiritualities* (in its broader and narrower senses), it seems clear that every conception of spirituality is a manifestation of the existence of a *spiritual motivation*, a universal human longing for the transcendent *higher spiritual good*. It is undeniable that there is a common human eagerness to find meaning of life, in life and after life, one that the world of matter alone cannot give. Therefore, it is important that *spiritual motivations* receive the recognition and respect they deserve.

Spiritual motivations: Worthy of universal recognition and respect

I am fully aware that, today, it is politically incorrect to talk about issues such as religion and spirituality in many public settings, and the same is true in scientific and academic spaces. For this reason, it is perhaps a subject that excites many young students because they are "taboo" issues. Of course, not everyone who attends my sessions is always excited; in some cases, the reaction is one of oddness, dismay or indifference. Why should we mention religion and spirituality in business- and people-management classes?

My attitude to the different reactions of dealing with these spiritual matters in class is always the same. I explain that this spiritual realm is true for millions of people (as we saw in the previous section); it is a realm referring to the mystery and meaning of human life that is universal and that demands some sort of faith. Given that such faith influences human motivations and behaviour, we should not be afraid of addressing this in our people-management classes.

On the contrary, we should be able to understand them, speak of them and understand why they are worthy of esteem. This is why I tried to explain the different conceptions of spirituality in earlier paragraphs and the reason why I now want to insist on the importance of respecting other people's spiritual motivations.

Many times, if not always, the answer to these transcendental spiritual questions is what makes the difference regarding the meaning we human beings assign to our entire life and work. It is precisely because of this that human spirituality and human motivations are worthy of universal recognition and protection. In fact, this is such a relevant domain of human life that, after World War II, the United Nations' Universal Declaration of Human Rights (1948) included a statement to protect the freedom of thought, conscience and religion, in Article 18:

> *Everyone has the right to freedom of thought, conscience, and religion; this right includes freedom to change his religion or belief, and freedom, either alone or in community with others and in public or private, to manifest his religion or belief in teaching, practice, worship and observance.*

As I like telling my students, the UN declared these universal rights because they are common human goods, not the other way around. Their goodness

104 *Exploring the region of higher human motivations*

does not come from their declaration, but the declaration of this right is a confirmation and the fruit of the universal understanding of the goodness of spirituality and religion.

Therefore, the spiritual good is one of those universal human needs at the highest level, or, as Maslow would say, they are meta-needs. They constitute the "deepest values and meanings by which people live" (Sheldrake, 2007). They are sources of inspiration and orientation in human life. They reflect "the extent to which an individual is motivated to find sacred meaning and purpose to his or her existence" (Tepper, 2003).

It is therefore crucial to recognise spirituality as a legitimate category of human needs and desires and that it deserves an open area in an accurate description or *map of human motivations*. That is why we added the category of spiritual good to the top row of the motivational grid, in addition to the useful, pleasant and moral goods (Guillén et al., 2015). Notice that the four rows or levels of the new version of the map refer to the four basic anthropological dimensions or realms of human nature: the *physical*, the *psychological*, the *ethical* and now the *higher spiritual* (see Figure 5.2).

As we discussed in Chapter 3, using the example of pushing the brown bear, our free and rational behaviour may be explained thanks to the understanding and knowledge of the different dimensions of human nature. To complete the example we saw then, if you push someone who had climbed onto the table, they may not move for *physical, psychological, ethical* but also *higher spiritual* reasons for example, because they are pacifists, and in their conscience they prefer not to conflict with anyone (see Figure 5.2).

It reminds me that, sometimes, participants in my seminars will comment that they always thought talking about these issues would end up leading to conflict and disagreement, but in fact the opposite is true. When these questions can be spoken about openly, precisely because they are reasonable, this is when mutual respect and the recognition of the freedom of consciences can take place.

Another way to explain the existence of these four dimensions in a more positive manner is by reflecting on the different types of human joy. In this sense, I was asked to give a talk to a group of undergraduates from MIT, Harvard, Boston College and some other universities in Boston some years ago. The topic of the talk was "joy at work", and I took advantage of my reflections on the *map of motivations* and the different realms of human nature to talk about four different meanings of joy.

I spoke to them about *physical joy*, which we perceive when we are physically well; the sensible *psychological joy*, that pleasure of feeling good; the moral or *ethical joy*, that we have when we know we are doing the right thing and, finally, the *higher spiritual joy*, which refers to the highest and most lasting joy and is related to the conviction to live a life full of meaning, worth living and full of love (see Figure 5.2).

A year later, when returning to the US, I had the chance to see some of the students that attended that talk again. They still remembered the content of

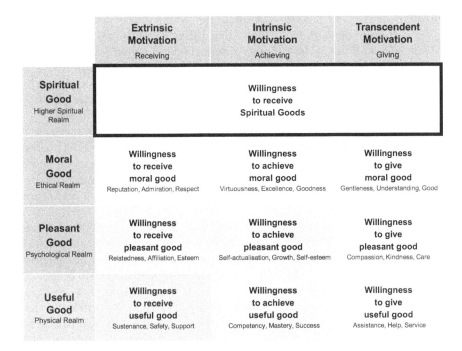

Figure 5.2 Mapping the territory of motivations: The spiritual motivations

the presentation. One of them told me that, being a religious person, it was that day when he profoundly understood the concept of spiritual joy for the first time. He found that his highest and most lasting joy was the result of considering God to be his Father who loved him madly and unconditionally. I told him that was quite a good example of what spiritual joy is all about.

Other students attending that talk told me that they were able to better distinguish the *physical*, *psychological*, *ethical* and *higher spiritual* realms in their own lives. Moreover, they loved the holistic view of human nature that this framework offered them (see Figure 5.2).

As we will discuss at the end of Chapter 7, this wider framework of motivations proposed here, while respecting and synthesising previous classifications, also provides an understanding of their diversity and interrelationship. My personal experience, after years explaining this *map of motivations*, proves that this proposal contributes to a more holistic understanding of human motivation by many people.

Moreover, it facilitates dialogue between different disciplines of human knowledge that have been fragmented in the academic world for centuries. As we saw in previous chapters, this framework is the result of the dialogue between psychologists, sociologists and philosophers. Now, we can also invite theologians to this conversation.

I recall a presentation of this map that I gave to a group of managers in Spain. When I finished the talk, one approached me, smiling, and said, "I'm an atheist and, believe it or not, I loved the framework you just presented". I was thankful and somehow surprised by the comment, so I asked him why he liked it. He answered, "Because your lecture helped me understand my own motivations and those of others, despite them being so different".

The recognition of the spiritual realm allows us to go beyond a narrow materialistic view of human nature. In an extremely competitive professional world, without time to stop, reflect, or meditate, it seems quite difficult to have a true inner spiritual life. With so much noise, pressure, and rush in today's world, spirituality and religion are almost a luxury for many.

Unfortunately, I don't think that, in modern times, many people have left spirituality because there has been an evolution or progression in our way of thinking, but rather because we have stopped thinking. It is not surprising that, in recent years, mindfulness and meditation practices are becoming ever more popular (Keng et al., 2011).

People are yearning for inner peace and joy of spirit, irrespective of a religious or non-religious context. As we will see next, the universal desires to receive, achieve and give *spiritual good* constitute the *extrinsic, intrinsic* and *transcendent spiritual motivations*. Let's now consider the particular case of the *extrinsic spiritual motivations*.

Extrinsic spiritual motivations: The willingness to receive spiritual good

I remember this young professional whose only thoughts were about success and earning money until he met a new friend, who was only twenty-two years old and who had already started an NGO and a social company. Thanks to the example of this person, he began to give a new purpose to his life and now wanted to spend it helping make the world better.

This is also the case of many students in my classes who admitted they were not environmentally aware. Thanks to the influence and advice of other classmates and friends, they now value the planet much more and connect much more spiritually with nature. Furthermore, many of my students have been able to find meaning in their lives and personal completion after meeting other friends who told them about their own experiences and set an example for them. This is something I have witnessed throughout my teaching career.

Using Maslow's own terminology, most human beings yearn for values of the spirit, such as *unity* and *simplicity*, and others related to *novelty* and *perfection*, such as *wholeness, fulfilment, uniqueness* or *completion* (Maslow, 1971). We could say that the desire to receive all these goods are examples of *extrinsic spiritual motivations* that practically every spiritual tradition, both *religious* and *non-religious*, would admit to being true.

Following the same logic that we applied in previous chapters to describe the different kinds of motivations, the *extrinsic spiritual motivations* can be defined as the willingness to receive spiritual good (see Figure 5.3). They refer to the human aspiration to obtain spiritual goods, such as life itself, practical wisdom, lasting happiness, peace and joy of spirit.

As Maslow would say, these "Being Values" are the highest values of the human spirit. In his own words, "I would go so far as to claim that these B-Values are the meaning of life for most people, but many people don't even recognize that they have these meta-needs" (Maslow, 1971, p. 43). These meta-needs, longings or highest ideals that all humans aim for could probably be summarised by the desire for the truth, beauty and goodness (the transcendentals) already described by ancient Greek philosophers, such as Parmenides, Socrates, Plato or Aristotle.

In our personal life, the discovery of *extrinsic spiritual motivations* (as some truth, beauty or goodness) could come from someone who taught us to have a nobler purpose in life. Questions about the ultimate meaning of human life demand a practical answer from every human being. Most people with the goodwill desire to reach the spiritual gift of *wisdom* and receive

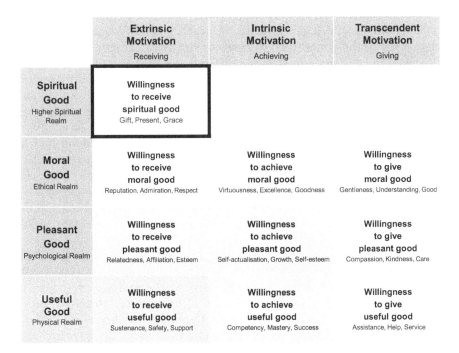

Figure 5.3 The extrinsic spiritual motivations

the appropriate *counsel* (both *spiritual goods*) succeed in the meaning they give to their lives (see Figure 5.3).

Wisdom and *counsel* to be able to judge and direct daily matters in accordance with our ideals and the truth of human nature, but also the gifts of *understanding, fortitude* and *knowledge* (three more *spiritual goods*), are necessary to get the strength of mind to do good and avoid evil in life. All these gifts of the spirit (wisdom, counsel, understanding, etc.) are longings or *extrinsic spiritual motivations* that can be found in non-religious and religious people (see Figure 5.3).

Of course, as I said before, they all request a certain kind of faith in the inner human capacity of spiritual development and growth and also a faith and trust in the different sources of those spiritual goods (oneself, other wise people, some religious traditions, such as the Hindu laws of karma, or God's revelation in the case of the main monotheist religions).

I recall attending a conference at the Harvard Divinity School. There, Bhutan's former Minister of Education was describing the way Buddhist spiritual motivations affect the way they care about the environment in his country. Given that they believe in reincarnation, they do not want to take the risk of hurting their reincarnated ancestors or families by treating nature poorly. Both the desire for a good reincarnation and the respect for reincarnated ancestors in nature would be spiritual goods or gifts of a Buddhist religious tradition, among others (see Figure 5.3).

Another illustration of *spiritual extrinsic motivations* that is shared by millions of human beings with religious beliefs is the willingness to receive eternal life or the desire to go to Heaven. Heaven, and what it represents, is conceived by many religions as a gift and a reward for a good life, one lived out of love for others and for those who believe in God, out of love for God. In the three Abrahamic traditions, Heaven is understood as the final union with God, the possession of God Himself, the truth, the good and the beauty, the highest human aspiration (see Figure 5.3).

It is important to underline that practically every spiritual good that is longed for by *non-religious* spiritualities is also an aspiration in most *religious* traditions. In the particular case of the three monotheistic religions, the origin of every spiritual gift is considered to be divine. In other words, all spiritual good comes from God, who shares it with human beings. Ultimately, when you are a believer, God is considered to be the giver of all material and spiritual gifts.

As we have seen, there are different examples of *extrinsic spiritual motivations*, depending on the tradition we observe. However, what is common to all of them is the openness to the realm of spirituality through different levels of faith and trust in their source. Moreover, once one accepts the existence of this spiritual domain, another two kinds of motivations can be displayed and defined on our map: the *intrinsic* and the *transcendent spiritual motivations*. Let's pay closer attention to the intrinsic ones.

Intrinsic spiritual motivations: The willingness to acquire spiritual good

The human longing for a deeper spiritual life demands a personal openness to the realms of the spirit beyond a materialistic view of human life and, again, some kind of faith on the existence of an intangible reality that human beings can access. Examples of these are those people who meditate to find inner peace or those religious people who pray to find a greater connection with God or to obtain the necessary strength to do good. We all yearn for an inner peace and joy of spirit that are normally fruits of a wisdom and personal spiritual growth whose origin is also spiritual.

It is interesting that both *non-religious* and *religious* spiritual traditions have this desire for inner peace and joy in common. This aspiration to access the *higher spiritual* realm constitutes *the intrinsic spiritual motivation*, the willingness to achieve *spiritual good*, to attain *spiritual* goodness, blessedness or *holiness* (see Figure 5.4).

However, such spiritual life and growth and all its fruits are only accessible when there is awareness of them and the desire to achieve them. This spiritual inner flourishing of the person would be the result of some specific practices, depending on the spiritual tradition considered. If we look at the two extremes of the continuum of spiritualities that I presented before,

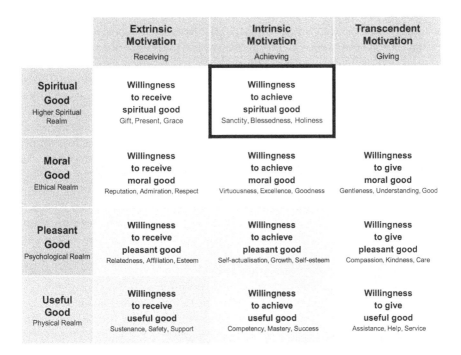

Figure 5.4 The intrinsic spiritual motivations

those who do not believe in God and those who believe in a personal one, the conception of spiritual growth varies.

For non-believers, spiritual growth is the result of higher levels of mindfulness, which leads to a deeper spiritual union with oneself, with others, the environment and the cosmos and to finding higher meaning in life. Learning to live in the present moment, appreciating its meaning and value, produces great joy, perhaps one of the clearest spiritual fruits of *intrinsic spiritual motivations*.

At the other end, for those who believe in a personal God, the spiritual growth and the finding of higher meaning in life are the results of a higher interior life of union with God, or of a higher love for God. The fruit in this case is then the perception of each present moment in life as a gift from a God who loves you. For those who have faith, this produces a kind of joy that only God can offer or, as Peter Kreeft described it, the most moving thing in life (Kreeft, 2004).

Unfortunately, as I said earlier, in an extremely competitive professional world without time to stop, reflect or meditate, it is quite difficult to maintain a spiritual interior life because this inevitably demands the necessary inner silence and quietness of the spirit; a tranquillity that is far from a reality in our modern society. Regrettably, today's hustle and bustle, hyperactivity and multitasking in personal and professional life make stress and anxiety commonplace.

For the past few years, I have been discussing the real case of a young manager named Vicente with my MBA students. As an executive in a large international company, Vicente[3] was having recurrent problems with stress and anxiety, which is nothing unusual in such settings, as I just said. He decided to ask for advice from one of his former MBA professors, a good friend of mine. It was clear that Vicente did not know how to say no to his boss and to the increasing demands of his job.

His intense eagerness to be successful, to get results for his superiors and to earn the appreciation of his subordinates, was destroying his health, his family and his social life. However, he was not entirely aware of what was going on, and he had no time for personal reflection or meditation.

Every time I discuss Vicente's case, many of my students feel as if I am talking about them. More so, some of them suggest that we should teach this case to their colleagues in their own companies because there are many Vicentes. As you may guess, we spend several intense sessions discussing how we could help him, or someone like him. The frenetic pace of life that we all usually experience has triggered the high levels of stress to which most professionals throughout the world succumb.

We live in the spotlight of never-ending deadlines and the excessive expectations of others. We spend more time thinking about the future than living in the present, and our minds are full of concern and noise. The inner world of the spirit and the spiritual motivation is drowned out by the many daily concerns.

People rarely stop to think about the big questions, about the meaning of life and work. As I mentioned, in light of this anxiety and "noise", mindfulness and meditation are becoming the modern tools with which to rediscover the spiritual realm and to achieve the spiritual goods of inner peace and joy. For those who believe in a personal God, the source of all spiritual good is God Himself and His divine Love (with a capital L). Therefore, in these cases, mindfulness would mean full awareness of God's presence, and meditation would mean a personal conversation with God.

In religious traditions, the holiest people are those who are more united with God, able to love with the Love of God Himself. In spiritual traditions that do not believe in God, the holiest people are those with a higher interior life, higher wisdom and higher goodness without reference to a divinity. In both cases, for believers and non-believers alike, a tangible manifestation of people's holiness is precisely their goodness, their capacity to do the good and their ability to transmit it to others.

As we will see next, the spiritual good seems to be contagious, exactly as happened with the moral good. This is what we will discuss next when describing *transcendent spiritual motivations*.

Transcendent spiritual motivations: The willingness to give spiritual good

Maslow makes very explicit references to the *higher spiritual* realm when describing transcenders, those motivated by the logic of self-giving. He states that they "speak easily, normally, naturally and unconsciously the language of Being (B-language), the language of poets, of mystics, of seers, of profoundly religious men, of men who live at the Platonic-idea level or at the Spinozistic level, under the aspect of eternity" (Maslow, 1971, p. 273).

As we discussed in Chapter 4, the universal self-transcendent quality of human beings was already described by the likes of Lersch (1938), Allport (1961) and Frankl (1966) and studied more recently by others (Cloninger, 2004). Moreover, Maslow himself devoted an important part of his posthumous book to explaining the concept of what he called the transcenders, those moved by the motivation of giving (Maslow, 1971).

Transcenders are not egotistic but the opposite. "Transcendence brings with it the 'transpersonal' loss of ego", he says and then states that "not only are such people lovable as are all of the most self-actualizing people, but they are also more awe-inspiring, more 'unearthly', more godlike, more 'saintly', in the medieval sense, more easily revered, more 'terrible' in the older sense. They have more often produced in me the thought, 'This is a great man' ". Moreover, "transcenders are in principle (I have no data) more apt to be profoundly 'religious' or 'spiritual' in either the theistic or nontheistic sense" (Maslow, 1971, p. 282).

The aspiration to share the goods and joys of the spiritual life with others is something that would be expected of people with more spiritual sensitivity, more "saintly" or "godlike" people, using Maslow's own words. It makes sense that people who are more holy have a stronger desire to transmit their inner peace to others and to promote that peace and joy to the entire world. Who could deny that this has been the case of holy notables, such as Mahatma Gandhi or Mother Teresa in India to give two well-known examples.

Transcendent spiritual motivation is the kind of motivation that consists of the willingness to give spiritual good to others. The existence of *transcendent spiritual motivation* is a fact that can be described and recognised. However, a quite different issue is the question of how often you find these saint-like people around your workplace (see Figure 5.4).

A good example of these *transcendent spiritual motivations* is seen today when a person suffers some adversity. For instance, I remember a time when I fell seriously ill, and my atheist friends wished me spiritual strength and positive karma. In fact, they sent me "positive energy" as a manifestation of their affection for me.

In the same situation, my Christian friends told me that they were praying for me, that they asked God to give me His strength and grace, which is also a kind of positive energy (what, in Christian tradition, is known as the communion of saints). Both attitudes, from believers and non-believers alike, are clear manifestations of my friends' *transcendent spiritual motivations*, their desire to bring me spiritual good.

As I noted before, people attending these sessions and students at the university are bemused that we talk about these issues on a business-management course or a seminar about motivations in organisations. I find it remarkable that we can talk about these human realities with total openness and respect.

Evidence of spiritual motivations

Unfortunately, I cannot give many examples of *spiritual motivations* coming from my own students as I did with the other kinds of motivations. I respect them and their privacy, so I do not ask them about their personal beliefs in public. Nevertheless, some students come to my office to ask for advice regarding their professional future. In order to help them to make better decisions, I normally ask them to use the *map of human motivations*. As a result, and after several years, I have been able to identify the most frequent spiritual motivations students have in mind.

In Figure 5.5, you can find some of the contents of students' own *maps of motivations*. I also include answers from some of the professionals who similarly ask me for advice. Among the *extrinsic spiritual motivations*, people usually mention their desires to learn from others' wisdom and find peace and joy at work, being able to connect with something greater than themselves. For people who believe in a personal God, motivations include finding God in their work, recognising His divine presence and seeing their work as a gift from Him and as a means of getting into Heaven.

	Extrinsic Motivation Receiving	**Intrinsic Motivation** Achieving	**Transcendent Motivation** Giving
Spiritual Good Higher Spiritual Realm	Willingness to receive spiritual good Gift, Present, Grace	Willingness to achieve spiritual good Sanctity, Blessedness, Holiness	**Willingness to give spiritual good** Sanctification, Salvation, Blessing
Moral Good Ethical Realm	Willingness to receive moral good Reputation, Admiration, Respect	Willingness to achieve moral good Virtuousness, Excellence, Goodness	Willingness to give moral good Gentleness, Understanding, Good
Pleasant Good Psychological Realm	Willingness to receive pleasant good Relatedness, Affiliation, Esteem	Willingness to achieve pleasant good Self-actualisation, Growth, Self-esteem	Willingness to give pleasant good Compassion, Kindness, Care
Useful Good Physical Realm	Willingness to receive useful good Sustenance, Safety, Support	Willingness to achieve useful good Competency, Mastery, Success	Willingness to give useful good Assistance, Help, Service

Figure 5.5 The transcendent spiritual motivations

The answers are very similar for *intrinsic spiritual motivations*, but this time people see their work itself as an opportunity to attain inner peace and joy while working, developing wisdom through their activities and being aware of being part of something greater than themselves. If they have faith in God, then they see their work as the place to unite themselves with Him, to show their love for God, sanctifying themselves and becoming holier through their work (see Figure 5.5).

Finally, when it comes to *transcendent spiritual motivations*, people see their roles as opportunities to bring wisdom, peace and joy to others – that they could contribute to something greater than themselves. For those with a more religious background, they find their work as an opportunity to pray for others and to help them find God and become holy (see Figure 5.5).

Some practical tips

These are all findings from my own experience as a mentor to many students and professionals over more than twenty-five years of teaching at the university. However, this goes beyond my own personal experience. It seems that in recent decades there has been a major transformation in organisations,

	Extrinsic Motivation Receiving	Intrinsic Motivation Achieving	Transcendent Motivation Giving
Spiritual Good Higher Spiritual Realm	- Finding God at work - Finding wisdom at work - Finding peace and joy at work - Seeing work as a path to Heaven - Connecting with something greater - Having the presence of God at work	- Developing wisdom at work - Being part of something greater - Uniting myself with God at work - Achieving peace and joy at work - Becoming holy while working well	- Bringing wisdom at work - Praying for others at work - Helping others to become holy - Bringing peace and joy at work - Contributing to something greater
Moral Good Ethical Realm			
Pleasant Good Psychological Realm			
Useful Good Physical Realm			

Figure 5.6 Examples of spiritual motivations

making room for the spiritual dimension, searching for meaning, purpose and a sense of community (Ashmos & Duchon, 2000).

Some researchers understand spirituality as a form of "spiritual intelligence" that gives a distinct capacity for transcendence; the ability to enter into heightened spiritual states of consciousness; the skill to invest everyday activities, events and relationships with a sense of the sacred; the aptitude to utilise spiritual resources to solve problems in life and the talent to engage in virtuous behaviours (to show forgiveness, to express gratitude, to be humble, to display compassion) (Emmons, 2000).

In regard to examples of the implication of spirituality in organisational leadership, Margaret Benefiel describes "the profound role that awareness of soul, or spirituality, can play in leadership and organization life" (Benefiel, 2005, p. 9). Her research presents several cases of managers whose priority is the growth and development of their employees by looking for the right thing to do, considering the effects of their decisions on people.

There are other recent studies, and a growing acknowledgement among scholars, that show how mindfulness promotes more ethical behaviours in organisations by improving the levels of people's awareness. This also serves as support for the development of moral virtues (Guillén & Fontrodona, 2018).

As Harvard professor Ellen Langer once said, "true well-being does not consist of going through life on autopilot, but being aware and present moment to moment to truly experience your life as it unfolds". Today's unbridled stress in the workplace is leading to a drastic reduction in our ability to pay attention to what is happening around us. Consequently, it lowers our sensitivity to do well and to do good (Guillén & Fontrodona, 2018).

Therefore, it is necessary (1) *to be aware of and pay attention to the environment in which we act and to be in constant connection with our values, the things we consider as really good*. By doing so, we will avoid acting automatically, or we will retain a reflective attitude when faced with behaviours or demands that we might otherwise simply accept because we are asked to act in that way or because "everyone is doing it" (Guillén & Fontrodona, 2018).

In today's workplaces, we get a lot of demands and requests. These are goals and values that, while useful in the business world, may not be best suited to our personal flourishing and spiritual growth. In this context, (2) *mindfulness – among others – may be useful as a tool to help us protect our inner world and to achieve greater awareness*. It will allow us to live in the present moment with greater attention to our actions (Guillén & Fontrodona, 2018). Even more, awareness of God's presence in every circumstance, meditation and prayer (for people with a faith in God), are also among the most powerful means of contributing to our moral and spiritual growth.

Finally, in a world of continuous technological innovation, the speed of our communications and the number of our connections grows exponentially. Moreover, the use of technology also contributes to increasing the immediacy of our expectations. We want to attain everything right here and now. All these factors contribute to the levels of stress, anxiety and hyperactivity we feel today, with the consequent loss of serenity and inner peace.

In this context, (3) *mindfulness and meditation (understood either as a technique or, for others, as a way of prayer) may improve the level of awareness of our surroundings, as it lets us connect to what is happening in an open manner* (Guillén & Fontrodona, 2018).

This is largely what *spiritual motivations* can do for us, according to recent studies. Nevertheless, and as far as I know, there is not much empirical evidence regarding the importance or effects of having spiritual and religious motivations at work, and its connection with physical, mental, moral and spiritual health. Maybe frameworks like that proposed here will help these studies to be more in depth in the future.

Undoubtedly, all the spiritual means we discussed here can help us perceive new dimensions in the situations around us. Moreover, spiritual mindfulness and awareness allow us to attain higher levels of empathy and compassion towards the people around us. When there is mindfulness and its resultant inner peace, each human experience becomes new, and we can forge deeper and more authentic connections with others, with something greater than us and also with God for believers.

Of course, each person will have different spiritual motivations because human beings are free to determine the reasons for their choices. Actually, and as I have insisted several times in this chapter, the *higher spiritual* realm is, in fact, the most human – the one that no other species can reach. Spiritual motivations are the highest kinds of motives of human conduct, the highest ideals and aspirations in life. The question then is, how often are we conscious of these spiritual drivers in our daily work and lives? To think about it, here are some questions that might help you find that out.

Some questions for reflection

1 *How often do I feel a lack of peace and joy in my life and my work?*
2 *How often do I sense a lack of serenity and balance in my life and work?*
3 *How often do I see my ordinary life as an opportunity to find peace and joy?*
4 *How often do I see my ordinary work as an opportunity to cultivate wisdom?*
5 *How often do I see my work as a contribution to something greater than me?*
6 *How often do I see my ordinary life as an occasion to grow in holiness?*
7 *How often do I pray for others in my daily life and my work?*
8 *How often do I seek God in my daily life and my work?*
9 *How often do I realise that I am in the presence of God during the day?*
10 *How often do I see my life in connection with something greater than me?*

A final critical thought on why the map is not yet accurate enough

As I mentioned right at the beginning of this chapter, the reason I decided to study the spiritual motivations was from the suggestion of a Spanish MBA student at the Harvard-RCC presentation. With genuineness, courage, and audacity, he made me realise that I was missing a group of motivations that are present in the lives of millions of human beings – the *spiritual* and *religious* ones.

Owing to the comments from this student, I spent a year studying, reflecting and in discussion with the two co-authors of the article (Guillén et al., 2015) that gave rise to the book you are now reading. During that year, we came up with the upper part of the grid comprising the group of *spiritual motivations* that we have discussed in this chapter. Nevertheless, the study of the different kinds of spiritualities, and the distinction between those *non-religious* and *religious* traditions, led us to the conclusion that we were still missing a group of motivations that were not included on the upper part of the map: the *religious motivations*.

It seems that the MBA student was right when he suggested that he was missing *spiritual* and *religious* motivations in the *map of motivations*. The distinction of both kinds of motivations (spiritual and religious), shows that for those spiritualities without God, there is no such thing as a personal relationship with Him; therefore, *religious motivations* would not make sense. This explains why people who do not believe in God would see no need to expand our map. The only reason that would justify expanding it would be to be able to understand the motivations of those who believe in God, which is why I wrote the following chapter.

If you are among those who do not believe in God, you can always skip Chapter 6 and go straight to Chapter 7. If you are curious, you can always go back. Nevertheless, I recall the fact that everyone attending the presentation of this *humanistic map of human motivations* liked it in its entirety. They found it useful and relevant. Moreover, those attending the sessions who consider themselves *atheists* and *agnostics* also valued the entire framework.

As I noted before, they kept saying that the explanation helped them understand everybody's motivations better. Ultimately, the existence of people with and without *religious* motivations is an outstanding manifestation of human freedom, and *religious motivations* as well as the *moral* and *spiritual* ones, are exclusively human.

Notes

1 These annual colloquiums, organised since 2013 by the Institute for Ethics in Communication and Organizations (IECO) and the Real Colegio Complutense (RCC) at Harvard University, bring together leading scholars and practitioners to shed light on what it takes to promote a workplace environment that brings out the best in people, creating not only trust but also organisations that thrive. On 3 April 2014, the second IECO-RCC International Colloquium addressed the topic "The role of moral and spiritual motivation in building trust in organizations". View the recordings of the event here: www.youtube.com/playlist?list=PL2SOU6 wwxB0splsmVkHIHWr2N0grP5M-j
2 To be more precise, Taoism and Confucianism arose as philosophical worldviews and ways of life. Unlike Confucianism, however, Taoism eventually developed into a self-conscious religion with an organised doctrine, cultic practices, and institutional leadership (see Encyclopedia Britannica, voices Taoism and Confucianism).
3 Vicente's Outcome. IPADE Business School Case. FE 08 eC 03. R – April, 2012.

References

Allport, G. W. (1961). *Pattern and Growth in Personality*. New York: Holt, Rinehart & Winston.
Ashmos, D. P. & Duchon, D. (2000). Spirituality at work: A conceptualization and measure. *Journal of Management Inquiry*, 9, 134–145.

Benefiel, M. (2005). *Soul at Work: Spiritual Leadership in Organizations*. New York: Seabury Books.

Cloninger, C. R. (2004). *Feeling Good: The Science of Well-Being*. New York: Oxford University Press.

Emmons, R. A. (2000). Is spirituality an intelligence? Motivation, cognition, and the psychology of ultimate concern. *The International Journal for the Psychology of Religion*, 10(1), 3–26.

Frankl, V. (1959). *Man's Search for Meaning*. Boston: Beacon Press.

Frankl, V. (1966). Self-transcendence as a human phenomenon. *Journal of Humanistic Psychology*, 6, 97–106.

Gotsis, G. & Kortezi, Z. (2008). Philosophical foundations of workplace spirituality: A critical approach. *Journal of Business Ethics*, 78, 575–600.

Guillén, M., Ferrero, I. & Hoffman, W. (2015). The neglected ethical and spiritual motivations in the workplace. *Journal of Business Ethics*, 128(4), 803–816.

Guillén, J. & Fontrodona, J. (2018). Mindfulness and its impact on ethical behavior in companies. In *Personal Flourishing in Organizations*. Cham, Switzerland: Springer, pp. 121–140.

Karakas, F. (2010). Spirituality and performance in organizations: A literature review. *Journal of Business Ethics*, 94, 89–106.

Keng, S., Smoski, M. J. & Robins, C. J. (2011). Effects of mindfulness on psychological health: A review of empirical studies. *Clinical Psychology Review*, 31(6), 1041–1056.

Kreeft, P. (2004). *The God who Loves You: Love Divine, All Loves Excelling*. San Francisco: Ignatius Press.

Lersch, P. (1938). *Aufbau der person*. München: Barth. (in German).

Maslow, A. H. (1971). *The Farther Reaches of Human Nature*, Ed. Arkana. New York: Penguin Books.

Mitroff, I. & Denton, E. A. (1999). A study of spirituality in the workplace. *Sloan Management Review*, 40(4), 83–94.

Nongbri, B. (2013). *Before Religion: A History of a Modern Concept*. New Haven and London: Yale University Press.

Pargament, K. I. (2013). Spirituality as an irreducible human motivation and process. *The International Journal for the Psychology of Religion*, 23(4), 271–281.

Pargament, K. L. & Mahoney, A. (2002). Spirituality: Discovering and conserving the sacred. In R. A. Giacalone & C. L. Jurkiewicz (Eds.), *Handbook of Workplace Spirituality and Organizational Performance*. Armonk, NY: M.E. Sharpe, pp. 646–659.

Petchsawang, P. & Duchon, D. (2012). Workplace spirituality, meditation, and work performance. *Journal of Management, Spirituality & Religion*, 9(2), 189–208.

Pew Research Center. (2008). Chinese believers in supernatural. 3 August 2008. www.pewforum.org/2012/12/18/global-religious-landscape-exec/#ftn6.

Pew Research Center. (2012). The global religious landscape. *Religion & Public Life*, 18 December 2012. www.pewforum.org/2012/12/18/global-religious-landscape-exec/#ftn6.

Pew Research Center. (2017). The changing global religious landscape. *Religion & Public Life*, 5 April 2017. www.pewforum.org/2017/04/05/the-changing-global-religious-landscape/.

Saucier, G. & Skrzypińska, K. (2006). Spiritual but not religious? Evidence for two independent dispositions. *Journal of Personality* (5), 1257–1292.

Sheldrake, P. (2007). *A Brief History of Spirituality*. Oxford, UK: Wiley-Blackwell.
Tepper, B. J. (2003). Organizational citizenship behavior and the spiritual employee. In R. A. Giacalone & C. L. Jurkiewicz (Eds.), *Handbook of Workplace Spirituality and Organizational Performance*. Armonk, NY: M.E. Sharpe, pp. 181–190.
Waddock, S. (2014). *Intellectual Shamans: Management Academics Making a Difference*. Cambridge, UK: Cambridge University Press.
Waddook, S. (2017). *Healing the World: Today's Shamans as Difference Makers*. New York, NY: Greenleaf Publishing/Routledge.

6 The *religious motivations*
Human longing for God's Love

Religious motivations: **A human reality**

I remember the first time I attended the global gathering of some leaders from the International Association for Humanistic Management (IHMA) at Fordham University in New York City after becoming part of this initiative a few months earlier. The purpose of this association is to promote human-centred organising practices, oriented towards flourishing and enhancing human well-being.[1]

One of the working sessions of this meeting involved producing a map that identifies the antecedents and consequences of a humanistic vision of management. In that session, I mentioned the role of spirituality and religion as a key element of a humanistic vision, and one person in the group, who introduced herself as an *atheist* at the time, did not initially like my comment. She argued that the humanistic approach should not be religious or confessional. This comment led to a very heated debate between the two of us on the subject of humanism and religion.

Of course, the humanistic approach cannot be religious or confessional, and in this I agreed with her, but I also insisted that humanism should not oppose the contributions of spirituality and religion. If humanism were opposed to religion, then it would cease to be humanistic because, since the beginning of human history, nothing has been more characteristic of the human race than its spiritual condition and religious practice. No other being in this world is capable of religious practices, something that demands an intellect to believe that which is "unbelievable" and the free will to access that which is "inaccessible".

My argument was that a humanistic management approach should not be confessional or ascribed to any particular religion, but neither should it oppose any reasonable contribution coming from religion and *theology* (from the Greek *Theos Logos*), the area of human knowledge studying God. In other words, humanism cannot be exclusive to *non-religious* people. A truly humanistic approach should be *inclusive*, consider everyone, believers and non-believers, the *religious* and *non-religious* alike.

It was clear that, from a humanistic perspective, it would not make any sense to impose any specific religion. That would lack respect for freedom and human dignity and therefore be inhumane. For the same reason, denying the existence of religion as part of human reality and its impact on human behaviour would also be a tremendous mistake and a lack of respect. Fortunately, we all agreed on this point.

Furthermore, the person with whom I initially had that disagreement ended up welcoming my suggestion to be more *inclusive*. We became good friends that day, and since then she has been the person within the IHMA who has helped me the most in promoting dialogue between believers and non-believers.

Perhaps you are religious or not, or maybe you don't know. In any case, this chapter, as with the book itself, is presented as a dialogue but now between religious and non-religious. For that reason, I strongly recommend keeping an open mind to reflect on this explanation with me so that we can jointly reach an inclusive vision of human motivations.

This entire chapter owes a great deal to this person[2] and will focus on explaining how religion is an integral part of human reality and the motivations for many millions of people. What do we mean by religious motivation, though? Did Maslow study this kind of motivation?

Religious motivations: A personal relationship with God

As we saw in Chapter 5, religious spiritualities in a broad sense comprise traditions such as Hinduism, Buddhism, Taoism, and many other traditional, native and aboriginal religions. They all believe in the universal human openness to an external reality that is greater than us. Nevertheless, even though many of them have faith in the existence of a divinity or divinities, when there is a god, it is usually an impersonal one. For example, in Buddhism, there is no god spoken of at all. In classical Hinduism, there is a god that is an impersonal cosmic consciousness rather than an individual loving person with intellect and will (Kreeft, 2004).

The study of comparative religions shows that the three Abrahamic traditions (Judaism, Christianity and Islam), unlike most other religious spiritualities, believe in one personal God, who revealed Himself in a historical moment to the Jewish people, establishing a bond, a covenant, with them. This personal relationship of mankind with God (*religare*) is what I have called "religion" or "religious spirituality" in its narrowest sense (Guillén et al., 2015).

This entire chapter will focus on the *religious motivations* related to the personal relationship with God that is typical of monotheistic religious traditions, and belonging to any believer in the existence of one personal God who created man out of divine Love. This is why I subtitled this chapter *Human longing for God's Love*.

Non-religious spiritualities share a commonality with religious spiritualities in that they consider *spiritual goods* intangible; things such as wisdom, peace and joy are immaterial. They are universal spiritual values or human aspirations that are shared by *non-religious* and *religious* spiritualities that could belong either to the natural *ethical* realm or to a *higher spiritual* one. Nevertheless, for those who believe in God, in a personal God, it is still possible to talk about another kind of motivation: the *religious motivation*.

What I argue in this chapter is that *religious motivations* are one of the most common manifestations of the universal human longing for Love. But, while this longing for Love seems to be universal, it is also true that not everybody believes in the existence of a God who is Love, a God that, for believers, is the answer to that universal yearning for Love, an idea that St Augustine graphically expressed in his famous sentence, "Because you have made us for Yourself, and our hearts are restless till they find their rest in Thee" (Augustine, 1961, n. 1).

The truth is that half of the world's population believes in this God and the other half does not, which is likely also the case for my students. Maslow accepted the idea of *spiritual motivations* as well as the *religious*, but was he a believer?

We can say for certain that Maslow included religion among "the spiritual life (the contemplative, religious, philosophical, or value-life)" that, for him, "is within the jurisdiction of human thought and is attainable in principle by man's own efforts" (Maslow, 1971, p. 312). However, what I describe here as *religious motivations*, Maslow would have included just among the realm of *spiritual motivations*, without distinguishing between *religious* or *non-religious*, believers and non-believers in God.

As Maslow himself recognised in his posthumous book, he abandoned his religious faith when he was young. "The form of religion that was offered to me as a child seemed so ludicrous that I abandoned all interest in religion and experienced no desire to 'find God'. Yet my religious friends, at least those who had gotten beyond the peasants' view of God as having a skin and beard, talk about God the way I talk about B-Values. The questions that theologians consider of prime importance nowadays are questions such as the meaning of the universe, and whether or not the universe has a direction. The search for perfection, the discovery of adherence to values is the essence of the religious tradition" (Maslow, 1971, p. 187).

As we can see, Maslow would not deny the existence of a *religious motivation*, but most probably for him it would be just another kind of *spiritual motivation*. In some sense, this is actually true. While not all *spiritual motivations* are religious, because there are millions of people who believe in spirituality but not in God, each *religious motivation*, understood as that of a personal relationship with God, is of a spiritual nature. *Religious motivations* are therefore a kind of *spiritual motivation* that explicitly recognise the existence of one personal God who revealed Himself to man, as the Creator of Heaven and Earth.

It seems that Maslow did not have these *religious motivations* himself. His personal view of the world, at the end of his life, was markedly Taoist, as much of his latest book reflects. He had faith, but not in God. There is no doubt that even a Taoist *religious spirituality* requires a kind of naturalist nontheistic faith. When things cannot be explained, then you trust fate. As he himself argued, faith then consists of a "willing and eager surrender, or yielding to fate and happily embracing it at the same time" (Maslow, 1971, p. 293).

Faith is believing in a kind of truth that surpasses human reason but is not irrational. The deepest human questions, related to the meaning of life, are a source of personal motivation, and they all belong to the realm of faith. For instance, it is not irrational to believe that one day we will see our deceased beloved ones again. This is a longing shared by millions of human beings, but it is also a mystery that can be true or false, a matter of faith.

There must be a truth about all the *spiritual goods* that are yearned by the human spirit, even for those coming from above, belonging to the mysterious *higher spiritual* realm, one that, for believers, has a divine content, a supernatural meaning. If these spiritual longings affect man's deepest motivations, it is because people believe them to be true. For believers, they are not mere dreams or the creations of children, fruits of human imagination or sentimentality. If that were the case, they would not become sources of the highest meaning in life, as they are for millions of people.

As we discussed in Chapter 5, the domain of faith is related to the things that are unknown, the mysteries of human life, and this realm is reasonable. Faith is not irrational, it is *suprarational* in the sense that the objects of faith, the realm of *spiritual goods*, exceed the human capacity for understanding, and accessing these mysteries involves taking a leap of faith, of accepting as true what cannot be demonstrated.

This is why we added this dimension to our *map of motivations* and why the declaration of human rights insists on the importance of respecting freedom of belief and religious freedom. Furthermore, this is also why the dialogue between faith and reason, as well as among all religions, is key.

There are spiritualities that believe in God and spiritualities that do not. Without entering into any theological debate, which is not the purpose of this book, religions that believe in God are clearly different from those that do not. Of course, most human beings would agree that there are *spiritual goods*, but not all would agree that these goods or gifts come from God, a divine Giver and Lover.

I remember a student who told me that he was spiritual but not religious. He told me that he believed in the spiritual soul, to which I replied that that soul must have a spiritual origin, a spiritual donor, and that donor is the one that even philosophers describe as God. This student said that this was one of the most compelling arguments he had ever heard for the existence of God, something I had never thought of myself. In the end, this student was more religious than he thought.

In other words, for believers, there are *spiritual goods* whose origin and nature are *divine*, they are *supernatural* goods coming from God (like the human soul and other divine graces or gifts), whereas, for non-believers, the spiritual goods would belong to a natural order, one of the highest moral value but not *divine* or *supernatural*. We might all accept that we are "spiritual" beings, but we do not all agree that we can also be "divine" beings, sharing God's supernatural spiritual life and Love, as monotheist religions do.

As Professor Peter Kreeft says, we "moderns" tend to feel that it is "narrow-minded" to claim that one religion must be wrong and another right, even if the two contradict each other. However, if two religions say the opposite regarding, for example, the existence of God and its nature, only one can be true. In other words, if God exists and is Love, not all religions are the same because not all religions defend this position (Kreeft, 2004).

To sum up, it makes sense to talk about the *spiritual motivations* because the majority of human beings believe in the spiritual dimension of human nature. However, it also makes sense to talk about *religious motivations* as a specific kind of *spiritual motivations* for those who believe in a higher spiritual being, a God capable of having a personal, loving relationship with mankind, which is the case of the three main monotheist religions. Let us stop now to reflect for a moment on these *religious motivations* and their place in our *map of motivations*.

Religious motivations: Discovering God's Love

I normally do not talk about Maslow's own spiritual motivations, as I just did in the previous section. Nor do I talk about my personal beliefs. However, it is also true that once I present the entire *map of motivations* in classes and seminars, it is not uncommon for one or more students or participants to approach me and ask about my own religious beliefs.

I have no problem answering people's direct questions about my own religious background. I am a Catholic, a Christian who believes in a God who is Love (1 John 4:8), but I do not normally mention this during my presentations out of respect for others. Nevertheless, now that I am writing this book, I think that sharing my own theological background and my religious personal experience is the most honest thing to do.

It is up to each believer in God, as well as each non-believer, to seek the final truth about God. In this sense, I want to emphasise that this book is not just about Christian motivations or any other specific *religious motivations* but is an inclusive view of all human motivations. I will therefore leave theological discussions to experts in theology and comparative religions.

In regard to the purpose of this book, in this chapter I will focus my interest on what is common to Muslims, Christians and Jews: the belief in the same one God and the human capacity to have a personal, loving relationship with Him, a relationship (of a religious nature) that, as we will see throughout this chapter, leads to the desire to serve, please, adore and praise Him.

To non-believers, this type of motivation may no doubt sound strange, or at least unfamiliar and distant. If only out of curiosity, I suggest non-believers and believers continue to read this chapter with a sincere positive critical spirit. As the "logic of love" is something universal, perhaps the use of this logic can help give non-believers and believers of different religions a better understanding of human religious motivations.

I found the findings of a recent comparative study about the three monotheist religions fascinating.[3] The authors explain that Judaism, Christianity, and Islam acknowledge Abraham as a common father and Moses as a genuine transmitter of their moral laws and values to their own prophetic traditions. The three faiths agree on specific laws initially provided to Noah by God – the Noahide Code – which include the belief in One Creator (God) and respect and reverence for Him by not blaspheming His name (Cowen, 2013).

It is promising that some Jewish, Christian, and Muslim leaders sought to find common ground in monotheists' moral, spiritual and religious goods. It is clear that at the heart of the commonality shared by the Abrahamic faiths is the idea of monotheism and of a God who took the initiative, out of Love, to reveal Himself to mankind. What I find really interesting here, however, is the dialogue among believers that share the same *religious motivations*.

As I mentioned in the previous section, it was my *atheist* friend at the IHMA who most helped me understand the importance of dialogue between believers and non-believers but also between believers in the same God. Only through sincere dialogue can we understand other people's motivations, even those we ourselves do not have. For this reason, I would like to continue this dialogue between psychologist, sociologist, philosopher and also theologian using a common language and a common rationality: the language of human love, or what I will keep calling from now on the "logic of love".

My personal experience for years has always been the same. The best way to explain *religious motivations*, even to those who do not believe in God, is through this logic of love, which I believe to be the main driver of all human motivations, as I will discuss in more depth in Chapter 7. I explain that *religious motivation* consists of the human correspondence to the Love of God, for those who believe in Him. Because this occurs within a personal relationship, the deepest source of this motivation comes from the personal discovery of God's Love for each person.

Of course, it is always possible to find people who claim to be religious but whose motivations are not out of love for God. Among other reasons, people can practice religion out of cultural or social customs, to look good in front of others, out of routine, duty or even out of fear of God, but not out of love for Him. If that were the case, when the response to God's Love is missing, something is wrong with those *religious motivations*.

It is true that not everyone understands *religious motivations* as a response to God's Love, not even all religious people. This is why it is so relevant to define the meaning of *religious motivations*. Strictly speaking, looking good, routine, fear, etc. do not seem to be genuine *religious motivations*. In fact, they don't sound very religious, pious, devoted, holy or even spiritual. They seem to be some other type of motivation, some of which we have seen before on our *map*. It seems clear, though, that they do not correspond to the Love of God that I describe here as *religious motivations*.

That God is Love is a distinctively monotheist biblical concept, which is missing in most other religions (Kreeft, 2004). Therefore, this is a conception of the three main monotheist religions. What I defend here is that the concept of *religious motivation* takes on its full meaning when understood as the loving personal response of mankind to the Love of its Creator.

Anyone who has been in love, and has had this love reciprocated, knows what it means to discover that someone loves you. This may not sound like a very academic argument, but there is nothing as real as human love. Who can deny that love is a source of motivation, indeed, *the* source of motivation? Love is the kind of motivation that gives meaning to human life. When you discover that someone truly loves you, a person that only cares about your good, it is unlikely that you will remain indifferent.

Just think about the millions of novels, poems and song lyrics describing human love. When someone loves you, that person wants all kinds of good for you, wants you to be the happiest person in the world. When a believer trusts in God's own revelation and discovers that God truly loves each person infinitely and unconditionally, that person can only reach the conclusion that God wants the best for each one of us.

God creates each human being out of Love. God is convinced that the world has become a special place because each person exists. A believer is convinced that God said, "How good it is that you exist", and He made it happen. He created me. This is what believers accept to be true; not just a philosophical truth, but the truth revealed by God Himself.

There are philosophers who sustain that God is a human creation, as is the case for Nietzsche, but the majority agree the opposite to be true, that humans are a creation of God. What believers believe is that it was God's initiative to create mankind and to reveal Himself to man, something that most philosophers and theologians can only verify but not prove. In other words, it is not irrational to believe that if God is omnipotent, the Almighty, He alone could create each person out of Love, and with the desire to be freely loved back by his creatures.

Again, all this remains a mystery, a matter of faith, and for those who have faith, the discovery of God's personal Love for them is what explains *religious motivations* in their deepest sense. The desire of the human heart to reciprocate the incredible Love of God for each person. This is how the logic of love operates in the minds of believers – paying for love with love.

This is why *religious motivation* makes sense to millions of human beings. It is a motivation that consists of a voluntary desire to return all good to God, who most believers conceive as Goodness Himself, a conception that conforms to the deepest philosophical definition of God as Truth, Beauty and Good (with capital letters). The *religious motivation* would then consist of the deep desire to return all love to Him who is understood as Love Himself.

I am not talking about love in a purely poetic sense – and much less, an erotic sense – as modern society does most of the time. Here, I am talking about love in its deepest and most philosophical sense. The desire for the good of the beloved one (well wishing). This is what the logic of love is about. It is a logic that, because it is universal, might allow a fruitful dialogue between believers and non-believers, as we shall see in the next section.

Religious motivations: It is all about love

I would like to show part of an email that I received recently from my atheist friend. I think its content reflects the logic of love that I have just spoken about very well. The subject of the email was, "love is the key", and in the message my friend wrote, "Hi – I just was asked a question – what do you do every day that makes you unique. I had no problem answering. I try to love. Love myself. Love my family. Love my friends and love everyone I come into contact with. Everything I do is about promoting love. Stopping bullying, it is about love. Humanistic management? It's about love. Teaching people humanistic philosophy – it's about love. Everything – is about love. It's my core motivation for everything".

She continued, "I feel like I've had an epiphany and you were the only person – aside from my husband and son and mother and sister – who I felt would really understand, so I wanted to share it with you. I hope you are doing well and that we can chat soon".

The last part of the message, that I'm not copying here, was about the way she had decided to change her professional life. Her epiphany drove her to a personal and professional conversion. Of course, I couldn't wait to reply to her and thank her for sharing her personal discovery about love being the centrepiece of her motivations. I told her that I fully agreed with her.

Who was going to say to my atheist friend that she had reached the same conclusion as Saint John of the Cross, one of the greatest theologians, saints and mystics of the Christian tradition? Saint John once wrote that "in the twilight of our lives, we will be judged on how we have loved". It sounds comforting to me to know that when we die, we will not be judged on our accomplishments, our fame or our triumphs, only on what we have loved.

128 *Exploring the region of higher human motivations*

Yes, my friend was right; I really understood her. What's more is that I think we understood each other, and very well. With that email, she summarised the entire map of human motivations that I have been trying to explain in this book. As we saw in previous chapters, human actions are always purposeful; they have an aim, a goal, an intention or motive. We act because we want to achieve something good, and since the desire for good is the simplest definition of love, we can say that what usually drives us to act is love.

We search for the things we love, those we consider good. Therefore, all human motivations are summed up in one: the desire for good or, what is the same, love. To be motivated in our lives in general, and specifically in organisations, we need to make sure that we receive, achieve, give and return love. This logic of love is always what is behind our motivations (see Figure 6.1).

As Figure 6.1 shows, and in line with what my friend wrote, love summarises all human motivations. What this map means is that the driver for every single human behaviour is the desire to either be loved by others, love ourselves, love others or, for those who believe in God, to love God back. The map can be abbreviated to one single and simple idea: that we are driven to act by the things we love.

Therefore, the more we love and feel loved, the greater our motivations will be at work and in our lives. This is exactly the "epiphany" my atheist friend had. Discovering the content of Figure 6.1 has also been one of those

	Extrinsic Motivation Receiving	Intrinsic Motivation Achieving	Transcendent Motivation Giving	Religious Motivation Returning
Spiritual Good Higher Spiritual Realm				
Moral Good Ethical Realm	**Receive Love**	**Achieve Love**	**Give Love**	**Return Love**
Pleasant Good Psychological Realm				
Useful Good Physical Realm				

Figure 6.1 Love as the summary of human motivations

"Aha!" moments for many of my students and a kind of personal epiphany for a few of them, too.

We are motivated daily with our family, work and communities when we know and feel that others care about us. They love us (first column of our map), and they help us to love ourselves (second column). We are also motivated by the chances we are given to care about others, to love them (third column). Finally, for those who believe in God, they are driven by a voluntary desire to match God's Love with personal love, and this is what *religious motivation* is about (see Figure 6.1).

Now, I know that my atheist friend understands what *religious motivation* means for me and for those who have it. For someone who has discovered God's Love, the natural reaction can only be to repay that Love with love. This return of love to God is a voluntary decision that constitutes not only an act of love but also an act of faith and hope.

As poetically expressed in the Book of Psalms, *religious motivations* are the answers to the question "What shall I return to the LORD for all his goodness to me?" (Psalm 116:12). The recognition of having received every material and spiritual good from God, as a gift, leads those who believe in Him to give all sort of goods back to Him: useful, pleasant, moral and spiritual (see Figure 6.2). Religious motivation is therefore the human willingness to return good to God: serving, pleasing, adoring and praising Him.

As Figure 6.2 shows, to consider these *religious motivations* in our map, a new fourth column has been added. One could say that the fourth column is a specific case of the third, the *transcendent motivations* of giving the good,

	Extrinsic Motivation (Receiving)	Intrinsic Motivation (Achieving)	Transcendent Motivation (Giving)	Religious Motivation (Returning)
Spiritual Good *Higher Spiritual Realm*	Willingness to receive spiritual good *Gift, Present, Grace*	Willingness to achieve spiritual good *Sanctity, Blessedness, Holiness*	Willingness to give spiritual good *Sanctification, Salvation, Blessing*	Religious Motivations: Willingness to to return good to God
Moral Good *Ethical Realm*	Willingness to receive moral good *Reputation, Admiration, Respect*	Willingness to achieve moral good *Virtuousness, Excellence, Goodness*	Willingness to give moral good *Gentleness, Understanding, Good*	
Pleasant Good *Psychological Realm*	Willingness to receive pleasant good *Relatedness, Affiliation, Esteem*	Willingness to achieve pleasant good *Self-actualisation, Growth, Self-esteem*	Willingness to give pleasant good *Compassion, Kindness, Care*	
Useful Good *Physical Realm*	Willingness to receive useful good *Sustenance, Safety, Support*	Willingness to achieve useful good *Competency, Mastery, Success*	Willingness to give useful good *Assistance, Help, Service*	

Figure 6.2 The religious human motivations

but instead of giving it to "the others", this time it is given to "the Other", to God the Spirit, the Higher Being, who for believers is a personal God.

I recall now a comment that a professor from Seville (Spain) made to me during a presentation I gave in that city. He told me that some people worship ideas, feelings or even things (power, fame, money, sports, etc.). He was asking me if I would include those objects of adoration among the religious motivations in the fourth column. My answer was simple: some people put things in the place of God, but for believers that would be idolatry.

This is why this fourth column is so relevant. *Religious motivations* refer to the return of love to God, a God who in the mind of believers is not a thing, a feeling, or even an idea, but a person with whom it is possible to have a personal relationship. As I said before, this is what the word religion (*religare*) means. Therefore, believers worship a personal God who is Love, not just the idea of Love. In other words, what believers believe is that God is Love but not that love is God. This distinction may seem like semantics, but it is not. If you say that love is God, you will worship love instead of worshipping God (Kreeft, 2004).

This is another reason why adding a new fourth column leaves no room for confusion. Through the logic of love, a love among persons, it is possible to better understand believers' relationships with God. At the end of the day, believing in God's existence and Love means trusting His own revelation and deciding to love Him back with the help of His own graces and gifts. This loving God back, returning love to Him, is the content of the fourth column, the meaning of *religious motivation*.

Adding *religious motivations* to the *map* favours the knowledge and mutual respect between non-believers and believers. It makes their different motivations clearer. Moreover, to ignore and exclude them would be unrealistic and render any systematic description of human motivations incomplete, non-inclusive and therefore inaccurate.

Let us now briefly review the types of *religious motivations* that can be distinguished by following the logic of the *map*. We start with what I call the *religious useful motivation*.

Religious useful motivation: Willing to return useful good to God

While reviewing the materials I had for when I could write this book, I recently came across an email from one of the attendees at a seminar on human motivations in organisations that I taught in Valencia. In her message, she was saying that, after having been away from God for years, she had decided to return to her religious practice as a result of the discussion during our seminar.

She explained that, while reflecting on her life during the session, she felt as if she was living a kind of "schizophrenic" double life. On one hand, she lived a competitive life during the week, ruled by the desire to receive and achieve as much as possible at work. On the other hand, she lived a very different kind of life on the weekend, guided mainly by the desire to do good and share her life with her family and friends. In the past, she had also gone to church, but lately her spiritual and religious life had somewhat cooled off. She was convinced that this abandoning of her faith was the reason for that schizophrenic double life and the lack of reflection.

As she explained, the hectic activity at work during the week and the need to rest and be with others on the weekend had, little by little, extinguished her interest in spiritual and religious matters. However, after listening about the logic of love, she also had her epiphany, now followed by her conversion, her resolution to match God's Love, to be faithful to that Love, not only on the weekend but throughout her life.

Of course, I'm grateful that the logic of this map helped this woman better understand her own faith. This was not the only case where a religious person had told me how much the framework had helped them better understand their own motivations. I'm grateful for the email she sent me, though, as it is a great example of how the logic of love is key to properly understanding *religious motivations*.

When this person stopped to reflect on how good God is to us, there was a moment of awareness, an enlightenment. After this personal epiphany, the next step in this logic of love was her conversion, as with my atheist friend. This time, however, the conversion involved a desire to match the goodness of God, an eagerness to be faithful to God's Love, to do His will and keep His commandments, out of love rather than fear or duty.

This is what happened to this woman. Her conversion involved this eagerness to be faithful to the Love of God. She wanted to answer His calling, cooperate with Him, serve Him and be useful to Him through her human actions. This is precisely what *religious useful motivation* is about – the voluntary desire or willingness to return the practical or useful good to God. This involves the desire to discover God's will and lovingly obey and fulfil it by answering His calling and doing His will. This is the kind of motivation that appears at the bottom of the new column we added to our *map of motivations* (see Figure 6.3).

As previously mentioned, not everyone sees religious practices and motivations as a response to God's Love. For some people, these motivations could be seen as a response to justice and the power of God. In this case, the reason for religious practices would be based more on fear or duty than on love. In some of these cases, we would still be talking about *religious motivations*, but in a negative or less positive sense.

As we will see in Chapter 7, the whole map of motivations can be interpreted positively, from the logic of love, or negatively, from the logic of fear and duty, which exist in the absence of the former. However, what most drives the human heart is love. Love is why so many religious people decide to do missionary work. They are sure that it is God's will for them, His

132 *Exploring the region of higher human motivations*

	Extrinsic Motivation Receiving	Intrinsic Motivation Achieving	Transcendent Motivation Giving	Religious Motivation Returning
Spiritual Good Higher Spiritual Realm	Willingness to receive spiritual good Gift, Present, Grace	Willingness to achieve spiritual good Sanctity, Blessedness, Holiness	Willingness to give spiritual good Sanctification, Salvation, Blessing	
Moral Good Ethical Realm	Willingness to receive moral good Reputation, Admiration, Respect	Willingness to achieve moral good Virtuousness, Excellence, Goodness	Willingness to give moral good Gentleness, Understanding, Good	
Pleasant Good Psychological Realm	Willingness to receive pleasant good Relatedness, Affiliation, Esteem	Willingness to achieve pleasant good Self-actualisation, Growth, Self-esteem	Willingness to give pleasant good Compassion, Kindness, Care	
Useful Good Physical Realm	Willingness to receive useful good Sustenance, Safety, Support	Willingness to achieve useful good Competency, Mastery, Success	Willingness to give useful good Assistance, Help, Service	**Willingness to return useful good** Obedience, Assent, Fidelity

Figure 6.3 The religious useful motivations

calling. They want to be useful to God, to cooperate with Him, to answer Him, to do His will.

As we can see, *religious useful motivation* will lead to discerning God's will and being useful to Him. To saying "Thy will be done" instead of "my will be done". To saying yes to God's call. This 'yes' to God's will, is a word of love, and the whole secret of worship, sanctity, contemplation, happiness, and peace for believers (Kreeft, 2004).

Within the logic of love, *religious useful motivation* leads believers to see life as a personal response to the goodness of God with faith, hope and love, trying to do his will, answer His universal calling to holiness and be united with Him by fulfilling the specific mission He has for each person in the world. In other words, every time God's Love is personally discovered by someone (an epiphany), the desire arises to faithfully match that love (a conversion), leading to a response to God's will as a personal calling (a vocation). These are indeed acts of faith, hope and love.

Furthermore, when this *religious useful motivation* is authentically human, this affirmative response of believers is not just a rational fulfilment of God's will but a sincere and joyful human response to the Love of God. It is therefore a kind, affective and sensitive answer full of bliss and joy. This sensitive desire of the human heart with the Love of God is what constitutes the *religious pleasant motivation* (see Figure 6.4).

	Extrinsic Motivation Receiving	Intrinsic Motivation Achieving	Transcendent Motivation Giving	Religious Motivation Returning
Spiritual Good Higher Spiritual Realm	Willingness to receive spiritual good Gift, Present, Grace	Willingness to achieve spiritual good Sanctity, Blessedness, Holiness	Willingness to give spiritual good Sanctification, Salvation, Blessing	
Moral Good Ethical Realm	Willingness to receive moral good Reputation, Admiration, Respect	Willingness to achieve moral good Virtuousness, Excellence, Goodness	Willingness to give moral good Gentleness, Understanding, Good	
Pleasant Good Psychological Realm	Willingness to receive pleasant good Relatedness, Affiliation, Esteem	Willingness to achieve pleasant good Self-actualisation, Growth, Self-esteem	Willingness to give pleasant good Compassion, Kindness, Care	**Willingness to return pleasant good** Gratitude, Thanks, Appreciation
Useful Good Physical Realm	Willingness to receive useful good Sustenance, Safety, Support	Willingness to achieve useful good Competency, Mastery, Success	Willingness to give useful good Assistance, Help, Service	Willingness to return useful good Obedience, Assent, Fidelity

Figure 6.4 The religious pleasant motivations

Religious pleasant motivation: Willing to return pleasant good to God

Religious pleasant motivation comes into play whenever *religious motivation* is fully human, noble, affective and all heart, and mostly when God is perceived not only as the Creator and the Almighty God but also as the One who wants to be acknowledged as Father. This motivation constitutes a human voluntary desire to return the pleasant good to God in order to be affectionate with Him. The purpose of the human heart before God as Father is then one of piety, appreciation, reparation, gratitude and thanksgiving. The human heart wants to please God affectionately and lovingly (see Figure 6.4).

In fact, the presence of this motivation somehow implies the fulfilment of the previous *religious useful motivation* while also being partly a consequence of it. For a believer, knowing that one is freely doing the will of God, who is a loving Father, leads to a kind of spiritual joy that drives the heart to give thanks and maintain a desire to keep pleasing Him (see Figure 6.4).

This explains the presence in almost all religious traditions of music through hymns, psalms and songs, often accompanied by musical instruments. As the Psalm goes, "I will sing of the LORD's great love for ever" (Psalm 89:1). The joy of music is part of the movement of a grateful human heart; it is part of the logic of love.

However, this grateful joy that is accompanied by music and celebration in front of the Giver of all goods is also compatible with believers' recognition that God is God, Creator of Heaven and Earth, the Almighty. This also explains the solemnity of sacred music and the gravity of the liturgy in so many religious practices. I must say that my non-Catholic friends, and even non-believers, are drawn to the beauty of the Catholic liturgy, as I have witnessed many times.

Believers are aware that God is all-powerful, ineffable and mysterious, and compared to Him, his creatures are worthless. Religious liturgy then calls upon the help of sacred music, of singing and the voices of creation in the sounds of instruments. Profound and true sacred liturgy is many times recognisable because it is cosmic, it sings with the angelic spirits yet at the same time is silent with the expectant depths of the universe (Ratzinger, 1997).

This explains the solemnity of music in the liturgy of so many religious practices in the face of the mystery of divine, but it also explains the third type of religious motivation: the *religious moral motivation*. The awareness of the divinity and infinite power of God leads human beings who believe in Him to prostrate themselves before their Creator, to adore Him as an act of justice, as the right thing to do in front of Him. This is the *religious moral motivation*.

Religious moral motivation: Willing to return moral good to God

In addition to practicing God's will and pleasing Him, a third kind of *religious motivation* can be described following the logic of our framework. This motivation is part of the ethical realm. It refers to the reaction among believers when they realise they are in front of a Supreme Being, the Creator of Heaven and Earth. The ethical or moral response of creatures in front of their Creator, as the right thing to do, is to recognise His grandeur and divinity by worshipping Him.

Following the logic of our map of motivations, *religious motivation* refers not only to the desire of believers to fulfil the will of God (returning *useful good*) and to please Him (returning *pleasant good*) but also to the duty of worshipping Him (returning *moral good*). It is the need to give back to God what is just, the reverence and respect that He deserves. In this sense, the *religious moral motivation* of believers can be described as the voluntary desire to return to God the moral good that is due to Him: reverence, veneration, worship and adoration (see Figure 6.5).

Adoration is the logical reaction of human beings when they perceive themselves in front of something greater than themselves, something mysterious and sacred. This is why this motivation is part of the sphere of moral or ethical good. The most correct response to God by a believer is to recognise His greatness, sacredness and divinity by worshipping Him. This sacredness, godliness or holiness is universally recognised by all who enter a sacred place, such as a synagogue, mosque, temple or church.

The religious motivations 135

	Extrinsic Motivation — Receiving	Intrinsic Motivation — Achieving	Transcendent Motivation — Giving	Religious Motivation — Returning
Spiritual Good Higher Spiritual Realm	Willingness to receive spiritual good — Gift, Present, Grace	Willingness to achieve spiritual good — Sanctity, Blessedness, Holiness	Willingness to give spiritual good — Sanctification, Salvation, Blessing	
Moral Good Ethical Realm	Willingness to receive moral good — Reputation, Admiration, Respect	Willingness to achieve moral good — Virtuousness, Excellence, Goodness	Willingness to give moral good — Gentleness, Understanding, Good	**Willingness to return moral good — Reverence, Adoration, Worship**
Pleasant Good Psychological Realm	Willingness to receive pleasant good — Relatedness, Affiliation, Esteem	Willingness to achieve pleasant good — Self-actualisation, Growth, Self-esteem	Willingness to give pleasant good — Compassion, Kindness, Care	Willingness to return pleasant good — Gratitude, Thanks, Appreciation
Useful Good Physical Realm	Willingness to receive useful good — Sustenance, Safety, Support	Willingness to achieve useful good — Competency, Mastery, Success	Willingness to give useful good — Assistance, Help, Service	Willingness to return useful good — Obedience, Assent, Fidelity

Figure 6.5 The religious moral motivations

This *religious moral motivation* constitutes human beings' deeply felt realisation of the smallness of all created reality in comparison to the Creator. As a consequence, it is also a manifestation of humility, of accepting human personal smallness before the One who infinitely transcends everything. That acceptance and the desire of recognition leads believers to this attitude of adoration – the most fundamental attitude of religion – that which consists of prayer and also sacrifice. The purpose of sacrifice is to offer God something, in homage to Him and as an expression of gratitude but also of interior surrender, obedience and respect to Him.

Even in the most ancient of religions, we can find glimpses and signs of these religious devotions of prayer, thanksgiving, adoration and offering or sacrifice. In the traditional religions of ancient Greece, Rome, Africa, Asia, the Americas and elsewhere, the reverence of images or statues has been a common practice, and cult images have carried different meanings and significance (Halbertal et al., 1992).

In this context, the revelation of God in a historical moment to the Jewish people is seen as an absolute change in man's relationship with the Creator, a gift received from on high and which is accepted by a believer with grateful acknowledgement and religious devotion. Therefore, faced with the revealed Word of God, and in this context of trust in God's revelation, only these attitudes of appreciation, gratitude and adoration are befitting. Moreover, in Christianity, Islam and Judaism, the worship of something or someone other than God as if it or they were God is idolatry, the "worship of false gods" (Doniger, 1999).

For believers, this attitude of adoration also belongs to the logic of love when it is not just pure submission but loving respect. Believers kneel before a personal God who took the initiative and revealed Himself as totally spiritual, sacred, transcendent, omnipotent and eternal – a God who decided to create the world and its creatures, to approach them out of Love and with Love.

Although I said a few paragraphs ago that the creature is worthless compared to his Creator, this is not entirely true for believers. In reality, for those who have faith, human creatures are worth a great deal because they were created from nothing, in God's own image, with an eternal soul. Man is loved by God, who as a loving Creator desires to receive love from His creatures as free beings, not as irrational animals, robots or slaves. The Lover wants to be united with each soul here and now on Earth and later for all eternity in Heaven.

The realisation of how much God loves each human being, and how He loves them infinitely, leads believers to the desire to praise Him continuously. That is what *religious spiritual motivation* refers to – the desire to acclaim His glory. As we shall see, this fourth religious motivation – that which synthesises and elevates all other *religious motivations* – is the most preeminent human motivation, the *motivation* par excellence.

Religious spiritual motivation: Willing to return the spiritual good to God

When I explain the map of human motivations in class and I reveal each square of the map, the last one I mention is the upper right corner. When I ask people to give me their definition of this *religious spiritual motivation*, it is very easy for them to build it. By now, everyone has understood the simple logic of each and every definition of this map.

Like all other motivations, this one is a voluntary desire or a willingness to return (because we are on the fourth column of the grid) the spiritual good (because we are on the fourth row). Therefore, *religious spiritual motivation* refers to the willingness to return the spiritual good to God. But what does this mean? Are the religious motivations not all spiritual?

Well, the answer is yes, but now, in addition to following the same logic as the rest of the map when naming each motivation, I want to underline that this is the highest human motivation, the most spiritual of all: to give back to God His own good, the spiritual or supernatural good. For believers, this is what He deserves the most, what is most appropriate for Him, even though He Himself gave everything to us first.

In fact, this is when the logic of love manifests itself as a mystery, even for believers, in their relationship with God, a mystery of love. To love God as He deserves, God gives man His own Love, He raises mankind to the supernatural plane. This is when human beings can then love perfectly, with the Love of God. It is an incredible mystery; to love God, one needs the gift of faith, hope and love that God Himself offers us. However, without personal freedom, not all of this would work. This mysterious capacity for man (finite) to enter in a personal relationship with God (infinite) is another manifestation of the immense human dignity for believers.

When I ask my students for a single word that summarises or synthesises the full meaning of this definition of *religious spiritual motivations*, almost none of them can think of a definitive answer. I fully understand that it is not a concept that arises spontaneously. It took a long time for my colleagues and I to understand what the upper square of this framework contained, but the truth is that once it was discovered, it made complete sense.

The word I was expecting students to say was "glory". In the context of faith, giving glory means paying back with praise all the good received from God, who deserves all the tribute and honour. According to most theologians, this is what the angels are doing in Heaven, giving glory to God. It is therefore the highest possible human motivation as spiritual beings. In other words, the *religious spiritual motivation* is giving back glory to the One who is Glory Himself and who wants to share His glory with His creatures, in eternity (see Figure 6.6).

It is interesting to note that the word "glory" is one of the most used and heard in the prayers of the three monotheist religions. The word, from the Latin *gloria*, mean "fame, renowned" and is used 148 times in the Bible (Isaacs, 2010). In Christian tradition, as in Judaism, to glorify Him means to acknowledge the greatness and splendour of His majesty through praise of which He alone is worthy because He is God of all.

Muslims use the term Subhanallah – also known as Subhan Allah – which could be translated as "God is perfect" or "glory to God". Subhanallah can

	Extrinsic Motivation Receiving	Intrinsic Motivation Achieving	Transcendent Motivation Giving	Religious Motivation Returning
Spiritual Good Higher Spiritual Realm	Willingness to receive spiritual good Gift, Present, Grace	Willingness to achieve spiritual good Sanctity, Blessedness, Holiness	Willingness to give spiritual good Sanctification, Salvation, Blessing	Willingness to return spiritual good Praise, Acclamation, Glory
Moral Good Ethical Realm	Willingness to receive moral good Reputation, Admiration, Respect	Willingness to achieve moral good Virtuousness, Excellence, Goodness	Willingness to give moral good Gentleness, Understanding, Good	Willingness to return moral good Reverence, Adoration, Worship
Pleasant Good Psychological Realm	Willingness to receive pleasant good Relatedness, Affiliation, Esteem	Willingness to achieve pleasant good Self-actualisation, Growth, Self-esteem	Willingness to give pleasant good Compassion, Kindness, Care	Willingness to return pleasant good Gratitude, Thanks, Appreciation
Useful Good Physical Realm	Willingness to receive useful good Sustenance, Safety, Support	Willingness to achieve useful good Competency, Mastery, Success	Willingness to give useful good Assistance, Help, Service	Willingness to return useful good Obedience, Assent, Fidelity

Figure 6.6 The religious spiritual motivations

also mean, "May Allah be raised" or "May Allah be free of any deficiency". In Islamic tradition, it is often used when praising God or exclaiming awe of His attributes, bounties or creation (Huda, 2019).

To give glory to God, to glorify Him, is a kind of motivation that is present in practically every religious theistic tradition, and, as in the case of the other religious motivations, human beings are unique in this possibility of voluntarily giving glory to their Creator. Only rational creatures can glorify their God directly, for they alone can know, or at least have a glimpse of His infinite grandeur, and be led to praise Him and to efface themselves before Him in loving subjection (Martínez, 2000).

The noblest *religious motivation* for believers consists then of perceiving that the main purpose of human life should be to give all the glory to God rather than to personal vainglory or self-glorification. In this way, life acquires a meaning that transcends the terrain.

Believers recognise that God is their Creator by serving, pleasing, worshipping and praising Him. Furthermore, in case there is any doubt that each person is not only looking out for themselves in their actions, there remains the possibility of frequently rectifying the intention by redirecting all the glory to God (see Figure 6.6).

Believers are convinced that everything created is the fruit of God's Love (cf. Gen. 1) and that God created each one of us because He loves us deeply. Then, it makes sense that the creature has a desire to recognise and proclaim God's grandeur and infinite goodness, and, paradoxically, the believer wants to return everything to Him out of love, everything meaning all the goods already received from God Himself (see Figure 6.6).

Within the logic of love, which is common to believers and non-believers, it seems easier to understand this kind of spiritual motivation, although, strictly speaking, it is really impossible to understand it because it is a mystery even for believers; it is a mystery of Love and, as such, requires faith.

It makes sense that when you love someone you only say good things about that person. Lovers would spend all day singing about their love, and they would like to spend their entire life telling their beloved how much they love them and how much they are worth. This is precisely what it means to give glory to God – sing His wonders, proclaim His greatness to the entire world.

As shown, the fourth column of the map includes all those motivations that, being spiritual, are related to returning all goods to God, in the context of a personal relationship with Him. In reality, among those who have faith in God, this relationship would include *returning* those goods but also *asking* for them, *achieving* them and *sharing* them with others. In other words, as I said earlier, all *religious motivations* are spiritual, but for believers, all *spiritual motivations* are also *religious*. They are part of the religious personal relationship with God.

Besides, this relationship of *asking*, *receiving* and *returning* goods to God is precisely the meaning of prayer in every religious tradition. Prayer of petition, as well as prayer of giving, is part of mankind's universal religious experience. The content of prayer, of human dialogue with a personal God, includes all these kinds of motivations: asking for material things and grace or for mercy and pardon, as well as giving material things and thanks, or adoration and glory.

Everything I have just described makes sense from a purely theoretical point of view. At least, this is what my atheist friends tell me when I explain these *religious motivations* to them. However, understanding *religious motivations* does not mean having them; as I said, they are a gift that, as such, has to be *asked* for, *received* and joyfully *shared*.

Only those who have experienced the *religious motivations* can say if this explanation is truly accurate enough because, at the end of the day, religion is not just something theoretical; it is a personal relationship of love with God. Therefore, every religious practice for believers constitutes a loving encounter – of the friend with his best Friend, of the brother with his loved Brother, the son with his loved Father. What seems clear is that everyone, believers and non-believers alike, appreciates that we have reflected together on these motivations from the logic of love.

We will return to these ideas in Chapter 7, where I will try to delve into the logic of love in this map to be better able to use it. In Chapter 8, we will reflect on how all of these motivations are connected to human work in organisations. Now, and to finish the presentation of the map, let us have a look at some evidence of these *religious motivations*.

Evidence of religious motivations

As in the previous chapter, I cannot give many examples of *religious motivations* from my undergraduate students. Out of respect, I never ask them about these issues directly. I just explain the logic of this taxonomy of human motivations to them and the map that emerges from this classification.

It is true, however, that once all the possibilities have been shown, including the *moral*, *spiritual* and *religious* motivations, some students and participants in the seminars approach me when I finish. Some of them ask me about my own religious beliefs, others share their beliefs with me and tell me how they could better understand their own motivations, but the truth is that I never ask first.

I think this map is ideal for personal examination and not so much for commenting on its individual content in public because it is very personal. Nevertheless, in recent years, I have received feedback from some students and many young professionals who have told me about their own motivations during their mentoring sessions. There are all kinds of spiritual and religious traditions represented among them. Figure 6.7 includes some examples of these *religious motivations*.

Among the *religious motivations* related to daily work, students and others tend to mention their desire to comply with the commands of God's law

140 *Exploring the region of higher human motivations*

	Extrinsic Motivation Receiving	Intrinsic Motivation Achieving	Transcendent Motivation Giving	Religious Motivation Returning
Spiritual Good Higher Spiritual Realm				- To start working at my best to glorify God - To think about Him and stop centring on my own vainglory - To rectify my intention to do everything mainly for Him and for His glory, not mine
Moral Good Ethical Realm				- To offer the hours of work to God - To present God with everything I do, detaching me from it - To give God the difficulties of the day as little sacrifices
Pleasant Good Psychological Realm				- To please God with everything I do - To give thanks to God for all the gifts I have received from Him - To be thankful to God for all the opportunities He gives me
Useful Good Physical Realm				- To serve God through my work and life - To comply with God's commands in all my deeds - To look for the will of God in everything I do

Figure 6.7 Examples of the religious motivations

in their daily deeds. Some of them go further and explain that they try to find out the will of God for them to fulfil it. For others, their ordinary work and life are seen as occasions to serve God. All these reasons fit within the category of the *religious useful motivations*, those related to the desire to fulfil the will of God, to answer His calling.

In addition, when believers talk about their relationship with God, some have the sense that they are pleasing God with their lives, or at least they are trying to do so, and they feel thankful for all the gifts they have received from Him. More so, some of them frequently give thanks to God for the opportunities He keeps giving them. These are all examples of *religious pleasant motivations*, those related to the desire to please God for all His gifts.

In all these cases, you can appreciate how these motivations affect the positive meaning these people give to their lives and work and the optimism with which they live their lives in general. Moreover, among the most religious people that I have met over the years in my mentoring meetings are those who regularly offer their work and their daily activities to God. They see their ordinary lives as occasions to venerate and adore God.

For those more religious people, some see the little difficulties and challenges of their daily circumstances as opportunities to offer them to God as small sacrifices. These are all clear examples of *religious moral motivations*, those related to returning to God the respect that He deserves in the form of sacrifice and self-offering.

What you can see with these people with greater religious sensitivity is that they are motivated by a higher *religious spiritual purpose*, the one of giving glory to God in everything they do. They frequently try to rectify their intention during the day in order to work and live for the purpose of giving glory to God. These kinds of *religious motivations* may only be found in people with a strong spiritual background and a deep faith, at least that has been my experience.

Obviously, this is not the case for most of those I mentor. Many have no religious background at all, and if they have it, and declare themselves believers in God, they recognise that they do not fully put their faith into practice. They agree that they barely reflect on the idea of God being part of their daily work or life.

Likewise, it is also striking that the devout believers I mentioned before are the type of people who are usually more interested in delving even deeper into this *map of motivations*. In fact, most of the students and young professionals who knock on my door to talk about motivations or to engage in mentoring sessions after attending a seminar are people who want to change the "schizophrenic" way they live or deepen their faith. This was the case of the person I mentioned earlier in this chapter who sent me that email after the seminar explaining that she had decided to go back to her religious practice.

This person, as a practicing Catholic, used to pray, study Christian doctrine and attend Mass frequently, but as she explained in her note, the excess of work-life and the interest for other lower-level *extrinsic* and *intrinsic* motivations, led her to abandon her relationship with God and her religious practices. Only after reflecting upon the *map of human motivations* did she decide to return to that relationship again.

On a personal level, this woman helped me a lot. First, because she had no problem telling me about her decision to return to her religious practice. Second, because she sincerely and humbly acknowledged that she had stopped reflecting and praying more calmly, and third, because she also shared with me that she felt great joy once she had decided to return to God. As I said earlier, joy is contagious, and the higher the joy the more contagious it is.

Who can deny that the matters of spirituality and religion are universal and that they impact on millions of lives? They are an essential component of the entire spectrum of human motivations. This is the reason I decided to include the fourth column referring to the religious domain in the *map of motivations*.

When someone suggests that, in order to respect those who do not have faith, I should not mention religious motivations, I explain repeatedly, as I did in my first meeting at the IHMA in New York, that the case is just the opposite. The only way to respect others is to be inclusive and take account of believers and non-believers.

Next, in practical considerations, I will stress the importance of respecting everyone's freedom of belief. After all, without freedom, you cannot love, and as I have wanted to show throughout this chapter using the logic of love, religion is basically a matter of love of God.

Some practical tips

The first piece of practical advice one could think of regarding *religious motivations* is probably the importance of freedom of belief and freedom of religion and religious practice. Every single human being should have the right to choose their spiritual and religious matters.

This is one of the most important decisions we as human beings should be able to make. We all have the ability to want the good and to choose it. This is what freedom is all about. We all want to make the right choices; we all want to engage in the true good, and therefore we should be allowed to look for it.

Given that spiritual and religious motivations belong to the domain of faith, and of truths that cannot or need not be proved, (1) *we must make sure that we always respect others' freedom, and more so, that we really care about every person's freedom of everything, including matters of religion*. This means acknowledging that they are the masters of their own actions and are responsible for them and that they are able to direct their own personal lives.

In the same vein, and for the same reason that we must respect the freedom of others, (2) *we should be able to exercise our own freedom in our own decisions, including our religious choices*. At the end of the day, we all have to take the "risk" of putting our freedom into practice that, in matters of faith, means deciding in whom we trust regarding religious beliefs.

In my case, I trusted my parents for years in matters of faith; then, when I was an adolescent, I had my own "crisis". You don't want to believe something because everyone believes it. Furthermore, believing in matters of religion means seeking the truth about the question of God, but it has also moral consequences; you want to be a good son of such an amazing Father. I finally decided to trust Him, as my parents had. However, the risk and responsibility of being a believer or not will always be mine.

This is the grandeur of the human soul, the ability to freely and responsibly look for the true goods and to choose them but also to reject them. Here, I recall the comment of a manager attending one of my presentations who, at the end of the session said, "Do you realise that the map of motivations you just presented can help people to be more free?"

I was shocked by the comment, but I guess he was right. The more we know about the good, and the kinds of goods we can choose, the better we can use our freedom. The phrase "the truth will set you free" really makes perfect sense. A third practical piece of advice would therefore be that, in order to be more free, (3) *we should make sure that we spend time reflecting on our motivations, on the good we normally search for, including that of the spiritual and religious orders*.

Of course, the clearest manifestation of the use of freedom on the religious level is the ability of human beings to pray. Along with the importance of finding time to reflect on our highest motivations, (4) *it is vital for those who have faith to find time for prayer, time for conversation with God, time for speaking, time for listening, time for silence. In short, time for personal encounters.*

As we have seen, freedom is related to the search for the truth and the good, the human true good, a universal aspiration that deserves to be respected, encouraged and protected, especially in matters of spirituality and religion. Moreover, together with truth and goodness, there is still a third longing of all human aspiration that was briefly mentioned throughout this chapter: the Beauty.

This third classic transcendental is also considered an essential quality of God for philosophers (believers and non-believers): the Truth, the Good and the Beauty. When my atheist friends ask me how to better interpret this chapter on religious motivations if you do not believe in God, I recommend they think in terms of Truth, Good and Beauty because God is all that. More so, I keep reminding them that because God is Love, He shows His Love for mankind with the beauty of His creation.

Contemplation of the beauty in the world has been the path for many to find their spirituality, as well as for many others to find God through the beauty of His creation. Unfortunately, in an increasingly mercantilist and technological world, the role of beauty in accessing the truth and the good has been marginalised, as the well-known Harvard professor Howard Gardner explained in one of his latest books (Gardner, 2012). We should not forget the phrase by Fyodor Dostoevsky: "Beauty will save the world".

Spirituality and religion are inseparable from artistic beauty. They are among the few walls of contention that prevent everything from being reduced exclusively to interest in material goods and physical pleasure, which are the lowest kinds of good in our map and the ones that prevail in most workplaces today. Contemplation belongs to the entirety of humanity, including believers and non-believers.

Therefore, (5) *contemplation must not be lost, not even in our work, if we want it to remain human.* We should be able to discover that there is always something "divine" in a job well done. In a job done for love, believers can discover God (who is Love). For those who don't believe in God, love at work offers glimpses of the Goodness, Truth, and Beauty belonging to the God of believers.

Contemplation of God is synonymous with contemplation of the good, the truth and the beauty. Therefore, for those who do not believe in God, the following final questions can be read by substituting these words. Let us consider if we are contemplative in our life and in our work. Let us think about it. Let us stop and reflect about how often the logic of love is part of our work. In other words, let us consider how often we contemplate the truth, good and beauty of our daily life and work. For believers, they are manifestations of God's Love, and for everybody, they are expressions of the highest dignity of human work.

Some questions for reflection

1 *How often do I think about the good, the truth and the beauty of the world, about God's Love for me?*
2 *How often do I give thanks for the goodness and beauty of the world, and for all the gifts God gives me?*
3 *How often do I see my life and my work as opportunities to promote the good, the truth and the beauty around me, to cooperate with God's creation?*
4 *How often do I try to do all my deeds and my work well to please God, and not just for myself or others?*
5 *How often do I see my life and my work as occasions to serve others and to serve God, to do His will?*
6 *How often do I think that my work has a transcendent meaning, that it matters to God, who loves me and cares about all the things I do?*
7 *How often do I do things intending to praise and give glory to God and not looking just for my own glory?*
8 *How often do I see difficulties in my work as opportunities to sacrifice myself and to give them to God as small offerings or tributes of love?*
9 *How often do I think about my ordinary life and my work as opportunities to love God, others and myself?*
10 *How often do I offer my work to God as an act of love, a tribute or sacrifice for Him?*

A final critical thought on why having a map is not enough

To conclude this chapter, I recall the comment of a graduate student who attended one of my seminars. He told me at the end of the session that he liked the map of motivations a lot but that he also perceived it as "too idealistic". He could not think of many people who would be driven by each of the motivations displayed in the entire map. Moreover, he said that he could not think of any organisation that tries to promote these moral, spiritual or religious motivations.

I really appreciate the honesty of young people like this student. He was quite right. The map of motivations can be characterised as idealistic because it includes all the human ideals. At the same time, though, I think this student was not representative of the majority of my students. Most of those to whom I have taught this theory loved it. I think that this is because the theory is idealistic and they are also idealistic.

What makes this *map of motivations* new for many people is that it includes all the ideals of the human spirit. However, the truth is that, nowadays, not many talk about all the motivations included on our map, and many fewer in the context of the workplace and organisations. Is this because we do not have ideals? Or is this because we do not bring them to our workplaces? Are we bringing all our motivations, all our ideals to our work? Is that not a problem of motivation in organisations?

To answer these questions, the third part of the book focuses on using this *map of motivations* to help us to better understand our motivations at work and to find higher meaningful work. To do this, I will explain why having a map is not enough. We should know how to interpret the *coordinates* of the map (Chapter 7) and then have a *compass* (Chapter 8) and a *roadmap* (Chapter 9). In other words, I will try to show how this theory of motivations can help in this journey in which we are all immersed in the search for a meaningful work-life balance.

Notes

1 *Humanistic* management differs from traditional, *mechanistic*, or *economistic* practices in that humans in organisations are seen as more than resources, stakeholders, assets or capital. Human beings are conceived as the means and ends, and the purpose of management is therefore to serve human flourishing in addition to wealth creation. To know more about IHMA you can visit its website: http://humanisticmanagement.international/
2 The person with whom I had that heated discussion when I first met her at the IHMA meeting is Jennifer Hancock, a member of the board of the Association. I have her permission to mention her in this chapter. I want to thank her again for helping me with this chapter and for teaching me how to use a more inclusive and universal language when talking about religious motivations.
3 This research project was primarily funded by the Attorney General of Australia and sets forth the common values on which Judaism, Christianity, and Islam agree. Three prominent theologians, one from each of the faiths, cooperated to publish this ground-breaking document. According to the authors, the shared values of these three Abrahamic religions are the "moral rules by which Abraham lived before these religions developed" (Cowen, 2013).

References

Augustine, S. (1961). *Confessions*. Harmondsworth Middlesex, England: Penguin Books.
Cowen, S. D. (Ed.) (2013). *An Education in a Shared Ethic: Common Values of Judaism, Christianity and Islam*. East S. Kilda, VIC: Institute for Judaism and Civilization Inc.
Doniger, W. (1999). *Merriam-Webster's Encyclopedia of World Religions*. New York: Merriam-Webster, p. 497.
Gardner, H. (2012). *Truth, Beauty, and Goodness Reframed*. New York: Basic Books.
Guillén, M., Ferrero, I. & Hoffman, W. (2015). The neglected ethical and spiritual motivations in the workplace. *Journal of Business Ethics*, 128(4), 803–816.
Halbertal, M., Margalit, A. & Goldblum, N. (1992). Idolatry. *Harvard University Press*, 1–8, 85–86, 146–148.
Huda. (2019). The definition and purpose of the Muslim word 'subhanallah'. *Learn Religions*. www.learnreligions.com/islamic-phrases-subhanallah-2004290.

Isaacs, R. D. (2010). *Talking with God: The Radioactive Ark of the Testimony*. Chicago: Sacred Closet Books.

Kreeft, P. (2004). *The God Who Loves You. Love Divine, All Loves Excelling*. San Francisco: Ignatius Press.

Martínez, L. M. (2000). *True Devotion To The Holy Spirit*. Manchester, NH: Sophia Institute Press.

Maslow, A. H. (1971). *The Farther Reaches of Human Nature*, Ed. Arkana. New York: Penguin Books.

Ratzinger, J. C. (1997). *A New Song for the Lord: Faith in Christ and Liturgy Today*. New York: Crossroads.

Part III
Using the map of motivations
Towards higher meaningful work

7 The map coordinates for motivations
The logic of love in organisations

The *logic of love* in life and work

On my arrival in Boston in March 2020, I had to go through customs control, as usual. A customs officer asked me why I was coming to the United States, and my answer was simple. I was there to finish writing this book as a visiting researcher at Harvard. He then asked me what the book was about, so I told him that the book was about motivations in organisations and the search for a meaningful work-life balance. To my surprise, he started to give me his opinion about it.

He told me, "I personally think that you are motivated in your work when you love what you do". I replied that that was the main premise of the book. He continued, "In my case, I am happy. My work is sometimes repetitive, but it is well paid, I have good holiday time, and time to be at home with the family". I told him that was the main question posed by the book, and it seems that he had it well resolved.

He kept saying, "Well, I'm lucky, but what about those who don't love their job?" I agree that this is the case for many people nowadays. Ideally, everybody should learn to love their work, whatever the job. I told him that being motivated is about finding reasons to love our work. He then said, "Well, good luck; it doesn't seem like an easy task", and added, "But in any case, it seems a very interesting book". He stamped my passport and let me in, while greeting me with a smile on his face.

That was incredible. In under two minutes, this officer understood and summarised the content of a book that I had been thinking about for more than ten years. My initial reaction was disheartening; so much work to explain something that is so evident, just common sense. Maybe it was not worth finishing writing the book, I thought.

I then realised that I didn't know of any academic book explaining that all motivations at work can be summarised by a *logic of love*, and I concluded that this book was worth finishing. The truth is that this brief conversation on the border gave me doubts that anyone would be interested in publishing this book.

150 *Using the map of motivations*

As the officer summed up brilliantly, we are motivated at work when we love what we do. This was exactly the same idea that my atheist friend shared with me not long ago in the email with her personal epiphany. The simple clue that all human motivations are summed up in one word: love. We are all driven to search for the things we love, those things we consider good. As we discussed in previous chapters, the map of motivations is just a snapshot of the whole spectrum of possibilities regarding human kinds of good or motives for love (see Figure 7.1).

Each of the four columns on our map of human motivations corresponds to four ways of looking for the good, or four ways of loving. We all aim to be loved, to receive love from others in our lives and work (*extrinsic motivation*). We also love what we do in our work, our activity and ourselves (*intrinsic motivation*). Moreover, we are capable of loving others in the workplace (*transcendent motivation*) and, in the case of believers, loving God in the workplace (*religious motivation*) (see Figure 7.1).

Maybe some of you will think that this explicit mention of love in an academic book is excessive or out of place. Talking about love in a scientific context and in a textbook about human motivations in organisations may seem not rigorous enough, or unscientific, in addition to being considered too *naive* an approach. However, the more I give presentations about this topic, the more I find that these ideas resonate with everyone in the audience, from professionals to students, irrespective of their age, country, race or beliefs.

My sense is that when teaching or studying these issues in academic contexts, we avoid the term "love" because it sounds too conventional,

	Extrinsic Motivation Receiving	Intrinsic Motivation Achieving	Transcendent Motivation Giving	Religious Motivation Returning
Spiritual Good Higher Spiritual Realm	Want to be **Loved**	Want to **Love Yourself**	Want to **Love Others**	Want to **Love the Other**
Moral Good Ethical Realm				
Pleasant Good Psychological Realm				
Useful Good Physical Realm				

Figure 7.1 Love as the summary of human motivations in organisations

commonplace or even banal and predictable. It might be seen as too abstract, philosophical or hard to measure. Perhaps we just fear the disdain and sarcasm that talking about this may bring. Of course, if you have MBA students, competitive managers or businesspeople in your audience, then irony, mockery and even cynicism are assured.

Although it may seem that talking about love as the engine of human motivations is too naive, I am convinced that it is true. If we don't talk about the concept of love, I don't think we're talking about true human motivations at all. Unfortunately, I guess that in our desire to teach this subject in an academic, technical or highly professional manner, we end up teaching human motivations in a rather inhuman manner.

To put this simply, a professor who loves teaching, who loves the activity of education itself, happens to be a good professor or teacher, and one who is highly motivated, regardless of many other factors. Who can deny that good teachers are those who love not just their work, the activity of teaching, but also their students? Good teachers care about their students and their good, and they want to be loved by them. At least, this has been my own experience and that of most, if not all, of my colleagues.

I am convinced that the logic of love as the core to explaining human motivations can be applied to any human activity, profession or job. A good doctor, police officer, boss or leader is one who cares about people and, because of that, is loved back and freely followed or obeyed, when required. This may also apply to a good mother or father who cares for their children; or to good friends, who care for those they love as friends.

As Aristotle elucidated many centuries ago, what motivates us is what we love. We move, we are attracted or moved – from the Latin verb *movere* – by the things we love. However, if this is true, why then is love not mentioned in the most recognised theories of motivation?

Why have we been teaching theories of motivation for decades without talking about the logic of love? Even though this is an issue that goes beyond the scope of this book, I consider that it needs to be addressed, albeit briefly.

The *logic of love* in the human sciences

As we saw in Chapter 3 – with the example of the brown bear – if we want to understand the phenomenon of motivation, we first need to properly understand the complexity of human reality. As we discussed at that time, Aristotle was one of the first thinkers who studied this complexity of human nature and its hierarchical order.

Starting from those philosophical reflections and in dialogue with other thinkers, we were able to distinguish the four hierarchical levels of our map of motivations: the *physical*, *psychological*, *ethical* and *higher spiritual* realms, referring to the useful, pleasant, moral and spiritual goods.

Unfortunately, in today's mainstream positivist view of the world, the only authentic knowledge would be scientific knowledge. As a result, the

152 Using the map of motivations

term "science" has been mainly employed as a synonym for *empirical science*. For that reason, topics such as human motivations have been explained exclusively in a scientific manner in schools and universities for decades. In other words, the phenomenon of human motivation has been studied solely from the perspective of the *natural* and *social sciences*, those considered proper sciences in the strictest sense.

This positivist view of human knowledge has led to the elimination of the findings of the *humanities* in explaining human phenomena (the classics, languages, literature, music, philosophy, history, religion and the visual and performing arts), something that is clearly appreciated in the case of the study of motivation. None of the typical contributions of the *humanities* is normally mentioned to explain human motivation.

As Figure 7.2 shows, the phenomenon of human motivation continues to be described exclusively from the perspective of "scientific sciences", including *formal* and *applied sciences*, such as physics and mathematics, and the *natural* and *social sciences*. This would explain why, as we saw in Chapter 1, when it comes to explaining human motivations, most researchers and teachers are still trapped in the lower-left quadrant (2x2) of our map. Mainstream theories refer exclusively to the *extrinsic* and *intrinsic* motivations, and only the *physical* and *psychological* or *sociological* realms are studied because they are observable.

The positivist view of human knowledge reduces its purpose to an observable reality, so only the findings of the empirical sciences are considered true. This fragmented and reductive view of the knowledge of reality, including the reality of human nature, calls all knowledge that is not material and

	Extrinsic Motivation Receiving	Intrinsic Motivation Achieving	Transcendent Motivation Giving	Religious Motivation Returning
Spiritual Good Higher Spiritual Realm	Willingness to receive spiritual good	Willingness to achieve spiritual good	Willingness to give spiritual good	**Comparative religions** **Theology**
Moral Good Ethical Realm	Willingness to receive moral good	Willingness to achieve moral good	**Philosophy** **Anthropology** **Ethics**	Willingness to return moral good
Pleasant Good Psychological Realm	Willingness to receive pleasant good	**Natural Sciences** **Social Sciences**	Willingness to give pleasant good	Willingness to return pleasant good
Useful Good Physical Realm	**Applied sciences** **Formal Sciences**	Willingness to achieve useful good	Willingness to give useful good	Willingness to return useful good

Figure 7.2 Disciplines involved in understanding human motivations

verifiable into question. Obviously, as Maslow himself acknowledged, the very concept of human nature is then also questioned (Maslow, 1971).

According to this positivistic view of science, the findings from *philosophy*, *philosophical anthropology*, and *moral philosophy* or *ethics*, among other human disciplines, would be no more than interesting reflections on human *values*, but not verifiable *facts*. From this perspective, it would make no sense to talk about an objective *ethical* realm in human nature, and, of course, *theology* would never achieve the status of a science and *comparative religions* would be reduced to sociological analysis. Clearly, this explains the neglected moral, transcendent, spiritual and religious dimensions of the theories of human motivation (Guillén et al., 2015).

Given that the findings of the *humanities* are outside the explanation of human reality, then the term "love" itself, as well as the "logic of love", can only be considered as a non-scientific issue or, at least, as a pre-scientific question. Furthermore, any *humanistic management* vision with its holistic outlook, and the entire *humanistic* theory of motivations presented in this book, would most probably be questioned or included among some pre-scientific findings.

It seems then that writing about these issues is risky and puts you on the edge of "science". I still remember what my doctoral supervisor told me many years ago. He said, "Whatever you decide to write and publish, it will remain in writing forever, so be prudent". I don't know if I'm following that advice right now, but given that I share the Aristotelian view of love being the engine of human motivations, and because I consider management and business organisation to be a human science, I decided to take the risk.

I understand the position of those who would rather take lesser risks in this area of knowledge. Here, I suggest they use alternative words, such as "care", "attention", "concern" or just "interest", instead of love when referring to this work. As long as we all understand the concept of motivation as the human voluntary desire for the good, the labels are relatively unimportant, but I will continue to use logic of love and now analyse it in the context of work in organisations.

The *logic of love* in human organisations

As this customs officer said in our brief conversation when I entered the US, all motivations at work can be summed up in one word: love. The entire rationality explaining our motivations in life and work could be summarised in one expression: the *logic of love*. We are motivated in our jobs whenever we follow this logic, and we consider we are receiving love when putting love into what we do, when we love those we work with and, when speaking of believers, we are returning love to God through our work (see Figure 7.1).

The type of love we are talking about, however, and the way this logic of love operates in our lives, the workplace and in organisations, is not obvious. There are many types of love: the love of lovers, the love of parents, that of children, of friends, colleagues, neighbours, etc. Obviously, I am not talking about love in a romantic or family sense, as I said earlier. Ordinarily, our colleagues at work are not our lovers, parents or siblings. Rather, I am talking about the *love of friendship*, the kind of love that can be part of all other types of love, a kind of love that contains all the ingredients of the logic of love because it is one kind of human love.

Who can deny that the ideal work environment would be one in which everyone would be a friend to everyone else? This is what most people mean when they speak of a "friendly" work environment. Of course, this is not always the case in real life, and anyone could argue that this is idealistic or even impossible for some. The truth is, though, given the choice, everyone would like to work in a friendly environment. Nobody likes to have enemies at work. This is what the logic of love means in an organisational setting: everyone cares about others' good.

The same could be said of an ideal family. The perfect family would be one in which all members would also be friends, just as the ideal community would be one in which everyone was friends. In the context of human relationships, friendship is probably the kind of human love that best expresses the human desire for the good of the other person, the friend in this case. Friendship refers to the common interest in happiness and human growth, as Aristotle was able to observe in his investigations of human nature (*Nicomachean Ethics* 8.3, 1156b7–11).

Friendship is a kind of human relationship based on the logic of love because it is a kind of love. It is driven by the reciprocal interest for the good of the other, that which looks for the union of both friends. As I said, while it is true that it is not possible to be friends with everyone, it is also true that we all would desire to live and work in friendly environments, those in which others care about us as human beings – not just as human resources – and where there is unity. This is precisely what characterises *ethically healthy organisations*, those that contribute to the human flourishing of their members (Bañón et al., 2012).

Understanding what true friendship means can better explain what it means to work in truly human or *humanistic* organisations, where everyone cares about the common good. In other words, exploring what true friendship looks like at work will help us better understand how the logic of love operates in truly human organisations. Therefore, reflections on love and friendship, as part of the humanities, can contribute to better understanding motivation in organisations from a humanistic perspective.

As we saw in Chapter 2, according to the Aristotelian distinction, there can be friends for three kinds of good – friends for *pleasure*, *utility* and *moral virtue* or *honour* – but not all are true friends. If friendship is based exclusively on utility or satisfaction, then it will only last until the relationship stops being useful or satisfying, which is what normally happens in many professional settings and relationships. For instance, just think about how many of your former classmates or workmates are still your friends.

Our professional relationships are mostly based on the reciprocal interest for utility and satisfaction, which is something good but also rather superficial on many occasions, and not that different from the way other animals organise themselves. True human relationships, based on a logic of love, have the capacity to take the person as a whole into account and not just exclusively as a resource or source of utility and satisfaction.

Aristotle believed that friends make us better people. Do our colleagues at work make us better people? If friendship is truthful and looks for the complete good of the entire person, it should make us and our friends better, more virtuous people. Therefore, truly human organisations that are based on this logic of love, caring for each person as a whole, should also make their members better, more virtuous people (Bañón et al., 2012).

This idea fits perfectly with the concept of virtue provided some centuries later by another classical philosopher, Augustine of Hippo. As in the case of Aristotle, he also asserted that our loves are the fundamental driving force of our wills, thoughts and actions. Following this same logic of love, but without using this term, he defined virtue as *ordo amoris*, or the "order of love", which means that virtuous people are those who love everything according to its proper value. They love what is worth being loved.

Therefore, friends love their friends for who they are, full of moral and spiritual goodness, and not necessarily for what they have (useful or pleasant goods). Because they love each other for their goodness, while loving the whole of their friend, they love them because they are worth loving. We love our true friends with their faults, although we would like to help them overcome their failings; we want them to be better and happier, but we love them the way they are, for being who they are, for their intrinsic moral and spiritual value. As a student once told me, that might be the reason why some rich people don't want to talk about their fortunes; they don't want people to love them because of what they have but because of who they really are.

In this sense, the more virtuous the friends, the more perfect the mutual friendship among them will be because they will contribute to the good of each other, not just in a more complete or integrative way but also in a more orderly manner. In other words, any real friendship, and therefore any truly human relationship that follows the same logic of love, entails an ordered mutual love. Therefore, and for the same reason, in truly human organisations, interpersonal relationships are founded on a reciprocal interest for the truly human good. It could be said that *humanistic organisations* are those that habitually seek the common good, the common "true good" (which is ordered).

Of course, the perfect *humanistic organisation* or *excellent ethical organisation* does not exist in the real world because in ordinary organisations neither people nor their actions and relationships are always perfect (Bañón

156 *Using the map of motivations*

et al., 2012). Unfortunately, we human beings do not always follow the logic of love, which would allow us to have perfect human relationships. Nevertheless, perfection constitutes the model, the reference, and for that reason, it becomes the ideal, the desire and the longing for an ideal *humanistic organisation*.

As we discussed before, we are all driven by ideals, we all want to be happy in our lives, and therefore in our human organisations. Who would not desire to work in an ideal organisation, one that contributes to our happiness? (Fisher, 2010). In the ideal organisation, all our *motivations* would be fulfilled because we would be *receiving, achieving, giving* and *returning* truly human good all the time. This is what the logic of love means in human organisations (see Figure 7.3).

As Figure 7.3 shows, the *map of motivations* that we have built throughout this book is actually a summary of what constitutes human happiness within some of the most well-known philosophical classical traditions.[1] *Receiving, achieving, giving* and *returning* the true good is the summary of all the potential aspirations or motivations of human beings. We all need to be loved, love ourselves, love others and return love to God (for believers), and therein lies happiness.

What we are doing in this chapter is applying these ideas to better understand what happiness at work means from a *humanistic* perspective. This is a subject that has grown in interest and popularity recently (Fisher, 2010). Therefore, in the following sections, we will study the *coordinates* for our *map of motivations* so we can identify where north, south, east and west

	Extrinsic Motivation Receiving	Intrinsic Motivation Achieving	Transcendent Motivation Giving	Religious Motivation Returning
Spiritual Good Higher Spiritual Realm	**Receiving** Truly Human **Good**	**Achieving** Truly Human **Good**	**Giving** Truly Human **Good**	**Returning** Truly Human **Good**
Moral Good Ethical Realm			
Pleasant Good Psychological Realm			
Useful Good Physical Realm			

Figure 7.3 The logic of love in human organisations

are, how the cardinal points are related and how far away each one is. In other words, once you understand the internal logic of the map, the logic of love in our case, you can better identify your position on the map. Let's start by reflecting on the first column of the map, the *extrinsic motivations*, our need to receive love.

Receiving truly human good in organisations

We all were born with a need for love because we all were born needed. As C. S. Lewis explains in his book *The Four Loves*, there is a kind of love that he describes as the "love of necessity", a spontaneous movement towards the good that comes first. As he says, this is the kind of love that propels a lonely, frightened child into its mother's arms (Lewis, 1991). From the day of our birth until the day we leave this world, we need others in every one of the human realms of our nature: *physical*, *psychological*, *ethical* and *higher spiritual* or *supernatural* (for believers).

Such love of necessity should not be dismissed as egoism because it is just a manifestation of the limitation of our human nature. No one will think that a child is egoistic for turning to its mother for food, help or consolation. Neither will anyone think that someone is selfish for seeking out food or a friend (Burggraf, 2012). We all need goods of all kinds, we all need to receive love, and this is what *extrinsic motivation* is all about, a manifestation of our incomplete human nature, always desiring to receive more and in need of fullness.

I remember a student who at this point suggested an analogy that he had heard from one of his teachers. She told them that we are all a *rechargeable battery of love* and that in our day to day, at work, and when we study, we discharge, and the level of love drops. For this reason, when we get home, we want to be with our loved ones to recharge with love.

When working in organisations, either for profit or not for profit, we all look for material provision, for salaries that are sufficient to support us and our families (*useful good*), but we also look for enjoyable and friendly work environments where there is companionship, or at least reasonably good human relationships (*pleasant good*). Moreover, we look for workplaces where they treat us with respect, justice and true interest (*moral good*), and if we are people of faith, we want it to be respected at work, so we can become holy while working (*spiritual good*). These are all *extrinsic motivations*, external reasons that explain why we go to work every day (see Figure 7.4).

As we discussed in Chapter 2, in addition to receiving material support and affection from others in organisations, we ordinarily want others to care about us. We need to perceive that we matter to others, that our colleagues and bosses will value us and our work, that they will recognise us as human beings with a unique dignity. Even if they do not show esteem or appreciate us, we at least hope they will respect us. Deep down, we all desire

158 *Using the map of motivations*

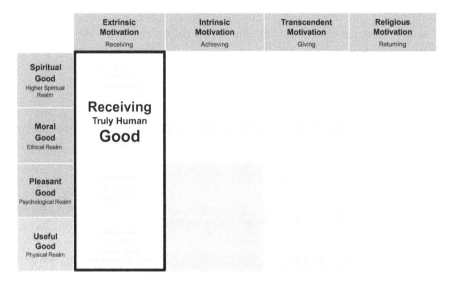

Figure 7.4 Receiving love at work

to be loved in our workplaces. We expect to receive goods at work, truly human goods (see Figure 7.4).

These considerations could help you to think about the kind of work you love, what kind of organisations could offer you that work, and what kind of tasks and responsibilities you would like to have. These thoughts might be useful for students thinking about their future jobs but also for young and not-so-young professionals reflecting on what their job can offer them.

Truly human goods are those that are in accord with our human nature. No one likes to be treated like an animal in the workplace or like a piece of machinery. Of course, we are animals, and we have the ability to behave as such when we forget the highest human goods (*moral* and *spiritual*) and we exclusively seek lower material *useful* and *pleasant goods*. Therefore, truly human goods are those of human beings, of beings that, as we discussed in Chapter 2, are spiritual bodies, or body spirits, in unity. For that reason, our different motivations, the different kinds of good we seek, can be distinguished into different types and categories, but they are not separable.

Truly human goods are not only those that consider the human needs as *inseparable* but also as *related* and *hierarchical*. As we saw in Chapter 3, there is a hierarchical relationship among the goods. They are all desirable in their own level, order or realm, according to their own nature, their own logic and their own purpose, which is inseparable and connected or related to those of the other realms, and they all contribute to our happiness.

As we discussed earlier, it means that the lower goods are subordinate to the higher ones, they exist for the sake of them. The *physical* realm allows us to fulfil the higher *psychological* level, and these two realms allow the *ethical* one to be fulfilled, and these three natural domains allow the *higher spiritual* one to be fulfilled for those who believe in it. As we saw, to make good *ethical* decisions with your mind, your brain needs to be physically and psychologically well.

In practical terms, the hierarchical order of truly human goods, the subordination of lower to higher goods, allows us to make common-sense decisions. For instance, if you don't earn a salary that is high enough to live decently, you won't care so much about a possible toxic work environment. Your first focus will be on earning enough before thinking about how to make your work environment more pleasant.

However, if another company offers you a job with a better salary and a good work environment, the most logical thing to do is accept the job, which allows you to achieve not only useful but also pleasant goods. If the new company tries to cheat you or treat you unfairly, the chances are that you will consider returning to the previous company, if they treated you fairly, even if the atmosphere was not so pleasant. You will choose the higher *moral good*, sacrificing part of the *pleasant*.

As Maslow inferred, it is logical to think that a certain achievement of the lower levels of good is necessary for the higher levels to function, at least at a minimum, but once these minimums have been attained, it is also true that human beings are capable of sacrificing inferior goods to achieve other superior ones. This is what we do when we encounter difficulties; we give up pleasant goods to obtain other higher, more desirable, human goods (family, friendship, etc.). It is love that gives meaning to sacrifice.

This hierarchical order of the different realms of human nature does not only affect the relationship between the different goods, it also affects their desirability. As Augustine of Hippo explained, not every good is worthy of being desired or loved in the same way; there is a hierarchical *order of love*, based on the hierarchical order of goods at stake. Higher goods are more worthy of love than lower ones.

To give a simple example, we all need physical *useful goods*, such as drinking water, but if it is a hot day, drinking a cold beer instead of just a glass of water might be a more *pleasant good*, it is more enjoyable. In addition, if we were with a friend while drinking, it would be better still. Friendship is one of the greatest *moral goods*. If that friend were a person of high spiritual standing, the meeting could also bring us wisdom, peace and joy (*spiritual goods*).

With this very basic example, you can see that all the goods at stake are attractive to us at their different levels. This is why we love them. We want them because we consider them good (*useful*, *pleasant*, *moral* and *spiritual*). In this particular case, we would love a beer, friendship, and holiness. However, there is no doubt that each of these goods is considered as good at a different level and from a different perspective, from their own different realms. It would be a tremendous mistake to confuse them.

Who would deny that friendship with someone (a *moral* good) is more valuable than a good drink (a *pleasant* good). Of course, if you can have both goods at the same time, it would be better. In fact, in real life, the same reality can be attractive to us because it is a *useful, pleasant, moral* and *spiritual* good all at the same time. As I just said, all the goods are inseparable, not only in our minds but in reality.

On the other hand, when there is doubt about which good to choose, it seems evident that the *moral good* of friendship is worth more than the *pleasant good* of a drink; however, as obvious as it may seem, we often end up loving *lower goods* in spite of the *higher goods*. This disorder is a manifestation of our freedom or, rather, our wrong way of using that freedom. Normally, when we do *moral evil*, we do it driven by the attraction of some other *inferior good*. Can you think of an example?

Mine concerns different managers I have spoken with throughout my career who, over the years, realised that they had spent more time seeking prestige at work than spending time with their families. They recognised that that was wrong. Unfortunately, seeking success and material well-being at any cost has become a compulsive behaviour all over the world. The attraction of inferior *pleasant goods* (prestige) leads to superior *moral goods* (family) being abandoned.

Perhaps the way we have been teaching motivations in business schools has something to do with this sad situation, but there is still time to correct our mistakes. There is no doubt that this disorderly way of loving has consequences. As Augustine defended, good loves lead to goodness, whereas evil loves lead to evil, which means that, at the end of the day, an individual is the sum total of their loves.

In the same vein, a modern philosopher described the current excessive dependence of many people for what others think about them. "The saddest thing is to encounter people who have obtained a deserved prestige in their professional lives, who have become competent doctors, great artisans, researchers, or artists and who, nevertheless, in the autumn of life – which should be a natural time of serenity and quiet – feel themselves unfortunate, unsuccessful, and lonely" (Burggraf, 2012).

Unfortunately, the theories we've been explaining for decades, while distinguishing *extrinsic* and *intrinsic* motivations, never explained how good or truly human these two kinds of motivations are. By understanding the logic of love, and the *inseparable, interrelated* and *hierarchical* nature of truly human goods, we can better explain that not all goods deserve to be loved equally. As Aristotle would probably say, a good teacher should be teaching the pupil how to love all good things in a way that is proportional to their goodness.

If we think in terms of people management in organisations, which has a similar role as teachers at times, good managers should always bear the hierarchical nature of human goods in mind. This has nothing to do with underestimating the lower goods, like the value of money, or overestimating the higher goods like being excessively good-natured with staff, but the opposite. The knowledge of what truly human goods are will make managers wiser and more respectful with others' freedom.

Imagine your boss corrects you in private about something you are doing wrong without even realising (like gossiping). Despite knowing that you are not going to like it – it will be unpleasant for you to hear, but *morally good* – the boss tells you. Managers need courage to correct others, but when done for the right motive and in the right way, it respects the hierarchy of goods and puts higher goods first. Someone doing so is a good teacher and certainly cares about you. I guess we all know when a manager, or a teacher, cares about us. We know when someone truly loves us. This is the foundation of moral authority of those in charge in human organisations, of *authentic leadership*.

Before moving to the next section, someone might ask how the higher *extrinsic motivation* of believers – regarding the *higher spiritual* or *supernatural* realm – works in human life in general and in organisations specifically. The French philosopher Gabriel Marcel said, "Being in the world means being loved by God" (Burggraf, 2012). A believer, who is convinced that what Marcel said is true, is someone with a different view of the world, a *supernatural outlook* that is based on faith and that affects motivations.

For a believer, all natural and supernatural good comes from God: life, freedom, wisdom, faith itself, etc. As we saw in Chapter 6, everything in this life is conveyed as a gift from God, made out of love, for someone who believes in God. Therefore, life is conceived as a gift and a task. More so, the meaning of life consists of freely *accepting*, *enjoying* and *sharing* every gift received from God, starting with God's Love. This is something that, for a believer, can be done at every moment, including at work.

Undoubtedly, this *higher spiritual* good of faith is a source of motivation for believers. As I mentioned in Chapter 5, faith is a very special source of joy for believers. Given that this matter is of a theological nature and goes beyond the purpose of this chapter, the way faith influences professional work and motivations in organisations will be briefly described at the end of the book. Now, we will reflect on how it is possible to achieve truly human good in organisations.

Achieving truly human good in organisations

As we discussed in Chapter 1, highly motivated people go to work not just to receive something *extrinsic* but because they also have an interest in what they do. They care about their professional activity. Those who are motivated see their work as worthy in itself. In other words, they love their work.

The insatiable human desire for the good, for love, is the driver of human motivations. We are seekers of the complete, people who relentlessly pursue whatever we think will ultimately make us content (Wadell, 1992). This yearning for good does not stop at our relationship with the external reality;

162 *Using the map of motivations*

it also includes our inner world, and this is what the *map of human motivations* shows. The *extrinsic motivation* is necessary but not sufficient; it demands the *intrinsic motivation*, the love for ourselves and for what we do, the desire to achieve our own good (useful, pleasant, moral and spiritual) (see Figure 7.5).

Without a doubt, our own desire for the good, our own self-love, also plays an essential role in explaining why we do the things we do in our life and at work. A love for ourselves that, as we will see, and following the same logic of love, should be truly human in accordance with the *inseparable*, *interrelated* and *hierarchical* nature of human goods. This time, the considerations of this section are not on what our jobs can offer us but on the attitude we want to have when working, which is something that depends exclusively on us.

To be happy at work, we should be able to achieve truly human goods in organisations. We should be intrinsically motivated and go to work because we love what we do, because we desire to keep achieving *useful*, *pleasant*, *moral* and *spiritual goods*, because we want to keep learning, enjoying, growing and flourishing, even to the point of becoming saints (see Figure 7.5).

At one extreme, there are people who love their work; on the other, you'll find those who hate it, and this is not an exaggeration. Unfortunately, it is a fact that nowadays around 85% of people say that they are not engaged in their jobs, and many of them hate their jobs (Gallup, 2017). As experience shows, when *intrinsic motivation* is lacking, instead of being a meaningful and joyful task, work becomes the opposite.

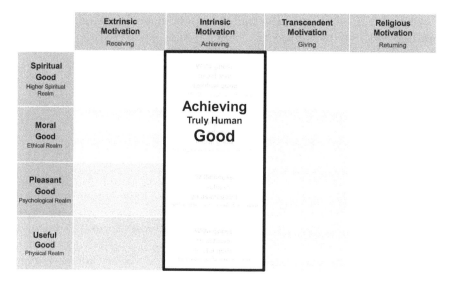

Figure 7.5 Achieving love at work

This is one of the reasons why reflecting on human motivation in the workplace from the perspective of the logic of love is extremely important. It is hard to say why people hate their jobs. It could be due to its external conditions and therefore related to *extrinsic motivations*, or it could be the absence or disorder of *intrinsic motivations*. I will discuss this question further in Chapter 8. Nevertheless, one thing is clear. If the *intrinsic motivations* are among the causes of people hating their jobs, the solution should come from them and not their bosses or colleagues. *Intrinsic motivation* comes from us, and we are free to decide whether to change it or not.

At this point, the issue gives rise to very lively conversations with my students, especially when I suggest they think about their own personal motivations. I tell them that if they do not like to study – that being their current job – they should not blame others (the professors or the content of the programmes). Of course, external factors are important reasons in explaining their higher or lower levels of motivation. Nevertheless, I suggest that they stop and think about how much their *intrinsic motivations* could change regarding their love for their studies and, therefore, for themselves and their own futures.

While it is hard for the students to change the content of their work once they have chosen it – their incentive system or the environment of their studies – they can do a lot to change their own inner motivations. We do not always like what we do, and there are aspects of our work that we probably enjoy less than others, but not everything is connected with what we like and what gives us pleasure. We should do our best to love our work unless it is impossible to be loved for some reason (it is inherently harmful, obscene, evil or sinful). This interest for the things we do, that we consider good in themselves, is what *intrinsic motivation* is all about.

If some of my students insist on telling me that they hate their studies, I recommend they pause and use our *map of human motivations* to diagnosis their deepest personal drivers. There are many reasons why they do not like what they do, including not having any other alternatives, but this does not depend on them. In fact, on many occasions, students discover that the reason they do not like their "job" is that they did not make a free decision when choosing it.

Sometimes the decision came from the pressure of others or was highly influenced by what others would say or think about them (*extrinsic motivation*). It is also true that sometimes what they wanted did not correspond with the opportunities that came their way, but more often than not, they did not stop to reflect seriously about their future or what they wanted to do with their lives. They postponed their decisions or made decisions based mainly on external influences. It seems that there is some kind of disorder here, specifically that they are not using their freedom well and not loving themselves properly.

Oddly enough, and as selfish or self-interested as it might sound, we all have to love ourselves properly. We have to use our freedom to choose what we consider good for us, not what others tell us we should choose. It seems logical that, even before we start friendships with others, we should be good friends with ourselves, so to speak. That's what happiness is about – the desire for our own happiness is the starting point in attaining it, achieving the highest possible good during our lives freely and responsibly.

The characteristics of self-love should be the same as what we described earlier in a perfect or true friendship with others; we should have a sincere friendship with ourselves. We should care for our own truly human good, whose nature is *inseparable*, *interrelated* and *hierarchical*. There is a right human way in our desire for self-love. This well-ordered, right or proper love for ourselves recognises all the good that we deserve, given our human worth and dignity. This is a kind of self-caring that some authors have described as "humble self-esteem" (Esparza, 2013).

A well-ordered self-love corresponds precisely to the universal human yearning to be happy that Aristotle claimed in the first chapter of his *Nicomachean Ethics*. It is the one that, during our lifetime, leads us to preserve our own being and to unfold it towards its perfection until it reaches its summit. This is the content of human life, and the day we stop loving ourselves is the day we start distancing ourselves from what makes us happy.

When we stop loving ourselves properly, we move to all kinds of disordered self-love. We start looking for selfish lower goods, or we become dependent on people's opinion and start trying to attract the attention of others, frequently begging for their love in an excessive manner. I am convinced that many problems related to psychological disorders nowadays, as well as drug consumption, alcohol abuse and other addictions (gambling, pornography, etc.) are related to this lack of ordered and truly human self-love, a "humble self-esteem" (Esparza, 2013).

It is important to understand this point to have the necessary truly human self-esteem. As we discussed in Chapter 3, given the natural hierarchy of human goods, the superior goods presuppose the inferior ones. Therefore, we should first take care of ourselves at the lowest *physical* level: caring about our food, our health, our sleep, our rest, etc. These are basic goods that, early in our lives, we obtain through our families, but as we become adults, we must be able to attain them by ourselves (see Figure 7.5).

This is why we should try to be competent in what we do, to achieve mastery. The capacity to attain these lower necessary goods by ourselves is one of the aspects that work provides us with and is the primary reason why a student should be a good student. If studying is a student's primary "job", they should study well. I tell my students that they should love themselves with a truly human self-love, even at work (see Figure 7.5).

When we do things well, and get the work done, we normally get satisfaction at the *psychological* level. The fulfilled task produces *psychological* peace, a peace that means tranquillity of order (Augustine, 1993). This phenomenon also seems to prove the idea that lower goods exist for the sake of higher ones. The *useful*, practical goods help us attain higher *pleasant* ones, and this enjoyment and peace – the result of the fulfilled task – will also contribute to our desire for other higher goods.

Our competence and mastery, and the satisfaction they produce, can also contribute to attaining moral virtues through the practice of work that is well done. In this context, while working well, one achieves moral virtues, such as optimism, order, industriousness, sense of humour or cheerfulness, among many others. The more we see our work as an opportunity to grow, to attain virtues, the higher the chances are of us thriving for greater ideals at the *ethical* level (see Figure 7.5).

This is what *intrinsic motivation* is about: a love for ourselves that, when rightly ordered and truly human, will contribute to our highest good. But of what does the highest good for us, and thus our well-being or happiness, consist? In Aquinas' view, what is good for us is something that remains good for us even if, for some reason, we do not recognise it as good. He states that what is good for us is necessarily good for us because it follows from our human nature (Feser, 2009).

Therefore, wealth, power, pleasure, fame, honour and the higher goods of the soul have their proper place in contributing to human happiness on their different realms (*physical*, *psychological* and *ethical*). Nevertheless, for this Christian philosopher, it is impossible for all these goods to be the highest or ultimate good to which every other good is subordinated. Aquinas states that God alone can be that good, at the *supernatural* realm (Feser, 2009).

Paradoxically, *godlikeness*, *holiness* or *sanctity*, the intimate union with God, would be the highest good a human being could reach and where the highest happiness would be found, according to the hierarchy of goods and the abundance of truly human self-love. If there is order in love for us, it will produce the best possible version of ourselves: a saint.

In short, thanks to our daily work done with the proper ordered love, we get the chance to attain self-actualisation, to become better people, to *flourish*. Even more, for believers, work may become a way of achieving the highest human spiritual potential, an opportunity to attain holiness (see Figure 7.5).

I remember one MBA student coming to me after I presented these ideas. She told me that she was a Catholic and that she had never thought that you could become a saint through your job. She was surprised after my explanation. She thought that wanting to be holy, or achieving godlikeness, sounded too high an ideal, maybe too bold or even too prideful as well as being something that wouldn't seem to be related with your daily work. My answer was simple. For someone who believes in God, ordered self-love implies attaining the greatest possible good, and this would be entering into a union with God, the greatest Good.

As we will discuss in Chapter 9, employing the *logic of love* in our daily life and work allows human beings to become competent, passionate, morally good and even saints, with God's grace (in the case of believers). As we have seen, in Aristotle's views, to love is to will the good of the person loved; he goes as far as to state that love for oneself is, in fact, a prerequisite to loving others.

In other words, self-love is truly human, as long as you love yourself not just for the sake of loving yourself but also for the benefit of others. For Aristotle, to love is conceived as wanting good for oneself and others (Konstan, 2008). Let us now consider what truly human good for others means.

Giving truly human good in organisations

During my discussions with undergraduates about truly human self-love, some students look perplexed. They cannot believe that the same professor, who had previously criticised current mainstream self-centred theories of motivation, is now suggesting that they should all love themselves as much as they can, infinitely in fact. They are astonished when I tell them that orderly self-love is a key human motivation that includes aiming for mastery, joy, goodness and even sanctity in their work and that without this *intrinsic* motivation, they will hardly know how to love others well.

As St Augustine explained, insisting on the complementarity of both self-love and others-love, to be able to love others, we first need to learn how to love ourselves. He questioned how you would be able to love your neighbour if you don't even know how to love yourself.

Likewise, Aquinas affirmed that the love one feels for another "proceeds from the love that one feels for one's own person". He explained the appropriateness of us humans loving our own good because we are made, by nature, to love all good, including our own. This natural love for ourselves is an urge that can neither be evaded nor renounced (Esparza, 2013).

The truth is that students start to better understand these ideas when they realise that recognising this necessity of ordered self-love does not mean denying the importance of ordered self-giving. Both self-love and self-giving are compatible and complementary. It was Aristotle who defended that they both need each other.

The *intrinsic* desire to be good at work, and to become better day after day (this ordered self-love), is a necessary condition to be happy, but being necessary is not sufficient. Only when that self-love is also open to others' good do *extrinsic*, *intrinsic* and *transcendent* motivations become truly human.

This is what Aristotle meant when he described human beings as social beings. To be happy, we need others. Human happiness is always *inclusive*, not *exclusive*. The exclusivity of self-love would give rise to a competitive, self-centred understanding of work and life, a proud and selfish outlook where others would not matter. This would be an inhuman or immoral behaviour. Therefore, the *transcendent motivation*, understood as self-giving, as the yearning for others' good or the love for others, is a universal human need. As Maslow would say, we are meant to be *transcenders* (Maslow, 1971).

When self-love is *inclusive*, open to sharing its own good with others, it leads to an even higher personal good being attained. For that reason, love is contagious, and it starts inside ourselves. The more we recognise our own human value and dignity, the more we want to share it with others. The discovery, appreciation and connection with our own dignity will also lead us to discover, appreciate and connect with others' dignity. In other words, "honoring dignity is love in action. Human connections flourish when dignity is the medium of exchange" (Hicks, 2018).

This is a human paradox that has been observed generation after generation. Any dedicated grandmother or grandfather could tell us a lot about this. The more one looks for the good of others, the higher the good and joy one ends up achieving. This need for self-giving seems to be a universal fact, one that Maslow was able to verify during the latter years of his career and a fact that is being proven by social scientists, as we saw in Chapter 4, including renowned organisational behaviour researchers (Grant, 2013).

Organisational and social sciences are proving what seems to be common sense. Most of us would rather work in places surrounded by people who are enthusiastic about their jobs, who love what they do and feel well about themselves because of that. It is always great to be around people who thrive in their work and lives because they are happy. Not even self-centred people would desire the opposite. If people around us love their work, we will also most likely end up loving ours, too, precisely because love is *contagious*.

Given the number of people who dislike their jobs, the chances are that we end up working in places where those around us also hate their jobs. This often explains why some people prefer to work alone. It seems obvious that we would all like to work in truly human or humanistic organisations, where people really care about others, trying to give truly human good. If you are a professor, a manager, or just someone working at the service of others, your motivation will be higher if you try to serve them with care, with goodwill and self-giving, rather than with coldness, disinterest or selfishness. This is what Figure 7.6 reflects.

The *transcendent motivation*, understood as true, well-ordered interest for the good of others, a truly human self-giving, opens a whole panorama for the reflection of those who hold positions of responsibility over others. This is the case of many of my Business Administration students. I keep telling them that, in any organisation, good leaders are those who are able to facilitate others moving and acting freely for the truly human good of the group, for the common good, because of *transcendent motivations*.

Since this kind of human *transcendent motivation* is a free human act that can only arise from each person's own initiative, the best way to promote such behaviour is to lead by example. True leaders are those who promote *transcendent motivations* around them because they are driven by these same *transcendent reasons* (Pérez-López, 1974). As we saw, *transcendent motivation* is as contagious as *intrinsic motivation*. Love begets love.

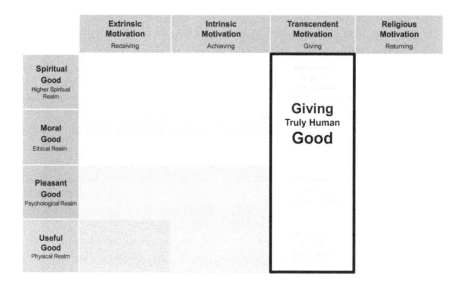

Figure 7.6 Giving love at work

Those who personally behave out of love for others "infect" others with the same caring nature. This is what happens in *ethically healthy organisations*, those in which *human dignity* is treasured and *human flourishing* is promoted (Bañón et al., 2012). When leaders encourage this logic of love, this truly human interest for others, in the workplace on a daily basis, they end up fostering more humane relationships in their organisations and enable others to be more generous.

This logic of love, which begets a logic of *gift*, expresses a deep truth about humans – that their *flourishing* is enabled through relationships of uncalculated giving and grateful receiving. But this logic also has practical implications for organisational management. When in harmony with the logics of *exchange* and *duty*, the logic of *gift* enables greater creativity, freedom and responsibility, inspiring trust and promoting commitment as no other incentive system can do (Baviera et al., 2016).

I don't wish to sound naive here, as this logic of gift, a part of *transcendent motivation*, is not inexorable and involves vulnerability, namely, the vulnerability of those who run the risk of giving for the good of others without expectations of receiving. This could result in others taking advantage of their goodness, or at least not caring and not thanking them for their good work.

Free and unconditional giving is not guaranteed to produce results beyond what the good (the gift) itself accomplishes. A fundamental aspect of unconditional giving is that it is not transactional; fulfilment is found in the gift itself. It is true that it might lead some people to be opportunistic, or it could bring about the opposite, a spirit of generosity in others, and thus generate further good, but this is not its purpose (Baviera et al., 2016). The purpose of *transcendent motivation* is a truly human interest for others.

When *transcendent motivation* is truly human, authentic and reflects a true desire for others' wellness, for its own sake, then it produces its own fruits: the good of the other. This is what human love and the *logic of love* are about. A true caring for others' *well-being* and *flourishing*, and it cannot be conceived as a management technique, much less a manipulative tool, to attain higher personal or organisational results. I always make sure my students understand that I'm not talking about management techniques here but about a *humanistic management* logic, a truly human interest for others, which is compatible with any good professional and transactional human relationship.

We should all desire to contribute to the greater good in our lives and at work. We all need to know that our work is useful for others, that it contributes to making others' lives more pleasant, humane and even divine (see Figure 7.6). Therefore, our leaders and organisations should know about that and help us achieve these noble ideals. Let us now briefly consider how this logic of love in organisations is connected with *spiritual* and *religious motivations*.

Returning truly human good in organisations

I remain aware that many people will think that the concept of motivations I present in this book is too idealistic, and I would agree that this whole approach is essentially idealistic. Human motivations are precisely that: ideals. Without ideals, we would not be motivated at all.

The problem is when we reduce our ideals to materialistic, self-centred, amoral and non-spiritual aspects of human life. I think this is the narrow conception of human nature that is embedded in the theories of motivation that we have been teaching for decades (Guillén, 2018). This is something that Maslow also seemed to have discovered in his final days.

I remember giving a presentation on this map of motivations to a large audience, including faculty members. At the end of the presentation, one colleague told me that my intervention had seemed "unscientific" to him and that he thought that because I mentioned *spirituality* and *religion* I was dedicating myself to "preaching". I could not contain myself and replied that, as teachers, we all preach.

I continued giving my argument to this colleague. The point is that some teachers "preach" theories that are supposed to be scientific, but the truth is that in their attempt to be scientifically neutral, their theories are, in fact, inhuman. I told him that we are educators, and as such, we need to be open to every reliable human source of knowledge, not just the empirical sciences. This is the *humanistic management* perspective, open to the knowledge

170 *Using the map of motivations*

provided by all the human sciences, including the *humanities*, as I discussed earlier in this chapter (see Figure 7.2).

This colleague was most likely concerned about the last column of the map of human motivations dealing with the *religious motivation* (see Figure 7.7). As I mentioned in Chapter 6, I have had people ask me to remove this fourth column from the map to make it more admissible and to consider those who do not believe in God, but I consider the map to be more inclusive when it considers all human motivations, including the *spiritual* and *religious*.

For those who do not have faith in a divine realm, this map confirms their position, telling them that they are not driven by *religious motivation* in how they behave. In these cases, some people will see their highest human values and their spiritual motivations reflected on the third level of the *map*, the *ethical realm*, or even in the upper *higher spiritual* level. In the case of believers, this is a *divine* or *supernatural* spiritual reality.

What is sure, though, is that for those who do not believe in God, the fourth column of the map does not apply to them. They do not "see" this column because they do not have faith in God. Therefore, this proves that the map allows people to identify the motivations they have but also those they do not have. The fourth column of the map makes a lot of sense for those who believe in a personal God, something I have been able to verify every time I have presented this framework (see Figure 7.7).

For believers, if everything you have in your life is a gift from God, then the most *humane* reaction is the desire to be thankful to Him. This is what this fourth column of *religious motivation* is all about: the yearning to give

	Extrinsic Motivation Receiving	Intrinsic Motivation Achieving	Transcendent Motivation Giving	Religious Motivation Returning
Spiritual Good Higher Spiritual Realm				**Returning** Truly Human **Good**
Moral Good Ethical Realm				
Pleasant Good Psychological Realm				
Useful Good Physical Realm				

Figure 7.7 Returning love at work

back to God the *useful*, *pleasant*, *moral* and *spiritual* good. The desire to serve Him, please Him, adore Him and glorify Him. In other words, the longing to return love to God, to *orderly* and *truly humanly* give Him back every kind of good (see Figure 7.7).

As I noted in Chapter 6, I have had many opportunities to talk about this last column with people who do not believe in God. To my surprise, more than once I have been shocked when these people thank me for the entire *map of motivations*, including the *religious* because it helped them better understand not only their own motivations but also those of others.

Both believers and non-believers can all make an act of faith regarding God's existence or non-existence, precisely because God is a spiritual being, and His existence belongs to the realm of faith. Faith is reasonable because, from a purely philosophical point of view, human reason can conclude that God exists. In other words, the qualities of the god discovered by the philosophers are also qualities of the God revealed to human creatures throughout the course of history, as the three monotheist Abrahamic religions believe and that their theologians study.

Believing in God is an act of faith that does not go against reason but surpasses it. This is why the right to freedom of thought, conscience and religion are protected as universal human rights. Faith is supra-rational. It is for this reason that there should be no contradiction between faith and reason. This is what theology strives for, the study of a divine reality using the sources of knowledge provided by philosophical reasoning, faith and revelation. Therefore, no scientist should fear accepting the existence of a faith that is consistent with reason.

As I said previously, this book is not a theological text, but this does not imply denying *religious motivations* nor confusing acceptance of religious reality with religious "preaching", as my colleague suggested. The fourth column of the map reveals the human desire of millions of human beings to have a personal relationship with a God they believe in. This is the meaning of the fourth column on our map, the desire to love God back, to return good to Him in a truly human way.

Moreover, in line with our previous reflections, this desire might be interpreted in terms of the *logic of love* belonging to a truly human friendship. The desire of the friend is to be loved back. "From our side to seek God's good is to want to do God's will. It is to adore and praise and worship God, to delight in God's goodness and to find joy in God's Love. It is to serve God because we are grateful, to be for God because we love" (Wadell, 1992, p. 72). This is precisely the content of the fourth column in the context of work (see Figure 7.7).

Returning truly human good to God, while working in organisations, means finding ordinary work as an opportunity to repay God's Love with human love. For a believer, this means transforming every moment of their life and work into occasions to love God, to serve, please, adore and praise Him (see Figure 7.7). In this way, the "schizophrenic" feeling of separation between professional life and spiritual life disappears, as most likely happened to the woman I mentioned in Chapter 6, who recognised she had this feeling.

I remember explaining this to a group of top American leaders in a presentation at the Harvard Kennedy School of Government a few years ago. A high-ranking military officer asked me about how to use this fourth column when directing and governing people. My immediate reaction was to tell him that *religious motivations* are very delicate, very *fragile*, because they belong to the most sacred sphere of consciences. Therefore, those who rule over people must not use them; they just need to respect them.

It seems logical that a "mechanistic" vision of management and government disciplines leads us to want to use theories as management tools. Precisely for this reason, I wanted to use the metaphor of a map to present the different types of human motivations from a *humanistic management* perspective. The advantage of a map is that it describes reality as it is, identifying different regions and areas but not telling you where to go.

This map has been conceived to help better understand our motivations in life and work and to understand the motivations of others. That is why this chapter tries to describe the *coordinates* of the map, to delve into the logic behind the map – a logic of love that explains the location of every kind of motivation as well as their *inseparable*, *interrelated* and *hierarchical* nature.

Once the coordinates are described, and the reference points are clear, we need a *compass* to understand how to move freely on the map, which will allow us to go to our chosen destination. This will be the purpose of Chapter 8, but before finishing, I would like to offer a final thought to give a clue about the map's coordinates. Not the vertical coordinates but the horizontal. Let me explain.

Thanks to Maslow's original insights and hierarchy of needs, we were able to understand the hierarchical order of human goods and motivations through a kind of "vertical" reasoning. The logic of love helped us identify some types of goods that are of a *higher* nature, more worthy of being loved than others. For this reason, thanks to this hierarchical vertical logic, the *rows* of the map present higher and lower orders of goods. What about the *columns* on the map, though? Is there any horizontal logic behind them?

The *order of love* and the *order of loves*

Some years ago, one of my students surprised the entire class with an incredible comment. After a couple of sessions in which I had explained and discussed the map of human motivations with them, this student asked me if he could share something with his classmates. When I approved, he said, "I know that I have been very talkative this past semester, and that I have been restless and seemingly inattentive in class, but it does not mean that I did not care. As you know, I am a nervous person. However, if I did wrong, it is not because I did not like the course content or because of you guys, but the opposite. Now, after attending these classes about human motivation, I better understand what's wrong with me".

At this point, I had to stop him. I told him that he did not have to talk about personal matters in class. Nevertheless, my comment was to no avail; he was determined to share. He went on to tell us that he was going through serious family difficulties. It was clear that they were also related to his self-esteem. However, what he wanted to tell the class was the news that now, after our discussions on human motivation, he understood why he was not able to behave as expected.

He had concluded that he did not love himself properly. In his own words, "I understood in these sessions that when you feel you are not loved by others, you are incapable of learning to love yourself properly, and then you just fight against everyone, including yourself".

He continued, "What I've got from this course is that in order to learn how to love ourselves, we need to be loved by others first". He explained that we need to feel an unconditional love, something that we do not always get. He continued, "My conclusion after our discussions is that the best way of solving this problem is by learning how to give our love to others". He was essentially applying the traditional Golden Rule, as he recognised.

I could not believe what was happening. This student was sharing his vulnerabilities and then helping others in the class comprehend the logic of the framework of motivations, which he had come to understand perfectly. After his comments, I told him that he was going to be a great entrepreneur because of his honesty and especially because of his capacity to love.

What this student had just described is something that I had tried to explain throughout the semester while revealing each column of the map of motivations. Once I finish explaining the entire map, I tell them that there is still a rule, the classic Golden Rule, that could help them understand the relationship between the different columns of the map, a kind of "horizontal" logic.

Of course, the Golden Rule is a maxim that can be found in many religions and in almost every ethical tradition in some form (Blackburn, 2001). It establishes that "you should not treat others in ways that you would not like to be treated", or, in positive terms, "you should treat others as you would like others to treat you".

This simple rule contains a profound wisdom about human dignity. The realisation that people possess a special and unique value gives us the reason to understand that everybody deserves special respect and treatment, starting with ourselves. Leaders of the world's major faiths endorsed the Golden Rule as part of the 1993 "Declaration Toward a Global Ethic" (Küng, 1993). Moreover, well-known authors have already studied this issue in the context of *humanistic management* (Pirson et al., 2016).

In practical organisational terms, this principle of reciprocity is priceless in order to make good managerial decisions, but we cannot stop here to consider this question. Regarding the interpretation of the coordinates of our map, the Golden Rule is also basic because it can help answer the question of how the columns are related. Should I love others more than myself, less or equally? In other words, which of the four columns goes first? Is there a kind of order?

The answer provided by the Golden Rule would affect the first three columns, referring to our relationship with others but not with the Other. Belief in God is not necessary to endorse the Golden Rule (Esptein, 2010). According to the rule, we must love ourselves as much as others or, to put it the other way around, we must love others as much as ourselves. So, the answer is that we should love others with a love that is equal to how we love ourselves.

Another question regarding the columns of the map is how many are necessary to attain happiness? Are all of them needed? This is a question that I am usually asked at the end of my presentations. The Golden Rule can again help us in the response on a natural, rational or philosophical level. I shall offer a few thoughts on the last column, and its necessity in attaining happiness, next.

We are all born with a natural self-preservation instinct, which corresponds to the *extrinsic useful motivation* in the left corner of the map. Therefore, there is no doubt that, as long as we are not mentally sick, we will try to do our best to care for ourselves. What the Golden Rule suggests is to not stop there but to move to the right, to care about others in at least the same way.

There is another interesting point here. The rule is to love others as much as we love ourselves, or to love ourselves as much as we love others. Therefore, we should not love ourselves any more or any less than we love others. Loving ourselves less than we love others would be a lack of ordered self-esteem, as the student I mentioned discovered, and loving ourselves more than others would be egoism.

These reflections could be much more nuanced, and, without a doubt, they are the source of very interesting discussions with students. We can't stop here either, though. The question that remains unanswered is: what about religious motivations? Are they needed? Is there a similar rule to the Golden Rule that can assist us here?

If there is a rule that helps interpret the role that corresponds to *religious motivation*, it can only come from religious sources. Obviously, if non-believers don't "see" the need for the fourth column because, among other things, the source of the column itself is God's revelation, then they don't need a rule that includes it either. As you have probably already guessed, though, there is indeed a rule for believers that comes from Abrahamic tradition and that complements the Golden Rule.

This rule is expressed in the primary Jewish prayer, the Shema, "Hear, O Israel: The LORD our God, the LORD is one. And you shall love the LORD your God with all your heart and with all your soul and with all your strength" (Deuteronomy 6:4–5). This religious law complements the

Golden Rule in that the Jewish tradition says, "but love your neighbor as yourself" (Leviticus 19:18). It is clear that the point of the whole law is love. It is a commandment of love, given in the Old Testament and repeated by Jesus Christ in the New Testament (Matthew 22:35–40).

If you have been paying attention, you will notice that these two commandments are the best summary of the entire map of human motivations described in this book. The map of motivations includes the four loves prescribed by this divine law. First, the love for God (fourth column), followed by the love for others (third column), which should have the same intensity as the love for ourselves and the love from others (second and first columns). Once again, faith and reason seem not to contradict each other at all (see Figure 7.8).

Even those without faith find these reflections fascinating and worth considering. As we look again at Figure 7.8, those "Aha!" moments come from many attending the sessions on human motivations. What we can now appreciate in the map is that, in addition to the vertical *order of love* that we discussed before, there is also a horizontal *order of loves*. Whereas the *order of love* refers to the hierarchical vertical order of each one of the columns in the map, the *order of loves* refers to the horizontal order of all the columns and answering which of them goes first.

This *order of loves* is precisely that described in the first and second Jewish commandments, which means that man should first love God and then others, as much as they love themselves. Therefore, it would be a disorder to firstly or exclusively focus on ourselves, as well as firstly or exclusively

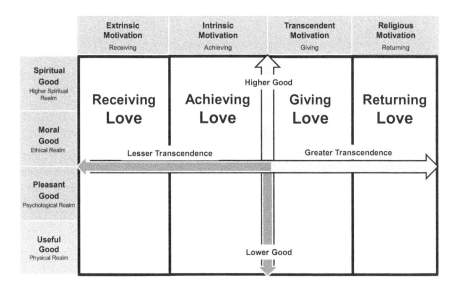

Figure 7.8 Map coordinates for motivations: The order of love and order of loves

focusing on others. More so, as we saw in Chapter 6, it seems that God is a zealous lover and, according to Abrahamic revelation, He asked men to freely love Him first. This is a mystery and a paradox, even for believers. Being God, He can do anything except force anyone to love Him.

This last reflection shows how valuable human freedom is for both believers and non-believers. What this map allows to be appreciated graphically is that not only does there seem to be an *order of love*, and an *order of loves*, it also proves the value of human freedom. This human capacity to choose and to want the good we decide to pursue.

Motivations are not inevitable external stimuli nor are they irresistible internal impulses, as that would be a reductive, *mechanistic* view of human motivations. As we will discuss in Chapter 8, a *humanistic* conception of motivations means that they are not given by the organisation but that we choose them freely. We decide the motives of our conduct freely and the meaning we want to give to our lives and to our work. Before moving to the next chapter, let us first stop to reflect on some of the questions we just discussed.

Some questions for reflection

1 *How often do I see my work as just a job to get ahead in life?*
2 *How often do I go to work with concerns and worries in mind?*
3 *How often do I complain about my work?*
4 *How often do I go to work with the desire to do something worthy for others?*
5 *How often do I see my work as an opportunity to serve and help others?*
6 *How often do I go to work with an enthusiasm and a desire to start working?*
7 *How often do I see my work as an opportunity to be happy?*
8 *How often do I see my work as a gift from something greater than me?*
9 *How often do I see my work as a gift from God?*
10 *How often do I see my work as an opportunity to serve God?*

A final critical thought on why having a map is not enough

After answering these questions, you might get the impression that there are some aspects of your motivations that could be improved in your work and maybe in your life; that is always my case. I guess that we can always improve our love for the things we do, for the people we work for and, in the case of believers, for God. It seems that there is always room for improvement and growth.

Through this book, we have found that our motivations are not good enough. The good news is that we can always rectify our intentions, correct our navigation and arrive at a better destination every day. Having a good map is always helpful, but the map is not sufficient. In order to arrive at any particular place, in addition to the map, we need a *compass*. We need an instrument to find the directions that always point to a fixed place to help us set the course to where we want to go.

Anyone who likes sailing, flying or hiking in the mountains knows perfectly well that a compass is an essential instrument to identify where we are on the map and to establish the course we want. In the case of human motivations, we can use the map to identify our position. Do we have an instrument to help us to identify where to go, though? The *compass* for our map is nothing more than the kind of *meaning* we want to give to our work. As we will see, there are different meanings of work, and knowing each of them will serve as a navigation tool to get to wherever we want to go.

Note

1 By classical, I mean based on the dialogue of classical Greek philosophers, such as Aristotle, Plato or Socrates, in dialogue with other later classical philosophers and theologians, such as Augustine of Hypona or Thomas Aquinas.

References

Augustine, S. (1993). *The City of God*. New York: Random House, pp. 690–691.

Bañón, A. J., Guillén, M. & Gil, I. (2012). Ethics and learning organizations in the New Economy. In *Human Resource Management in the Digital Economy: Creating Synergy Between Competency Models and Information*. Hershey (Pennsylvania, EE.UU.): IGI Global, pp. 67–79.

Baviera, T., English, W. & Guillén, M. (2016). The 'Logic of Gift': Inspiring behavior in organizations beyond the limits of duty and exchange. *Business Ethics Quarterly*, 26(2), 159–180.

Blackburn, S. (2001). *Ethics: A Very Short Introduction*. Oxford: Oxford University Press.

Burggraf, J. (2012). *Made for Freedom*. New York: Scepter.

Esparza, M. (2013). *Self-esteem Without Selfishness*. New Rochelle, NY: Scepter.

Esptein, Greg M. (2010). *Good Without God: What a Billion Nonreligious People Do Believe*. New York: HarperCollins.

Feser, E. (2009). *Aquinas. A Beginner's Guide*. Oxford, England: Oneworld Publications.

Fisher, C. (2010). Happiness at work. *International Journal of Management Reviews*, 12, 384–412.

Gallup. (2017). *State of the Global Workplace. Gallup Report*. New York: Gallup Press. www.gallup.com/workplace/238079/state-global-workplace-2017.aspx.

Grant, A. (2013). *Give and Take: A Revolutionary Approach to Success*. New York: Viking.

Guillén, M. (2018). Creating better human motivation theories for personal flourishing in organizations. In *Personal Flourishing in Organizations*. Cham, Switzerland: Springer, pp. 49–65.

Guillén, M., Ferrero, I. & Hoffman, W. (2015). The neglected ethical and spiritual motivations in the workplace. *Journal of Business Ethics*, 128(4), 803–816.

Hicks, D. (2018). *Leading with Dignity: How to Create a Culture That Brings Out the Best in People*. New Haven and London: Yale University Press.
Konstan, D. (2008). Aristotle on love and friendship. *SCHOLE*, II(2), 207–212.
Küng, H. (1993). *A Global Ethic: The Declaration of the Parliament of the World's Religions*. New York: Continuum.
Lewis, C. S. (1991). *The Four Loves*. Orlando, FL: Hartcourt Brace & Co.
Maslow, A. H. (1971). *The Farther Reaches of Human Nature*, Ed. Arkana. New York: Penguin Books.
Pérez-López, J. A. (1974). Organizational theory: A cybernetic approach. *IESE Research Paper*, July 1974, WP n° 5.
Pirson, M., Goodpaster, K. & Dierksmeier, C. (2016). Guest editors' introduction: Human dignity and business. *Business Ethics Quarterly*, 26(4), 465–478. https://doi.org/10.1017/beq.2016.47.
Wadell, P. (1992). *Primacy of love. An Introduction to the Ethics of Thomas Aquinas*. New York: Paulist Press.

8 The *compass* for motivations
Searching for a meaningful work-life balance

Meaning in life and motivations

In Chapter 7, we saw how the *logic of love*, or the logic of our desire for truly human goods,[1] allowed us to better understand the coordinates of our map of motivations in life and work. Following this logic, we concluded that some goods are higher than others, more worthy of being loved or more truly human (friendship, virtue, holiness, etc.). In addition, there are goods that come first (service, gratefulness, worship, etc.) due to their being more "transcendent", involving others and not just ourselves (see Figure 7.8).

Now, once the internal logic of the map has been shown, and its coordinates identified, I usually recommend students use the map to diagnose their personal motivations, in their lives in general, and not just with their studies. This exercise allows them to see for themselves to what extent this theory is useful, contributing to their personal self-knowledge. Furthermore, the map will eventually allow them to reflect on the meaning they give to their lives.

Without a doubt, taking a hard look at our motivations is a complex task. Each of our actions can be motivated for a multitude of reasons, and all of them are interrelated and fluctuating. For this reason, I encourage students to use Figure 8.1 as a framework to look for specific evidence that justifies the presence of the different kinds of motivations in their decisions, those that they find in their daily behaviours and in their ordinary life.

Normally, the best way to look for evidence on what moves you to act (what motivates you) is to think about the time dedicated to different kinds of activities every day. It seems logical that we spend more time on the activities that interest us the most, on what we love the most, but this is not always the case. For example, students who go to class out of duty or obligation or to pass their exams because they have no other choice are not positively motivated. For this reason, as well as considering the time dedicated to each activity, I ask students to think about the reason or reasons behind them, to think about the motives that lead to them spending time doing that activity.

At this point, students prepare their own lists of the things they do on a daily basis and the motivations behind them before adding the evidence to

	Extrinsic Motivation Receiving	Intrinsic Motivation Achieving	Transcendent Motivation Giving	Religious Motivation Returning
Spiritual Good Higher Spiritual Realm	Receive **Grace** from God	Achieve **Holiness** through God's action	Give **Light** to others	Return **Praise** to God
Moral Good Ethical Realm	Receive **Respect** from others	Achieve **Excellence** through our actions	Give **Good** to others	Return **Adoration** to God
Pleasant Good Psychological Realm	Receive **Esteem** from others	Achieve **Satisfaction** through our actions	Give **Joy** to others	Return **Gratefulness** to God
Useful Good Physical Realm	Receive **Support** from others	Achieve **Competence** through our actions	Give **Service** to others	Return **Fidelity** to God

Figure 8.1 The map of motivations and the meaning in life

the corresponding boxes on the map. Some use a Likert-type scale, rating items on a level of agreement (Strongly agree, Agree, Neutral, Disagree and Strongly disagree); others add plus and minus signs, and some employ a traffic-lights system.

For example, using Figure 8.1 as a pattern to fill up her own map, one student shaded boxes in green (as having those motivations) related to achieving competence and satisfaction in the second column. In her comments, she said that she would like to learn and enjoy life. She added green to the achievement of excellence, because she wanted to become a better person at the same time. In addition, she also included "give joy" and "give good" as green in the third column. The remaining boxes were red. She did not consider them to be her important motivations, the ones giving meaning to her life.

As I have said, this exercise is personal, and I never ask students to share it with the class. If they share it with me, it is always of their own volition as part of our mentoring sessions during my office time. Normally, for them to learn how to do this exercise, we analyse the real case of a third party, such as Vicente, who I mentioned in Chapter 5. When doing this exercise, many practical issues arise related to people management and their motivations.

Among the many reflections that this type of exercise allows, one of the most important is realising that motivations are always personal, in the sense that they belong to the entire person. Nevertheless, motivations are always intangible, which means that in order to be known, they have to be shared and communicated. We can always guess, but we will most likely make big mistakes as managers. Therefore, we should never guess what others' motivations are; we should ask them. Good managers judge subordinates' actions but not their intentions. If they want to know motivations, they should ask and listen.

If this can be applied to the management of other people in organisations, even more so should it be applied to the management of our own motivations. Stopping to reflect on your own motivations using the map is an exercise that all those attending my seminars have always appreciated. This explains why many say that this is a very practical theory. As for the students, they all seem to be thankful for having learnt about this map and having used it for their own personal reflection.

The student I quoted a moment ago wrote at the end of the course, "This map has been a great help to me in realising what motivates me. Stopping to think and reflect on it has made me realise that, in my case, the motivations that led me to study management and my personal motivations in life do not coincide. I have decided that from now on I will not stop looking for what makes me happy, what I am good at and what really motivates me". The reason she was able to differentiate between her personal and professional motivations is that I asked her to compare them both.

As we will see in the coming sections, one of the key reasons why it is not easy to find a balance between personal and professional life is precisely because of the tension between the different motivations in play. Before discussing the balance between work and personal life, let us pause for a moment to consider the most common motivations and meanings in work that I have found among those attending seminars and classes on people management.

The meaning of work and motivations

As the courses and seminars I usually teach are about people management and business organisation, our goal is to understand people's motivations in organisations. For this reason, once the students have understood this *humanistic theory of motivations* in general terms, as well as the *map of motivations* and its internal logic, I ask them to go back again and use this tool to analyse their own motivations and the meaning they seek in their work.

On this occasion, the question I ask is along the lines of what they usually look for in their work. What moves them to go to work every day? Obviously, in terms of their content, the answers of the professionals who attend the seminars are usually different from those of students. However, as we will see, the responses between them are not so different regarding the most common type of motivations at work.

As I did before, I suggest that students and professionals use the map in Figure 8.1 as a pattern to help them answer this question and to diagnose their motivations at work. It makes sense that the motivations and meaning of work are not the same for students with no real work experience as

182 *Using the map of motivations*

they are for mid-career senior managers, at least concerning the reasons that move them to go to work daily.

The purpose that leads a young student to work (studying, in most cases) is usually related to things such as obtaining a degree that allows them to get a well-paid job, doing what they enjoy the most and, less frequently, learning or becoming competent for their future jobs. These have been the most common answers from the majority of my students since I started using this tool in my classes several years ago. All these responses (to be paid, to enjoy and to learn) are found in the lower-left quadrant of the map of motivations that refers more specifically to work (see Figure 8.2).

The responses of MBA students differ slightly from those of undergraduates, but not by much. What moves them to study an MBA is to earn a good salary, but they also add the idea of achieving a good job with high social status and that gives them prestige. Of course, they also want to be professionally competent and to be among the best in their areas of expertise. Once again, all the responses (to be paid, to be esteemed, to learn and to enjoy) are located in the lower-left quadrant of the map (see Figure 8.2).

Finally, the answers that mid-career managers often give for what moves them to go to work is to achieve financial security or to earn a good salary that allows them to support their families and enjoy life. In this case, it is evident that senior professionals go to work to be paid, but they have the need to serve in mind, to support the other members of their family. Many of them seek to maintain status (to be esteemed), although not all recognise it. What is striking is that, in most cases, they do not mention that they go to work to learn or to enjoy (see Figure 8.2).

	Extrinsic Motivation Receiving	Intrinsic Motivation Achieving	Transcendent Motivation Giving	Religious Motivation Returning
Spiritual Good Higher Spiritual Realm	To Be Sanctified	To Be a Saint	To Sanctify	To Honour
Moral Good Ethical Realm	To Be Respected	To Flourish	To Do Good	To Worship
Pleasant Good Psychological Realm	To Be Esteemed	To Enjoy	To Please	To Thank
Useful Good Physical Realm	To Be Paid	To Learn	To Serve	To Be Faithful

Figure 8.2 The map of motivations and the meaning in work

It is evident that the findings I get from those attending my classes and seminars are not necessarily representative; however, the purpose here is not so much to offer a global and rigorous map of what the motivations are at work today but, rather, to help those attending the sessions to know their own motivations better and to interpret them. The purpose here is to show what the most common motivations are in these cases and to learn how to read the map. If these findings were truly global and could be generalised, what would they be telling us? How can we interpret the position they indicate on the map? Before conducting more in-depth research with this map, it is necessary to know how to use and interpret it.

For this, we need some instrument to help us, to interpret the different positions that can be found on the map. The instrument that normally serves this purpose is the *compass*. Is there a *compass* that tells us where we are on our *map of motivations*? As we will see next, the answer is yes. The *compass* that allows us to interpret this map comes from understanding the different meanings of work. How do we conceive our work, what purpose or meaning do we give to it? Is it just a *job*, is it a *career* or is it a *calling* or *higher calling*?

The meaning of work as a *job*

In April 2019, I was invited to attend an interdisciplinary conference at Harvard on the meaning of life. The event had a significant impact on my understanding of human motivations and on the content of this book. Until then, I was planning to write a book exclusively about a *humanistic* approach to motivations in organisations, just the first and second parts of this book that you are reading now, but it was then that I decided to connect the map of motivations to the meaning of life and work. At that conference, I understood that these issues are inseparable, and I started to become familiar with the literature on the meanings of work and its relationship with the meaning of life. It was there that I decided to write the third part of this book.

At that conference, I learnt more about the origin of meaningful work theories. It seems that they draw their inspiration from Durkheim's (1897) sociological analysis of suicide. I read this in a text published by Michael F. Steger of Colorado University, one of the world's experts on purpose and meaning at work and who I was lucky enough to meet personally at that conference. I owe him everything I have learnt in this area of knowledge.

In one of his works, Professor Steger explained that it was Durkheim who "argued that one cause of suicide was unemployment because it deprived people of their function and their opportunity to contribute to society" (Steger, 2017, p. 61). More than one hundred years after Durkheim's observations about the direct impact of losing one's place in society through the loss of work, we still see the importance of having a meaningful *job*.

As Professor Steger explained, "meaningful work is viewed as a way to bring harmony, if not balance, to the busy lives of workers, providing workers with well-being at the office and providing organizations with enhanced productivity, performance, and dedication" (Steger, 2017, p. 60). In his view, meaningful work seeks to understand the meaning and value work provides to people.

Given the growing body of research in this area, it seems that "meaningful work holds the promise of being the 'next big thing' among organizations seeking a lever for improving organizational performance" (Steger, 2017, p. 60). Even though scholars have differed on how they formally define this concept, "the common thread across all definitions is the idea that for work to be meaningful, an individual worker must be able to identify some personally meaningful contribution made by his or her effort" (Steger, 2017, p. 60).

As we saw in the previous section, undergraduates, MBA students and senior managers all want to have a job. There is nothing wrong about conceiving your work as a *job*, in fact, just the opposite. When we go to work with a "job" mind-set, we work for the money. We are extrinsically motivated, for practical and useful reasons. Work is seen as a means to an end, to financially support life outside of work, and therefore is a basic necessity, a kind of need that is universal. This is the first basic purpose of the majority of jobs: to support us and our families.

We all need an occupation, so, again, there is nothing wrong with having the concept of our work as a *job*. What would be wrong is not to be able to get a job, or to only have access to bad, inhuman or unfair jobs. This is why I always advise my students to make sure they start looking for a good job as soon as they can. I suggest they find employment capable of helping them and their future families satisfy their *extrinsic useful motivations*. We all need and want to receive useful good. The starting point of any good work should be its capacity to contribute to the satisfaction of our basic needs (see Figure 8.3).

It is true that work is a means to an end and is why we all need to have a job. However, this statement is not entirely accurate. To be more specific, we should say that work could be a means to many possible and different ends, goals or purposes. This is what we have been discussing in this chapter; there are different *meanings* we can give to our work, different reasons or purposes we look for when working. One of these purposes is related to obtaining *useful goods*, the lowest meaning of work, but the first and necessary one, as Figure 8.3 captures.

For most people, having a job, daily occupation or task, is an essential ingredient in a fulfilled and healthy life. These were precisely Durkheim's findings regarding the negative impact of losing one's place in society through the loss of work and the resulting number of people committing suicide (Steger, 2017). Unless one is ill, ageing or incapable of working, having a job or looking for one is crucial to fulfilling life. This is why whenever I meet former students who are unemployed, if they ask, I suggest they think of their search for employment as a job in itself.

The compass for motivations 185

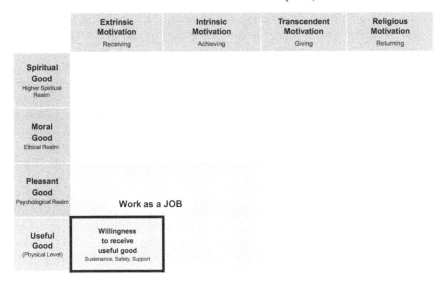

Figure 8.3 The meaning of work as a job

When work is seen as just a job, it is progressively perceived in a negative light. It is just the price you have to pay to receive other higher goods later and in some other place. People will look for other activities outside their job to fulfil their other higher *motivations*. This is why so many people, when they go to work, dream about the upcoming weekend. They don't love their work; in fact, only 15% of the world's one billion full-time workers are engaged at work, the other 85% are not engaged (Gallup, 2017).

Even though having a job is necessary, reducing the meaning of our work exclusively to its useful purpose, seeing it as "just a job", is neither the only nor the best possible alternative. What the literature on meaningful work in recent decades seems to keep proving is that being stuck in such a limited mind-set of work is counterproductive. People who see their work as just a job "tend to be dissatisfied, finding little meaning in what they do. They also are generally looking for something new" (Barnett, 2012).

In addition to making money, there are many other *higher goods* at stake in our work in human organisations, precisely because they are human. Organisations cannot be reduced to their technical or financial functions; in the case of business organisations, they are not simply moneymaking machines as some might pretend. The meaning we give to our work can be greater than just a way of paying our bills or making a lot of money.

When the only good at stake in an organisation is the practical, *useful* one, the vision of human work remains limited to just its practical or technical dimension. In these cases, effectiveness and efficiency become the only criteria that seem to matter in making decisions. Incentive systems are then centred mainly on monetary rewards, premiums, bonuses and all kinds of financial return. This is often the case when the purpose of the organisation is reduced to its bottom line: making money.

Of course, the managers in charge of running companies know that, in addition to money, most people would rather work in a friendly environment, have fun and become masters at what they do. This simple reason would explain why the concept of work promoted in most companies and business schools is the meaning of work conceived as a *career*. What does work focussed on a professional career consist of? Let us now consider this.

The meaning of work as a *career*

When work is perceived as a *career* opportunity, it is then a kind of stepping-stone to reaching a higher-level goal related to more success. This gives work a higher meaning, not only because it pays (as a job) but also because it produces prestige, satisfaction and advancement (Barnett, 2012). The entire idea of conceiving of our work as a *career* is encapsulated visually by the first two columns and the first two levels of our map of human motivations. This visual representation also allows the concept of work as a *career* to be compatible with that of work as a *job* and in the majority of cases will include it (see Figure 8.4).

Within this career orientation, one generally aims to impress others, so one tends to strive for the next promotion and greater prestige (*extrinsic pleasant motivation*). It makes one look for personal satisfaction, a feeling

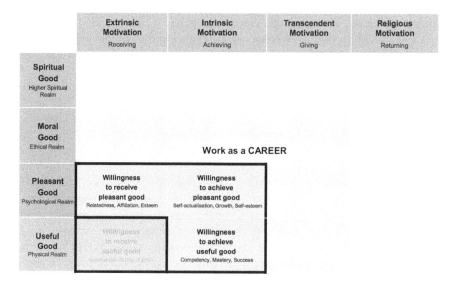

Figure 8.4 The meaning of work as a career

that one is "winning" when achieving some goal and measuring most things in terms of competition, success and excitement (*intrinsic pleasant motivation*) (see Figure 8.4).

Of course, this *career* view demands more training and aiming for continuous personal advancement (*intrinsic useful motivation*). These are the kinds of motivations that are captured as we move inside the second grouping of our map of human motivations. As we discussed earlier, lower levels of goods in our map are necessary and subordinate to higher-level goods. In order to have a *career*, you first need to have a *job* (see Figure 8.4).

It is clear that the concept of work as a *career* is higher than a *job*. Now, work is not only seen as a means to obtain financial support, it is not just a way to get the resources needed to enjoy our time away from the *job*; it now becomes an end in itself. We have higher interests and ambitions that are expressed through doing the work itself. That is why the *intrinsic motivations* become the cornerstone of this meaning of work, as we saw in Chapter 1.

When we see our work as a *career*, we have a deeper personal investment in it. We mark our achievement not only through external monetary gain, but also through achievement in the work and advancement within the occupational structure. This advancement often brings a higher social standing, increased power within the scope of one's occupation and higher self-esteem (Wrzesniewski et al., 1997).

This concept of work as a *career* is the most widespread in today's world of management education, in particular, and in most professional training in general. Schools, colleges and universities have become places where people look for the necessary qualifications and skills for their future professional careers. Within this generalised social framework in Western countries, work success is measured mostly in terms of salary and prestige (*extrinsic motivations*) but also in terms of competence or mastery, power and self-satisfaction (*intrinsic motivations*).

As we discussed in Chapter 1, *intrinsic* motivation is presented currently as the key factor in explaining higher levels of motivation, engagement and commitment in the workplace. Everyone has a permanent natural desire to look for the things they consider good, this is precisely the substance of our motivations, and these goods constitute the purpose or *telos* of our actions. We are insatiable purpose seekers, good seekers, and having a *career* brings more goods than just having a *job*, as we have just discussed (see Figure 8.4).

Because we are insatiable purpose seekers, we have the tendency to look constantly for higher and wider goods in our lives, and that means that we have the tendency to look for higher and wider meaning in our work, too. This explains that, when we care about having a job, we also start caring about the work itself, its *intrinsic* meaning. We then have the desire to enjoy and improve in our work, to become better at what we do, to improve our *career*. Furthermore, and because of this permanent desire for higher and wider goods, things do not stop there.

As we saw in Chapter 7, given that we want to achieve as many goods as we can, we have this tendency to move up and to the right in our map of motivations. If we love what we do in our work, the inner tendency is to then transcend our own good and try to reach out to others to share that good with them. As we discussed in Chapter 4, the *intrinsic motivation* is contagious. As the medieval philosophical adagio goes, *bonum est diffusivum sui* ("the good diffuses itself"). The good always tends to disseminate, and this is probably what explains the tendency of so many to conceive work as a *calling*. But what does it mean to conceive our work as a *calling*?

The meaning of work as a *calling*

Those who fall into the *calling* category often see their work as more meaningful. People who have a calling view their work as one of the most important parts of their lives and a vital part of their identity. Their source of motivation comes from the fulfilment that doing the work brings them. "They see their work as a positive end in itself. They feel good about what they're doing. They give more to their work. They get more from it. And here's a secret about people with callings: Not only are they happy and fulfilled, they're often very successful, sometimes bringing financial rewards" (Barnett, 2012).

A well-known example of this higher meaning of work is the story about the answer that a janitor gave to President John F. Kennedy while on a visit to NASA in 1962. He saw this janitor mopping the floor and asked him what his job was at NASA. He replied, "I'm helping send a man to the moon". He didn't say he was cleaning that area to earn some money (seeing his work as a *job*), or because he liked it, or that it would help him get a better job (seeing his work as a *career*).

No, his answer was related to a higher purpose, a bigger meaning. He was contributing to a project that was greater than he was, and he felt proud of his work because of that. This is precisely what it means to conceive our work as a *calling*. We see a higher purpose behind the work. We feel it is highly rewarding and inspiring.

When we see our work as a *calling*, the content of the work is relativised; it does not matter if it is big or small – mopping the floor or landing on the moon – its value will depend on the meaning that each person gives to the work. Because each person is unique, each must discover the unique gift that they can give to the world. We will reflect on this in more detail in the final chapter.

Research proves that those seeing their work as a *calling* are most likely to feel a deep alignment between their professional aptitude and who they are as a person. They are enthusiastic, have a sense of transcendent purpose and are willing to work harder and longer to make a contribution. They make helping others a higher priority. Unsurprisingly, this group is often the most satisfied with their professional situation (Barnett, 2012).

Not long ago, I had a conversation with a colleague in Boston. When I told her about my passion for teaching and my desire to write this book, she told me, "It is clear that you are listening and answering to your *inner calling*". At first, it sounded quite weird to me, mostly because we do not use that expression much in Spanish, but then I suddenly understood what it means to conceive our work as an *inner calling*.

An inner calling is something you have to listen for, to understand and to answer. The calling is something that comes to someone and is individual to that person. It is something that calls out to everyone in a different way in our consciences if we listen to it. You don't hear it once and then immediately recognise it. It takes time to discover it. You've got to attune yourself to find it because it is something internal and deep within your conscience, a reflection, intuition or desire to discover the meaning of what we do, why do we do it and for what purpose.

The inner calling that my colleague was talking about is related to the concept of moral conscience that I described in Chapter 3 – the judgement of our reason whereby we recognise the moral quality of our actions. In our conscience, we can judge the reasons we go to work and why we keep working as we do. This is related to discovering our own talents, our own capabilities and our own potential to contribute to a greater good.

When we see our work as a *calling*, we tend to think that the things we do in life, be they great or small, make a difference as if we had been called to do it. Moreover, once we find our calling, we have a higher meaning, a sense of transcendent purpose or a mission in our work and in our lives. In our later years, we will be able to look back to see the impact we made on the world, an impact that some will measure exclusively in terms of the money they made in their *job* and the fun they had outside it. Others will also value that impact in terms of their *career* achievements. Others will view their time in terms of personal human growth and service to a *calling*. These are all different meanings that we can freely give to our work and lives.

As you probably remember, I mentioned a colleague in Chapter 7 who once told me that it seemed that I was preaching more than teaching because I talk about motivation, meaning and purpose beyond its economic scope. I replied that, as teachers of management, we are supposed to teach how to make good decisions. Therefore, by providing a wider view of what "good" means, beyond strictly material good, we enhance our students' capabilities to make better decisions. We can help them be better and freer in finding good *jobs*, in pursuing good *careers*, but even more importantly, in better hearing their inner *callings*.

As the map of human motivations shows (see Figure 8.5), the material good is necessary, but it is neither the highest nor the only good at stake in the workplace. This is why this book is part of a *humanistic management* series. Only by considering other higher levels of human good can a manager understand the higher meanings that people give to their work.

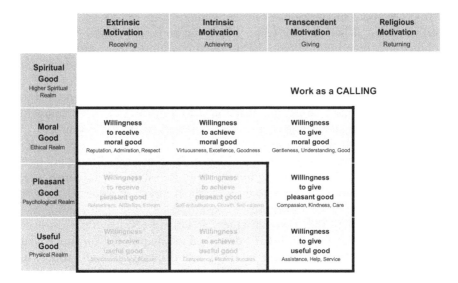

Figure 8.5 The meaning of work as a calling

As Figure 8.5 shows – looking at the third row from the left – when we try to find our *calling*, we are then open to receiving advice from others who care about us (*receiving* moral good). We want to find the best version of ourselves (*achieving* moral good). We desire to contribute to the well-being of others (*giving* moral good) that includes their entire humanness. It means that we care about their moral human flourishing but also – now looking at the third column going downwards – about making their life more pleasant (giving *pleasant* good) and helping them through our work, by serving them (giving *useful* good).

Again, I reiterate to my students that the meaning of our work refers to the purposes we choose to follow when working. We may decide to see our work as "just a job", or we can choose to move towards a more meaningful view of our daily work. Either way, we are the ones finding meaning in what we do; no one else can find that meaning for us.

As we saw in Chapter 7, our insatiable desire for the good corresponds to our desire for love, for truly human good, even in the workplace. Therefore, we can say that the deepest meaning of our work depends mainly on the love with which we look at it, on the love with which it is done and on the love or the true human good that it produces. Of course, this meaning is affected by the nature of the work itself, by the organisation in which we work and by the work environment in general, among other things. Nevertheless, it is in our hands to give a greater or lesser meaning to our work.

Clearly and simply stated, it is our choice to work with more or less love, to make the work more or less human.

Meaningful work itself represents an opportunity to transition from organisational practices that simply seek to maximise effort and output to those that also contribute to a more humane work that best fits with a *humanistic management* view.

The literature on meaningful work again proves that different people give different meanings to the same jobs and that more meaningful work is not concentrated in particular occupations or positions in organisations. Besides, what seems to also be a universal fact is that people giving higher meaning to their jobs are healthier and happier, capable of finding a better work-life balance (Steger, 2017).

A higher meaningful work perception augments employees' motivation, attitudes of ownership, responsibility and citizenship towards their organisation. It provides greater well-being, health and belongingness inside the organisation (Steger, 2017). People engaged in meaningful work report greater job satisfaction and work enjoyment; they increasingly value their work highly and believe that it plays a more central role in their lives (Steger, 2017). This is precisely what the meaning of work as a *calling* provides to people in their workplaces.

As noted before, attending this conference on the meaning of life at Harvard in 2019 had a major impact on my understanding of the connection between human motivation and meaningful work. While there, I learnt more about a popular model among specialists in this area of knowledge. The model draws upon a three-dimensional orientation towards work and was first presented by Bellah and colleagues (Bellah et al., 1985). I will describe the model now, and then you can best decide to what extent the model fits with the logic of the *map of motivations*.

First, the model describes people who see their work as a *job*. Those who perceive their daily tasks as an avenue towards financial or material compensation. These people have little or no concern for whether work is meaningful or significant; for them, it is just a way of living. Second, people who perceive their work as a *career*. They focus on work as a path towards gaining a sense of achievement, mastery, status or advancement within the organisation. Once again, they have no particular interest in meaning. Third, and in contrast to the previous concepts, there are those who see their work as a *calling*. Their work orientation is mainly focussed on the fulfilment, prosocial benefits and sense of purpose that their daily tasks provide. They are those who are trying to make the world a better place (Steger, 2017).

This *calling* orientation model is relevant to theories of meaningful work because of how scholars have relied on it since it was first published. For example, the later work of Wrzesniewski and colleagues framed their research in the same terms of *calling* as Bellah and found similar results regarding the three concepts of work (Wrzesniewski et al., 1997). On the other hand, authors like Pratt and colleagues proposed that Bellah's classic calling orientation model could itself be further understood as a combination of three independent dimensions (craftsmanship, serving and kinship) that may exist outside the parameters of calling and would be related with work orientation (Pratt et al., 2013).

What all these studies have in common is a multidimensional understanding of the meaning people give to their work. Moreover, and regarding how the model fits with the logic of the *map of motivations*, if you look at the map in the form of expanding rectangles, starting from the lower-left corner (see Figure 8.5), what you see is that each rectangle corresponds exactly to the three work meanings described decades ago by Bellah et al. (1985).

The first rectangle includes the motivations behind a concept of work as a *job*. The second, which includes the first one, gathers the motivations behind a perception of work as a *career* and the third embraces the previous two to include all the motivations that justify a view of work as a *calling* (see Figure 8.5).

This amazing coincidence between the groups of motivations in our map and the kinds of work orientation does not seem to be pure luck. It supports the idea that, as I endorsed in Chapter 6, the map we have seen throughout this book is an accurate taxonomy of the entire range of human motivations. Moreover, this happy coincidence seems to reflect that, following the logic of the *map of motivations* described in Chapter 7, the classification of work orientation understood as a *job*, *career* or *calling* could also be understood in a hierarchical order.

Therefore, we could say that there are work orientations that are higher and better than others in terms of the kinds of good they pursue. In other words, they are greater manifestations of the interest for truly human goods and, for that reason, are more desirable. Here, I defend an even bolder thesis that the different work orientations are not incompatible but are, in fact, complementary, and the ideal one would include them all in a fully integrated manner. What about the final rectangle, then? Can we still talk about a higher meaning of work, a *higher calling*?

The meaning of work as a *higher calling*

People viewing their work as a *calling* think that it contributes to making the world a better place. They are those who "find that their work is inseparable from their life. A person with a Calling works not for financial gain or career advancement, but instead for the fulfilment that doing the work brings to the individual" (Wrzesniewski et al., 1997, p. 22).

Therefore, the concept of *calling* refers to a view of work that is personally meaningful, that is motivated by an interest in serving a prosocial benefit and, additionally, responds to a summons to work that comes from the personal conscience but that could also come from transcendent sources. Such sources could be as different as some perceived external societal need, some respected authorities or some other spiritual reasons, and for those with faith in God, the desire to fulfil God's will, conceived as a *divine higher calling* or *supernatural vocation*.

As the research by Wrzesniewski and colleagues explains, the word "calling" was originally used in a religious context (Wrzesniewski et al., 1997). Nevertheless, as they themselves recognise, while some may consider the modern sense of "calling" to have lost its religious connection, there is evidence that the religious connection still matters (Davidson & Caddell, 1994).

In a religious sense, the concept of *higher calling* or *vocation* (from Latin *vocātiō*, meaning "a call, summons") refers to the call received from God to do His will, to follow a specific path or carry out some *mission*. It is usually understood as stable state of life, permanent over a lifetime. For centuries, the concept was applied mainly to members of formal religious Christian institutions, such as pastors, priests, monks or nuns, and only by analogy to other secular forms of callings.

Only more recently has the religious concept of *vocation* been applied universally to laypeople. Well-known examples of professions that are still today understood as vocations, given their higher levels of social service, are those of doctors, nurses, teachers, the armed forces, police officers and firefighters. The word "vocation" is still used in a religious context with a spiritual meaning, whereas in secular contexts, the use of the word *calling* is more frequent.

Therefore, it is possible to distinguish between, on one hand, the secular concept of *inner calling* (or just *calling*), which is internal and of a moral nature and, on the other hand, the concept of *higher calling* (or *vocation*), which is of a spiritual nature and of a supernatural or divine origin. I find it important to make this distinction because there are several lines of research under the rubric of *calling* that do not include the spiritual content.

Even though the term higher calling is not univocal and may include various motivations of the spiritual and supernatural realms, it is still different, compatible and complementary with the one of just *calling*. Therefore, it is important to distinguish between them and understand the difference.

On one hand, the concept of *calling* captures the idea of a higher meaning of work that makes it personally expressive and with high moral standards to benefit others. It refers to a plausible inner calling to give a higher and more transcendent meaning to our work, and its origin is in our moral conscience (see Figure 8.5). On the other hand, the concept of a *higher calling* or *vocation* captures the idea of a calling whose source is higher, and has a spiritual, transcendent or supernatural origin. This concept demands faith in a spiritual realm, or even faith in the existence of God, the Giver of such a divine supernatural *vocation*, in the case of believers (see Figure 8.6).

The truth is that there is not much empirical evidence for the role of this meaning of work conceived as a *higher calling*. Nevertheless, there is

194 *Using the map of motivations*

	Extrinsic Motivation Receiving	Intrinsic Motivation Achieving	Transcendent Motivation Giving	Religious Motivation Returning
Spiritual Good Higher Spiritual Realm	Willingness to receive spiritual good Gift, Present, Grace	Willingness to achieve spiritual good Sanctity, Blessedness, Holiness	Willingness to give spiritual good Sanctification, Salvation, Blessing	**Work as a HIGHER CALLING** Willingness to return spiritual good Praise, Acclamation, Glory
Moral Good Ethical Realm	Willingness to receive moral good	Willingness to achieve moral good	Willingness to give moral good	Willingness to return moral good Reverence, Adoration, Worship
Pleasant Good Psychological Realm	Willingness to receive pleasant good	Willingness to achieve pleasant good	Willingness to give pleasant good	Willingness to return pleasant good Gratitude, Thanks, Appreciation
Useful Good Physical Realm	Willingness to receive useful good	Willingness to achieve useful good	Willingness to give useful good	Willingness to return useful good Obedience, Assent, Fidelity

Figure 8.6 The meaning of work as a higher calling

evidence that people who see their job as sacred (i.e. a vocation) experience higher job satisfaction, more commitment to their organisation and a lower intention of quitting their job (Walker et al., 2008).

Another study of highly educated working mothers, found that those who declared "sanctification of work" among their purpose predicted higher positive emotions and job satisfaction and lower life-work conflict beyond other measures of religiosity (Hall et al., 2012). In the same vein, another more recent study indicated that the sanctification of work was a significant predictor of job satisfaction, turnover intention and organisational commitment after controlling for personality, spirituality, religiosity, psychological safety and demographic variables (Carroll et al., 2014).

To be precise, this concept of sanctification of work has been measured as a psychological construct that includes every process through which people perceive aspects of life (in this case of work-life) to possess a spiritual character and significance. As we will see in Chapter 9, this concept fits with the religious idea of a universal call to sanctity, to be perfect in love, with the help of God in ordinary life and daily work.

What empirical research seems to keep proving is that, for those who have faith, understanding work as a *higher calling* has a positive impact on a number of work-related outcomes. These studies also show the need to distinguish between the meaning of work understood as a *calling* in a secular sense and the one understood as a *vocation* or *higher calling* in a spiritual or religious sense. What the *map of motivations* allows is a better understanding and distinction between those two different concepts of work meanings.

The fourth row from the left in Figure 8.6 shows that when work is perceived as a *higher calling* or a *supernatural vocation*, it is seen as source of spiritual gifts and, for those who have faith, as an occasion to have an encounter with God at work (*receiving* spiritual good). Moreover, it becomes an opportunity to attain holiness (*achieving* spiritual good) and a chance for self-giving and prayer for others (*giving* spiritual good). For those who have faith in God, now looking at the fourth column of the map going upwards, work also becomes an occasion to serve, please, adore and glorify God (*religious* motivations).

At the beginning of this chapter, we recognised that to understand our motivations at work and in organisations, simply having a map was not enough. We saw that, in addition to the map, some instrument was needed to help us read the map and interpret the different positions one could take on it. Such an instrument would serve as a *compass*, a navigation tool helping to identify a fixed reference point, giving direction. Such a reference point is the different work meaning each person wants to have.

Consistent with the findings of scientific literature on meaningful work, the internal logic of our map of motivations allows us to distinguish between four meanings of work conceived as a *job*, *career*, *calling* and *higher calling*. Therefore, knowledge of these different points of reference or purposes at work should allow us to define a *roadmap* for our personal and professional life's journey. Reflecting on this *roadmap* will be the purpose of the final chapter, but we still need to answer the question of how this *compass* can help us find a meaningful work-life balance.

Searching for a meaningful work-life balance

At the beginning of this chapter, I mentioned a student who, after using the map to diagnose her motivations in life and at work, discovered that those motivations did not match. The motivations that led this person to study business administration and her motivations in life were quite different. This mismatch between motivations at work and in life is not something unique to this student.

I have encountered this same phenomenon every time I have asked students and seminar attendees to use the map to diagnose their motivations in life and then at work. For example, as I said earlier, the purpose that leads young undergraduates to work (study) is usually related to the lower-left quadrant of the map (see Figure 8.7). They all want to get their degrees to access well-paid jobs, to be competent and to enjoy life. However, when they read the map and think about their life's purpose, higher and more transcendent motivations appear. Almost all of them want to change the world and make it better; many want to start a family, and they all want to mature, grow humanely and be happy. The misalignment of the motivations is evident, and it is what the double-headed arrow in Figure 8.7 tries to reflect.

196 *Using the map of motivations*

	Extrinsic Motivation Receiving	Intrinsic Motivation Achieving	Transcendent Motivation Giving	Religious Motivation Returning
Spiritual Good Higher Spiritual Realm	Receive **Grace** from God	Achieve **Holiness** through God's action	Work as a HIGHER CALLING **Light** to others	**Praise** to God
Moral Good Ethical Realm	Receive **Respect** from others	Achieve **Excellence** through our actions	Work as a CALLING **Good** to others	Return **Adoration** to God
Pleasant Good Psychological Realm	Receive **Esteem** from others	Work as a CAREER **Satisfaction** through our actions	Give **Joy** to others	Return **Gratefulness** to God
Useful Good Physical Realm	Work as a JOB **Support** from others	Achieve **Competence** through our actions	Give **Service** to others	Return **Fidelity** to God

Figure 8.7 Searching for a meaningful work-life balance: Compass for motivations

Something very similar occurs with MBA students. What moves them to finish their Master's programme is to earn a good salary, get a prestigious job, be among the best and do what they like. Once again, all the MBA students' answers about work purpose are in the lower-left quadrant of the map (see Figure 8.7), but they respond very differently regarding their motivations in life. The ideals of MBA students are very similar to those of undergraduate students. Whereas some are only interested in succeeding in life (again in the lower quadrant of the map), most want to change the world, to contribute to making it better and to be happy. Again, a mismatch of motivations shows up.

I have had numerous conversations with MBA students who told me about their desire to not make the same mistakes as their parents. Many have witnessed family crises caused by this tension between personal and professional lives. This is consistent with the response that mid-career managers give about their motivations in life and work. I have also seen the tension among them between both the personal and professional spheres.

What moves most senior managers in their jobs is to achieve financial security for themselves and their families. It is very striking, though, that many of them recognise that they have also been carried away by status, looking good, having luxurious cars and good houses. Worst of all is that they recognise they are not happy (see Figure 8.7). For older people, the mismatch or imbalance of personal and professional motivations produces concern, stress and tension, a tension that usually ends up having consequences in the different spheres of human life: *physical*, *psychological*, *moral* and *spiritual*.

As I said before, the findings I obtained from those who attended my classes and seminars are not necessarily representative, but it is also true that others have reached the same conclusions in recent years. Most successful people in professional settings are not happy in their personal lives (Wilson & Wilson, 1998).

Moreover, as technology continues to change the shape of work in our lives, by increasing competition in the job market, increasing globalisation and increasing the intrusion of workplace communications into personal time, people struggle with the challenge of trying to balance the demands of work with life's priorities (Steger, 2017).

The question is how we manage this tension between personal and professional motivations. How can we find a more meaningful work-life balance? Of course, the answer is not easy, but I am convinced that the solution has at least three stages: being aware of the problem, wanting to solve it and making the appropriate decisions to change the situation. I call these the three Cs: consciousness, conversion and change. These are the three stages I have seen repeatedly in the lives of the many people I have met while teaching about human motivations in organisations, so I recommend my students reflect carefully about those three Cs.

Some examples of these three stages have been mentioned already, for instance, with the person I mentioned in Chapter 6, who decided to return to her religious practices after hearing about the *map of motivations*. She first realised she was living a "schizophrenic" double life, personal and professional, and she became aware of it because she took the time to stop and reflect, to examine her conscience. It was a personal epiphany, a moment of *consciousness* for her, followed by a *conversion*, a deep desire and resolution, which ended in real *change*.

This is just one of the many examples I have observed over the years. All of them show that the tension between personal and professional motivations is a universal phenomenon, the reality behind the lack of a meaningful work-life balance. It is a reality that explains the frustration of many students who do not succeed in their future professions or young professionals who are absorbed by work and end up destroying their family lives or that of so many mid-career crises, which lead to many people radically changing professions.

Finding a meaningful work-life balance is neither a one-day task nor an easy one; in fact, it is probably a challenge we all face every day. As with sailors, this imbalance requires regular course correction. The three Cs I mentioned, *consciousness*, *conversion* and *change* require us to spend time thinking, making decisions and getting down to business.

As we have seen, the knowledge of the map and the use of the compass have allowed us to know where we are, to be aware of our position (consciousness). In the example I cited, the *map* and the *compass* allowed for an

198 *Using the map of motivations*

epiphany. However, to carry out the necessary course changes (conversions) and to move to our destination (changes), it would be very helpful to have also a *roadmap*. In fact, how the compass helps us find a meaningful work-life balance is by helping us interpret our own *roadmap*, one that might allow us to change course whenever necessary.

The last chapter of this book will be dedicated to the *roadmap*. For now, and to conclude this chapter, I would like to suggest some questions to help us consider the kind of meaning we give to our work. We can use these to figure out where we are on the map right now. I recommend everyone use the map to diagnose their *personal* and *professional* motivations and compare them.

If you find tension between your personal and professional motivations, or if you are conscious that you are located in a place that is not good enough, you can still have your personal conversion and change your situation. As we will see in the final chapter, we can always search for a higher and more balanced meaning in our work and lives.

Some questions for reflection

1 *How often am I concerned about not earning enough money in my current job?*
2 *How often do I think about finishing my job and rushing off to do other things I like more?*
3 *How often do I think about my prestige or whether others are going to praise or criticise me at work?*
4 *How often do I think about the higher professional position I want to get in the future?*
5 *How often do I think about my personal satisfaction at work, putting my career before the service of others?*
6 *How often do I think of my work as an opportunity to put into practice my talents and skills?*
7 *How often do I think of my work as an opportunity to serve and give my best to others?*
8 *How often do I think of my work as an opportunity to make a positive contribution to society, to build a better world?*
9 *How often do I think of my work as an opportunity to become a holy person?*
10 *How often do I think of my work as an opportunity to serve and please God?*

A final critical thought on why having a map is not enough

As I said before, if you discover that your position on the *map of motivations* at work is not good enough, you can always change it. The meaning of your work is not something given by your boss, the organisation or even the work itself. It is a free personal decision. You can always search for higher meanings and purposes.

Moving from a *career* understanding of our personal work to a *calling* brings the opportunity to keep growing personally and to find more and better ways of serving others through our work. Furthermore, for those who have higher spiritual aspirations, finding a sense of *higher calling* in our work promotes higher levels of inner peace and better ways to contribute to something greater than ourselves.

In the end, different people give different meanings to the same work. We all have the freedom to seek the meaning of work we want, the one we deem most appropriate. As one of the attendees to my seminars once explained in a very logical way, the more we know about the goods we can achieve through our daily work, the higher our capacity to freely want and choose those goods.

The final chapter of this book will focus on the importance of stopping to reflect, looking at our own *roadmap* and choosing our next steps. To be motivated means being moved to do something because we want to do it. Therefore, the more we know about the goods we want, the freer we become. This capacity to lead our own lives and get to our destination also helps us to be good leaders at the service of others.

Note

1 As I said previously, I would understand the position of those who would rather take lesser risks in the context of work in organisations using alternative words, such as the logic of caring or the logic of attention instead of the logic of love. Again, as long as we all understand the concept of motivation as the human voluntary desire for the good, the labels are relatively unimportant. To avoid an excessive use of the term "love", some may decide to use "truly human good" and the "logic of truly human good" to refer to the same ideas.

References

Barnett, B. (2012). Make Your Job More Meaningful. *Harvard Business Review Online*. https://hbr.org/2012/04/make-your-job-more-meaningful.

Bellah, R. N., Madsen, R., Sullivan, W. M., Swidler, A. & Tipton, S. M. (1985). *Habits of the Heart: Individualism and Commitment in American Life*. New York, NY: Harper & Row.

Carroll, S., Stewart-Sicking, J. & Thompson, B. (2014). Sanctification of work: Assessing the role of spirituality in employment attitudes. *Mental Health Religion & Culture*, 17(6).

Davidson, J. C. & Caddell, D. P. (1994). Religion and the meaning of work. *Journal for the Scientific Study of Religion*, 33, 135–147.

Durkheim, E. (1897/1951). *Suicide: A Study in Sociology*. Glencoe, IL: The Free Press. The World's Broken Workplace.

Gallup. (2017). *State of the Global Workplace. Gallup Report*. New York: Gallup Press. www.gallup.com/workplace/238079/state-global-workplace-2017.aspx.

Hall, M. E. L., Oates, K. L. M., Anderson, T. L. & Willingham, M. M. (2012). Calling and conflict: The sanctification of work in working mothers. *Psychology of Religion and Spirituality*, 4(1), 71–83.

Pratt, M. G., Pradies, C. & Lepisto, D. A. (2013). Doing well, doing good, and doing with: Organizational practices for effectively cultivating meaningful work. In B. J. Dik, Z. S. Byrne, & M. F. Steger (Eds.), *Purpose and Meaning in the Workplace*. Washington, DC: American Psychological Association, pp. 173–196.

Steger, M. F. (2017). *Creating Meaning and Purpose at Work. The Wiley Blackwell Handbook of the Psychology of Positivity and Strengths-Based Approaches at Work*. Chapter 5, Eds. Lindsay G. Oades, Michael F. Steger, Antonella Delle Fave, & Jonathan Passmore. West Sussex, UK: John Wiley & Sons, Ltd.

Walker, A. G., Jones, M. N., Wuensch, K. L., Aziz, S. & Cope, J. G. (2008). Sanctifying work: Effects on satisfaction, commitment, and intent to leave. *International Journal for the Psychology of Religion*, 18(2), 132–145.

Wilson, L. & Wilson, H. (1998). *Play to Win. Choosing Growth over Fear in Work and Life*. Austin, TX: Bard Press.

Wrzesniewski, A., McCauley, C. R., Rozin, P. & Schwartz, B. (1997). Jobs, careers, and callings: People's relations to their work. *Journal of Research in Personality*, 31, 21–33.

9 The roadmap for motivations
Always searching for higher meaningful work

Searching for higher meaningful work

Most people, at some point in their career, struggle with the challenges of balancing work and family life and finding an appropriate meaning to their work. This challenge is intensified during moments of transition or opportunity, such as a promotion with greater responsibility that leads to a greater salary, relocation, etc. Many have rethought the hours spent at work as their families grow. Is there a correct answer to all these questions? The issue is not easy to solve, but it seems that searching for a higher meaningful work-life balance is a universal aspiration.

I recall a comment made by a law student, who was working to pay his way through university, during a seminar I gave on human motivations in organisations. He told me that trying to help everyone to have a meaningful work-life balance is a colossal and unattainable task. He told me that this approach was "too idealistic", something I have been told many times, as you have read throughout the book.

According to this student, given that most people work because they have no other choice, they mostly see their work as an obligation, a way to earn money and possibly get ahead in life. Therefore, because most people perceive their work as just a *job*, it would be naive to try to get them out of such a mind-set. He argued that there is no such thing as ideal work. Today's working conditions are far from being ideal in most parts of the world, and, in many places, even finding a job is difficult, so finding the ideal is all but impossible.

While it is true that working conditions are less than ideal in many places today, and even though I respect his arguments, I do not agree with such a pessimistic view because it places the blame on third parties for something that largely depends on us and the meaning we want our work to have. The meaning of our work does not come exclusively from the working conditions (the salary, our boss, the organisational environment, etc.) or from the work itself (the nature of the tasks, the difficulty, etc.).

These important external factors shape the meaning we give to our work, but, at the end of the day, the meaning depends solely on us. We are the ones who decide the final motives of our own conduct in every minute of our daily work and lives. Even in the worst possible scenario, with dire working conditions, we can always find a meaning, a higher meaning, to what we do (Frankl, 1959).

Of course, I am not advocating giving up the fight for better working conditions in our organisations. We all should desire and promote the best possible working conditions, and that is one of the goals of a *humanistic management* approach to business administration. In fact, it is one of the first steps to finding meaning, as I will discuss next.

What I want to underline here is our capacity to freely give a higher meaning to our own work, to personally search for higher meaningful work or higher and better motivations. The meaning we give to our work and lives is not exclusively reliant on external factors, or even internal feelings and moods, but mainly relies on our free will, our capacity to choose our attitude and what we really want. We must not confuse motivations with just external stimuli or with a greater or lesser passion for doing things.

Naturally, motivation is related to external incentives and internal feelings, but it mainly refers to the personal desire to do what we do and to keep doing it freely for a purpose; even though at times it may not be pleasant, it is still good. Human motivations, if truly human, are free human acts and, above all, refer to our positive attitude, to our voluntary desire for good and to the logic of love as we have seen throughout this book.

Human motivation is not just an animal motivation only or primarily about responses to stimuli and instincts, as that mechanistic or emotive concept of motivations would reduce all human drivers to just the lower levels of the *map of motivations*. When what prevails is the reaction to external or internal stimuli, then one leaves the *logic of love* and enters the *logic of fear*, which is behind much of the tension students feel when making decisions about the future as well as among experienced managers.

As we saw in Chapter 7, we can freely decide to seek those things we consider valuable in our work, those we consider worthy of being desired and loved. Therefore, as the customs officer told me, "we are motivated in our work when we love what we do". We have the capacity to love our work, and that is where the reason for our motivation lies or, to put it succinctly, where it should lie. Unfortunately, we are often moved by fear, just a feeling, instead of love, which is a feeling and a voluntary desire.

While love is related to the feeling and free desire of "winning" goods, fear is the feeling of losing them. We fear a coming evil, the loss of a good or the inability to achieve one in the future. We fear an evil that is future, threatening and nigh impossible to avoid or overcome (St Thomas, STh II, II, 125).

Before considering how to improve our motivations at work or how to achieve more meaningful work, we need to stop and consider the difference between the *logic of fear* and the *logic of love* because the *roadmap* to higher meaningful work means leaving the *logic of fear* and returning to the *logic of love*.

From the logic of fear to the logic of love

Understanding fear is another of those issues that most people love to discuss in seminars on human motivations in organisations and that helps us better understand our *map of motivations* and how to manage our concerns. This question is inseparable from the search for a higher meaning in life and work. When our work-life balance is compromised, it is often accompanied by tension, stress and worry.

Fear is found both in human beings and in animals. It is a natural feeling; it is what conflicts with the normal tendency or desire for good, such as the fear of death, and affects the four realms of human life. We all fear *physical* death and sickness, and we should also fear *psychological*, *moral* and *spiritual* death and sickness. The fear of suffering, the fear of contempt or even of offending God, in the case of believers, is something human and reasonable if it is ordered and tends towards love (St Thomas, STh II, II, q 125, art.2).

Moderate fear is a stimulus to the mind, an emotion that triggers you to act. For this reason, this is a kind of motivation that affects every human being to a greater or lesser extent, but the problem is when fear is not ordered,[1] not healthy, sane, appropriate or holy. A disordered fear normally produces an excessive, unavoidable or obsessive tension that is wrong because it does not lead to an ordered love. An example of disorder in love would be excessive timidity, as well as excessive vanity.

For the same reason that we were able to describe a reasonable order in *love* in Chapter 7, it is also possible to talk of a reasonable order in *fear*. In other words, as well as there being goods that are more worthy of being loved than others, there are also evils that are more worthy of being feared. The reason for this is that fear is always linked to evil, which is nothing more than the absence of good. The cause of fear is the threat of losing what we love, or the impending failure to gain what we desire and love.

When we studied the *logic of love* behind the *map of motivations*, we saw that the reasons why we are motivated could be summarised as the desire to *receive*, *achieve*, *give* and *return* truly human good or love (see Figures 6.1 and 7.1). Now, following the reverse logic, the logic of fear, we could say that other reasons why we are demotivated, or motivated not to act or to avoid some behaviour, are summarised as those related to the fear of *not* receiving, achieving, giving and returning truly human good or love (see Figure 9.1).

This logic of fear becomes clearer when the *map of motivations* is seen from a negative perspective instead of a positive one (see Figure 9.1). The columns on our map can be read as motivations in negative terms rather than positive. It is like contemplating heads and tails of the "coin" of motivations. For example, if we look at the lower-left corner of the map, the reason that would lead us to act is a fear of losing or not obtaining some useful good (a basic salary, for example). Instead of the positive desire to obtain a

	Extrinsic Motivation	Intrinsic Motivation	Transcendent Motivation	Religious Motivation
	Fear of Not Being Loved	Fear of Not Loving Ourselves	Fear of Not Loving Others	Fear of Not Loving God
Spiritual Good *Higher Spiritual Realm*	Fear of Being **Condemned**	Fear of **Sinning**	Fear of **Embarrassing** (others)	Fear of Being **Irreligious**
Moral Good *Ethical Realm*	Fear of Being **Blamed**	Fear of **Wrongdoing**	Fear of **Scandalising** (others)	Fear of Being **Irreverent**
Pleasant Good *Psychological Realm*	Fear of Being **Disliked**	Fear of **Suffering**	Fear of **Displeasing** (others)	Fear of Being **Impious**
Useful Good *Physical Realm*	Fear of Being **Underappreciated**	Fear of **Failing**	Fear of **Unavailing** (others)	Fear of Being **Unfaithful**

Figure 9.1 The logic of fear: A map of negative motivations

useful good, the motivation here is the negative fear of disapproval, of not obtaining the necessary support.

There are many forms of fear. In fact, there are as many kinds of fears as there are positive motivations or desires. Some other examples (now in the second column of the map) would include fears of failing or wrongdoing, like when speaking in public. This is very frequent among my students, and many of them overcame this by using the map. There are also all kinds of anxiety that cause dread of possible evils when making decisions, such as a student making a mistake when choosing their future profession or the possibility of losing a job in the case of those in the workforce (see Figure 9.1).

As we will see, knowing how to face reasonable fears becomes an opportunity for growth and love. Nevertheless, it is always useful to have a map showing the origin of those fears. Once you identify which goods are at stake in your human growth, you can also identify the different kinds of fears in your imagination related to losing or not attaining those goods. Let us briefly review what fears arise from each of the types of motivation shown on our *map*.

Starting with the first column, *extrinsic negative motivations* show reasons for acting out of fear of not being loved properly. These include the fear of being underappreciated, dismissed or not being well paid in our jobs (a useful good); the fear of looking bad or being disliked (a pleasant good); the fear of blame, contempt or denunciation (a moral good) and the fear of being punished or eternally condemned (a spiritual good). For the same reason, *intrinsic negative motivations* are reasons for acting out of fear of not loving ourselves properly. What moves us to act here is the fear of failing (losing a useful good); suffering (losing a pleasant good); wrongdoing (losing a moral good) or sinning (losing a spiritual good) (see Figure 9.1).

Transcendent negative motivations are those that lead us to do good to others out of fear and not out of love. This would be the case when things are done for the fear of being useless or unavailing (not useful); displeasing (not pleasant), scandalising (not moral) or embarrassing and overwhelming to others (not spiritual). Finally, the fourth column includes *negative religious motivations*, those that lead to practicing religion not out of love for God but out of the fear of being separated from Him. The motive to act would then be the fear of being unfaithful to God, of being impious, irreverent or irreligious (see Figure 9.1).

This way of interpreting the *map* by referring to negative human motivations complements the description and understanding of the previous description of human positive motivations on the same *map* (see Figure 7.1). Furthermore, it clearly shows that the *logic of fear* and the *logic of love* are opposites. In other words, if the main motive for human action is fear, then love cannot be present. Therefore, when the goal is to increase motivation, the first thing to do is overcome the unjustified fear and move towards love, to move from negative to positive motivations. This is why this section was necessary before we could proceed further in better understanding our motivations and the tension behind the search for higher meaningful work.

According to the logic of the *map of motivations*, searching for higher meaningful work involves looking for higher and better positive motivations, leaving the *logic of fear* and moving to the *logic of love*. For that reason, now that we have a complete understanding of the map and its logic, as well as a compass to interpret the map (the four meanings of work), we can reflect on a *roadmap* that we can use in our life's journey, in our work in organisations.

As the border police officer would say, it is about finding a way to work with greater love, or a more perfect love. Ultimately, the *roadmap* is about finding a way to work with a higher desire for true good, with a higher and better meaning and purpose. Let's start by looking for a higher meaning in our work.

In search of a higher meaning in a *job*

As we discussed in Chapter 8, most human beings agree that having a job, daily occupation or task is an essential ingredient for a healthy life. There are millions of people all over the world, though, who stay at home because they take care of their house, family or an ill or elderly loved one. These are all serious occupations, even if they are not widely considered as such.

All those occupations that are not considered "jobs" and those others that are indispensable but not well paid (cleaners, shop assistants, etc.) usually go unnoticed but are real roles that fill the day and give meaning to many people's lives because they have a meaning and purpose.[2] Even those who are ill or retired are able to find a sense of purpose in their situation because the meaning we give to our actions and lives comes not from the outside – from social considerations or external circumstances – but from our interior freedom – from our deepest intentions or motivations.

External circumstances influence our lives and our work, but they are not decisive. We are neither machines nor irrational animals that must obey our circumstances blindly and instinctively. As I said, that would be a simplistic *mechanistic* view, not a *humanistic* one. We are rational and free beings able to get away from an unjustifiably excessive *logic of fear*. In fact, finding a higher meaning entails being able to freely look for more and better kinds of good in what we do because we want to.

People should not blame external situations for the lack of interest or motivation in their daily occupations. Of course, there are exceptions, such as having hostile colleagues who you don't want to spend hours with or vile and abhorrent bosses who are able to discourage even the most committed person. If that were the case, and people worked in organisations where the environment was so flawed that they bring out the worst in people, they are probably in what has been called an *ethically unhealthy organisation* (Bañón et al., 2012).

I hope this is not your case and your organisation is not ethically harmful or corrupt so you can stay in your current job. The question then is how to stop hating or fearing your job and start loving it, how to find a higher meaning in your job. As we considered in Chapter 8, three stages are normally needed to improve or learn: *consciousness*, *conversion* and *change*. Put in other words (and as we discussed in Chapter 3), to recover trust you need to *recognise* what is wrong, *rectify* the direction, and *repair* the wrongdoing (the three Rs).

Being aware of the meaning that we give to our current job is the starting point. If we want to foster a more meaningful job, awareness of the situation and the logic behind our job motivations right now is key. If we were ensconced in a *logic of hate* or a *logic of fear*, we should know. Therefore, we must stop and reflect on whether the job is contributing to supporting us, our livelihoods, our existence and our well-being. Am I well paid? Is the job lucrative enough? If the answers are no, that would explain feelings of sadness, resignation and even stress, especially when there is no job stability.

In these cases, where survival is at stake, what prevails is a logic of fear, one that prompts individuals to interact for an immediate instrumental purpose. In this case, working is understood as a way of giving (hours of work) in order to receive something of value later (money), within the framework of a contract, also following a certain *logic of duty*, but mainly inside a *logic of transaction or exchange* (Baviera et al., 2016). Inside this logic, you only think about earning more, achieving better working conditions and attaining some stability.

Until these issues are accomplished, the *logic of fear* will want to prevail over the *logic of love*, but even in these negative cases, it is possible to give more meaning to our jobs with the courage to face fear. For that reason, whenever I find people in these circumstances, I recommend they read *Man's Search for Meaning* (Frankl, 1959) because if someone can find meaning in a Nazi concentration camp and also later in life – having lost his father, mother, brother and wife – we should be able to find meaning in an unstable or difficult job situation with courage while always looking for a higher and wider meaning.

It is true that, in many cases, the job we have does not match our deepest personal desires or abilities. What I want to underline here though is that having a job is something good in itself. Being optimistic, having a positive attitude towards the job, is something you can freely decide upon, even in the worst possible scenario. This awareness of the good means having a job can be a source of certain peace, courage and joy for any employed person because it provides some material basic goods, even if it is not the ideal job.

I hope everybody can find a basic job in their lifetime and that everyone answered yes to the previous question about having a job that contributes to their personal livelihoods. If that is your case and you have a well-paid job that contributes to your well-being, to your personal and family livelihoods, then you should have the courage to recognise it.

We should be aware and acknowledge it if we have a good job and even celebrate it from time to time. Even the possibility of using the money and free time to look for other higher kinds of good in other activities outside the workplace is good in itself. This is what defines the *logic of love*. The awareness and acknowledgement of having a job has all the benefits from the types of good that the job itself provides (salary, occupation, stability, security, etc.) Recognising the goodness of having a job is key to leaving the logic of fear with courage (a cardinal virtue) and starting to love our work, increasing interest in our profession (see Figure 9.2).

As we analysed in Chapter 7, the key to understanding our motivations is recognising that we are insatiable seekers of the good, that we are moved by the things we love, but for that we need courage. If we don't love our job enough, we will end up complaining, dreading it and trying to escape from daily reality by searching for love somewhere else. This is why, as I said earlier, so many people spend the week looking forward to the weekend or just looking for compensation outside of the job.

If we are among those who see their job as just a *job*, the first thing we must do is recognise that this work contributes to our livelihoods. At the same time, we should be realistic, aware of its goodness but also its limitations, knowing that material goods are always limited and, as such, can provide material well-being and the money to attain other kinds of useful and pleasant goods.

For that reason, having a good salary is always good, but there are other sources of goodness in that same job. One is the career opportunity that

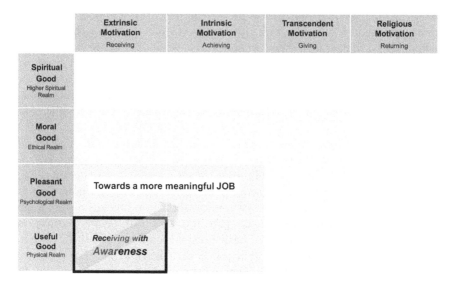

Figure 9.2 Fostering higher meaningful work as a job

most jobs offer. Is it possible to find a higher meaning in a *career* than in just a *job*? It seems obvious that it does, as we dicussed earlier, but let us stop for a moment to think about its consequences and its connection with our humanistic understanding of motivations.

In search of a higher meaning in a *career*

As we saw in Chapter 1, the majority of theories of motivation that are taught in business schools and universities today can occupy the lower quadrant of our map. They only consider the *extrinsic* and *intrinsic* motivations, the useful and pleasant goods. Motivations at work would then be reduced to making money (*extrinsic useful* motive), achieving prestige (*extrinsic pleasant* motive), being competent (*intrinsic useful* motive) and achieving personal satisfaction (*intrinsic pleasant* motive). These would be the motivations enclosed in a vision of work conceived as a career, as we saw in Chapter 8.

When we are in this lower quadrant of our map, the meaning of work as a career becomes a path towards success, status, mastery and achievement. The main logic behind this concept of work is once again a logic of exchange in order to "win" all these goods within the rules of the "game", a contractual relationship, that also demands a logic of duty to be followed.

"These two logics of action – exchange and duty – are in some sense universal, but they are particularly salient within business contexts" (Baviera et al., 2016, p. 161). Paradoxically, when only the two logics described are at stake in our motivations in organisations, instead of resulting in feelings of success, they produce feelings of fear. Yes, as paradoxical as it might sound, the more you think in terms of success, the more you enter the *logic of fear*.

In the book *Play to Win! Choosing Growth over Fear in Work and Life*, the authors describe the scene of a dinner they held for some of the top-performing second-year salespeople in the US insurance industry. When the event organiser asked them how they felt about their success, there was a deathly hush. "They were terrified, they said – the more successful they became, the more pressure they felt to be even more successful" (Wilson & Wilson, 1998). Something had gone wrong.

As the authors explain, the concept of success is primarily defined by external measures, such as how much money you make, your seniority and the respect you get. Unlike success, though, the concept of human fulfilment is largely defined by internal measures and related to the deeply felt sense that your life is full, whole and complete (Wilson & Wilson, 1998). Following Victor Frankl's ideas, these authors defend that it is possible to be successful but not fulfilled in life and vice-versa; someone could be a failure, socially speaking, and yet be fulfilled.

This idea of desiring to win instead of not losing matches the *logic of love* described in this book. We should follow our desire to win the good above all and focus less on the fear of losing it. As they say, if you have a fear of failure, just try "doing your best, not being the best".[3]

Unfortunately, we all can be trapped by the *logic of fear* in a conception of our work as a *career*, as these authors foresaw more than two decades ago. To avoid this reductionist vision, what they propose is the same as I suggest here, moving from the *logic of fear* to the *logic of love*, to understand the tension produced by the logics of exchange and duty in this conception of work and then search for a more meaningful career.

Fostering a *logic of love* in our career means having a voluntary positive attitude that looks at our daily work (a *job* but also a *career*) through appreciative eyes for the goodness of what we have. It is by valuing the good we receive and achieve in our *jobs* and *careers* that we start to enjoy it in a different and higher way, as an "adventure" where you discover and learn new things every day because you allow yourself to be surprised by the good that surrounds you.

For example, just think about the people who smile at you when you enter the workplace. You do not always pay attention to all the positive and good around you. Have you thought about the interest that others pay every day to your needs in such small details that you often don't even realise? To think about how others normally care about you and your dignity, I recommend revisiting the ten elements of dignity proposed by Dr Hicks as mentioned in Chapter 2 (Hicks, 2011).

Maybe we are not mindful of the many gifts that we receive daily. The attitude of trying to be attentive to everything that is worthy of being loved

210 Using the map of motivations

around us, of valuing the good surrounding us, is what "play to win" means. This is the rational way in which we can foster a higher meaning in our careers. A greater meaningful career should move us to a permanent attitude of gratitude, which will reinforce that greater meaning in our career and in our life. In this way, thankfulness for our *job* and *career* becomes one more step in our journey towards a more meaningful work-life balance (see Figure 9.3).

The attitude of thankfulness that allows us to conceive our career in a less fearful and more meaningful way is the effective and affective recognition of all the good we receive, an attitude of gratitude that is freely decided, even if what we are receiving is exactly what we deserve. Unquestionably, we should always receive what we deserve from our peers, supervisors and organisations.

Remember, this desire to receive some kind of good is what defines *extrinsic motivation*, a desire that normally includes what we deserve as part of our career development. Even in those cases where we are given nothing more than what we are supposed to receive, we may always be thankful, a gratitude that makes us value our *career*, the *job* we choose and the organisation in which we work.

This attitude of gratitude, of thankful appreciation for the things we receive from others in our work, applies not only to material useful things (a good salary, a good retirement plan or a safe workplace, for instance). This positive outlook also applies to the other *extrinsic motivations*, as is the case with the pleasant ones. Feeling the esteem of our colleagues and having a

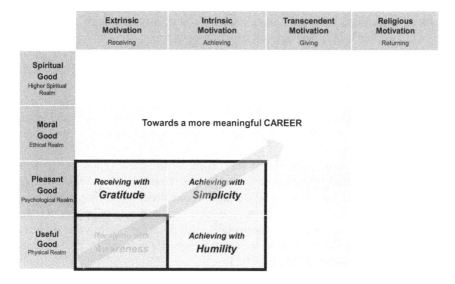

Figure 9.3 Fostering higher meaningful work as a career

grateful sense of belonging to the organisation are pleasant *extrinsic motivations* worthy of recognition and appreciation (see Figure 9.3).

A thankful outlook for our work can reinforce a higher concept of our occupations in a more humane way because we freely choose to want that which we consider good. In fact, seeing our work as a *career* is a higher manifestation of love than just considering it as a *job* (see Figure 9.3). Loving our career means loving what we do, what we achieve through that work and what we receive from others in that work. There is nothing wrong therefore with getting a good job and pursuing a good career with a noble professional ambition and an enthusiasm for what we do in our work.

When we deal with this issue in class, students ask me how they should succeed in choosing their career, which leads me to talk to them about another basic attitude that is necessary to foster a more meaningful career: humility. It may sound bizarre, but humility is a key human quality that we all need to be able to grow, to be better. To grow personally and professionally, we all need the humility to recognise our virtues but also our faults and limitations. We must recognise the strengths and weaknesses of our character, the talents and skills that we have and those that we do not (see Figure 9.3).

As the Spanish writer Theresa of Jesus once said, "humility is living in truth", a truth that starts with sincere self-knowledge. "This self-knowledge leads to the appreciation of what we do well – for having developed certain skills, strengths, or being gifted in certain ways in areas that we find meaningful. Focusing on what we do well can provide a sense of contribution to our identity" (Rey, Bastons, & Sotok, 2019, 102).

Paradoxically, if we are humble enough to see our limitations but also the things that we are capable of achieving – our true potential –we will be able to find ways to actively and frequently use them in our daily tasks, and we will perceive greater meaning in our work (Littman-Ovadia & Steger, 2010). Once again, this humble attitude regarding our career removes a jealous, envious and fearful attitude in those who see others as competitors because they only seek to excel, to be the best.

We also need humility in looking for a career that really fits with the rest of our life's projects, with the meaning we want to give to our lives as a whole. It means choosing a career that is consistent with not only our real capacity and true potential, but also consistent with our other dreams, feelings, desires, beliefs and values. This kind of personal simplicity, clarity or consistency reflects personal coherence, maturity and "unity of life" (see Figure 9.3).

Simplicity or consistency, like humility, is a human virtue, but seen from a technical point of view, the specialised literature on meaningful work calls it "integration", a concept that "builds on research showing reciprocal relationships over time between the meaning people find at work and the meaning they find in the rest of their lives" (Duffy et al., 2014; Steger & Dik, 2009).

Integration refers to the desirable consistency, simplicity and harmony between our work and our internal drivers, a personal and professional authenticity, which is the opposite of a fearful attitude. Simplicity, like humility, is related to the cardinal virtue of temperance, of measure, statement and self-knowledge. It is a manifestation of ordered self-love, a kind of "unity of life" or sincerity of behaviour in which the motivations of our work are consistent and in harmony with those of our life (see Figure 9.4).

This integration or personal simplicity allows work to become an important path to meaning in life. Therefore, as meaning in life is thought to partly express a person's values (Steger, 2009), integration points to the potential importance of engaging in value-congruent activities while at work, both in terms of the actual tasks required and in terms of the overall values of the organisation (Hoffman et al., 2011).

Unfortunately, many students and seasoned managers believe these reflections arrive too late for them, even though they recognise the importance of these findings concerning the meaning of work. "Nobody told me about these issues before", they say. As students, they made decisions about their professional careers in a very intuitive manner highly influenced by the opinions of third parties (family, friends, cinema, media, role models, etc.).

Decisions that are crucial for our future are frequently made without deep reflection on our talents and capabilities but, most importantly, without thinking much about the meaning we want to give to our future work and life. Of course, this will have a huge impact on our daily motivations in organisations for the rest of our lives, but why do we talk so little nowadays about those personal aspirations of our students? Why don't we talk more about motivations and the sense of calling?

I don't think it is ever too late to think about our professional calling, our vocation, our suitability for a particular occupation and career. As we will see, it is by finding our inner calling and by fostering its higher meaning that we become highly motivated in our work and our lives. Let us now reflect about this new step in our search for higher meaningful work.

In search of a higher meaning in a *calling*

Every time I recall the law student's comment that the entire theory of motivations was too idealistic, I am reminded that finding a higher meaning in our work is inseparable from having ideals. Human "ideals" are the keys that explain humanity's greatest achievements. The greatest human endeavours are the fruit of the ideals of those who led them. The great conquests, the greatest inventions, the most successful businesses, all these human achievements were led by people with ideals, with great motivations.

Unless students have great ideals, they cannot be enthusiastic about carrying out great projects, and they will not be able to find more meaning in their jobs and professional careers. This is true for everybody; we all need to answer questions, such as: what activities do we feel we have a natural ability to give our best to? What do we enjoy doing? What especially motivates us, and what work do we love? These are issues that refer to the meaning of work as a *calling*, as a vocation.

Thinking in terms of *calling* is not only about our personal interests; it also means considering the contribution that we can provide to society. Understanding our work as a *calling* means discovering the role we are called to play in this world, the unique contribution we can make with the talents we have.

By unique, I mean irreplaceable, not necessarily important, big or complex. Work becomes unique because of the meaning we give to it, because of the love we put into it. Consider the janitor mopping the floor at NASA. He knew his work was unimportant, small and simple, but he was "helping send a man to the moon".

We all should be able to answer the question regarding the contribution we make to others with our work. But we should also be able to respond to the question of how our work contributes to making us a better person because we are now reflecting at a moral level. Seeing our work as a *calling* for growth and contribution is a higher manifestation of love for ourselves and for others than seeing it as just a *job* or as just a successful *career*.

This explains the importance and necessity of talking to students about finding their *calling*, their professional vocation. At the end of the day, though, the final word on students' vocations must come from themselves. They may ask for advice and trust in those who love them and care about their happiness, but this decision about following a vocation is always personal. It involves using your own freedom with practical wisdom (another cardinal moral virtue) to ask and receive good advice and the responsibility to make that personal decision. No one else can decide our higher motivations (see Figure 9.4).

Wisdom in receiving advice and help regarding our work means being able to ask the right people, those who really care about us and who can give the best advice. In fact, trusting the advice of those who care about us is synonymous with maturity and confidence on the benevolence of others. Nevertheless, at the end of the day, we need to be convinced of the goodness of our own motivations and decisions; that is why we ask for the best possible advice from the best possible advisers. In doing so, we are fostering a higher meaning to our own calling because we will always be able to say that we got the best advice possible (see Figure 9.4).

Although we must be open to the best advice, the decision must always be our own. This is what it means to be free. If we make a mistake, that will be our mistake, not the mistake of the one giving us the advice in the first place. Unless we are clear about this, we will never be able to make our own decisions freely and responsibly. It is this sense of freedom that will move us to make our work truly our own. We do what we want because we want to. We take ownership of our decisions because they are genuinely and fully ours.

214 *Using the map of motivations*

	Extrinsic Motivation Receiving	Intrinsic Motivation Achieving	Transcendent Motivation Giving	Religious Motivation Returning
Spiritual Good Higher Spiritual Realm	\multicolumn{4}{c}{Towards a more meaningful CALLING}
Moral Good Ethical Realm	*Receiving with* **Wisdom**	*Achieving with* **Responsibility**	*Giving with* **Exemplarity**	
Pleasant Good Psychological Realm	*Receiving with* *Gratitude*	*Achieving with* *Simplicity*	*Giving with* **Cheerfulness**	
Useful Good Physical Realm	*Receiving with* *Awareness*	*Achieving with* *Humility*	*Giving with* **Generosity**	

Figure 9.4 Fostering higher meaningful work as a calling

Unsurprisingly, this sense of ownership or personal responsibility of our work is also part of the path to higher meaningful work. This is what the specialised literature calls "personalisation". It means bringing more of ourselves to work, bringing our humanness, goodness and moral qualities responsibly to the workplace and aligning our work with our feelings, desires, values and virtues, making it more personally expressive (Steger, 2017). This is another loving attitude that distances us from fear when we foster a higher meaning in our calling.

Adopting an ownership mentality of our work also means having higher personal responsibility regarding our contribution to the organisation. By taking our work seriously, with responsibility, and by fulfilling our duties, we do our work better. Work centrality then increases, and it becomes more expressive of who we are (Steger, 2017). Unless we have a competitive or proud attitude, fear should not fit in this approach, only the desire to do the greatest possible good, of loving our work more.

Because work is the axis around which a large part of our existence revolves, the way we work affects the way we live and the kind of people we become. Being good as human beings, we do better work, and from good work, we can become better people (Gardner et al., 2001). When we want to do our work right, when we want to work well and with responsibility, then we have the right disposition to grow morally in our work. Through our jobs, employing moral virtues while working, we become better human beings.

This personalisation of our work not only helps bring out the best of ourselves in our work but, paradoxically (and as we saw in Chapter 4), it drives us to give our best to others (Steger, 2017, p. 75). This desire to give good to others (*transcendent motivations*) is what the literature on calling describes as "expansion", seeking ways in which our work can be expanded to benefit some greater good and expanding our concerns to embrace broader interests beyond ourselves. This is what moral reasoning would describe as "generosity", the quality of being willing to share.

I was invited to give a keynote speech at the 23rd Annual Conference of EBEN (The European Business Ethics Network) in 2019. It was titled "University Academic Work: Just a Job or a Vocation of Service?" and I presented these same ideas, but this time I applied them to the work of those teaching at university. When I finished, I was approached by someone who said, "I need you to come and explain what you told us today to all my students and colleagues".

A year later, I visited her university in Malaga (Spain) to give a similar presentation on the map of motivations to her colleagues and students. The room was packed that day, and I could appreciate in a practical way what I had written. When we find something we consider good, it drives us to give it to others, to be generous – the opposite of a fearful attitude of losing some good. This is what this lecturer did. When we care about our work, we have this human tendency to transcend ourselves, to expand our love for our work to others, to expand the good and make it "resonate".

In fact, in addition to expansion, or generosity in moral terms, the literature about calling suggests "resonance" as another way to foster this higher meaning in our work. This term means making our own personal values and purpose align with the organisation's core values and mission or purpose. Then, leaders in organisations are not followed out of fear but out of love, of recognising interest for the truly human good of their followers. "Resonance builds on research showing that leaders who can express a vision and purpose for an organization make it easier for workers to find meaning in their efforts" (Judge & Piccolo, 2004).

From the perspective of our *map of motivations*, this concept of resonance might have two different dimensions: moral and affective. On one hand, we could talk about a *moral resonance*, which would refer to the ability to transmit the higher human or moral components of the organisation's vision and purpose to others. This moral resonance would consist of not only the transmission of some moral principles and values shared by the organisation but also on its practice being uplifting, with exemplarity (see Figure 9.4).

On the other hand, we could talk about *affective resonance*, referring to transmitting those values and principles with a personal passion for our work to others. It would include our capacity to genuinely show our enthusiasm, to resonate with the practices of the organisation, transmitting its vision and purpose around us with cheerfulness (see Figure 9.4).

While this cheerfulness responds to the contagious nature of our own satisfaction with our work in the organisation, of our gratitude and simplicity, exemplarity responds to the contagious nature of our moral wisdom and responsibility, of our moral qualities aligned with the organisation's purpose. In other words, cheerfulness is the resonance in others of our affective simplicity, while exemplarity is the resonance in others of our moral responsibility (see Figure 9.4).

Unsurprisingly, most of the attitudes and behaviours in the workplace described above are among the most important predictors and correlates of meaningful work. This is what positive psychology professor Michael Steger has described as the SPIRE model,[4] one that contributes to fostering higher meaningful work conceived as a vocation (Steger, 2017, p. 64).

It is striking to see the qualitative leap involved in the meaning of work as a *calling*. In this conception of work, the *logic of gift* now joins the *logic of duty* and *exchange*. A new kind of transcendent motivation or rationality shows up, and its purpose is to contribute, to give for the sake of giving, seeking some good beyond ourselves in a gratuitous and unconditional manner (Baviera et al., 2016, p. 168).

When work is conceived as a *calling*, the three logics of *exchange*, *duty* and *gift* start to operate together at work with their own strengths, weaknesses and complementarities. Of course, this is a human art, and "the three logics have to be played altogether as in a symphony". "The hope is for organizations to be more humane, to become communities with meaningful social and moral bonds among members, which can inspire generosity and common purposes that transcend instrumental self-interest or mere duty and elicit the best that people have to offer" (Baviera et al., 2016, p. 168).

We could therefore say that people see work as *calling* when they have a clear identification with the job, are moved by a transcendent guiding force and have a sense of meaning and value-driven behaviour (Hagmaier & Abele, 2012). Such a meaning of work is amplified when some positive attitudes or moral virtues are promoted (wisdom, responsibility, exemplarity, cheerfulness and generosity). Unsurprisingly, when we have these positive and transcendent attitudes towards our work, we are moved by higher kinds of motivation.

This phenomenon shows that the hierarchical concept of human goods that follows from the logic of our map is fully consistent with a hierarchical understanding of the different work meanings described by the literature of meaningful work as a *job*, *career* and *calling*.

As we saw in Chapter 8, there is also empirical evidence for the role of a meaning of work conceived as a *higher calling*, as a spiritual vocation. Moreover, for believers, and for those who see their job as sacred (i.e. a vocation), they might experience a higher motivation from this higher meaning (Walker et al., 2008). In the next section, I will briefly reflect on how the perception of this spiritual vocation, or *higher calling*, might affect motivations at work and in organisations.

In search of a higher meaning in a *higher calling*

In Chapter 6, I spoke of a woman who felt she was living a kind of "schizophrenic" double life until she stopped to reflect on her motivations during one of the seminars on motivations. Her professional, social and family life was separate and distinct from her higher spiritual inner life, from a life related to God as the Christian she was. Learning about the *logic of love* behind this framework helped her better understand the separation between her faith and her life and work. It was the discovery of her love for God that made her become *conscious* of the situation, *challenge* herself and *change*, looking for growth instead of fear (Wilson & Wilson, 1998).

Her reaction was not one of fear or duty but was a desire out of love to reciprocate God's calling with fidelity. This is a wonderful example that explains how believers can find *higher meaning* in their work, founded on faith. From a believer's point of view, all human creatures have been called to love a God who is Love Himself, here on Earth, and later for all eternity in Heaven. This is a universal calling to holiness, to an encounter with God in ordinary life and work.

As one of my students told me recently, when you have faith, the mindfulness of God's love and His presence gives a very different meaning to every second of your life and work. Here, the concept of *mindfulness* is relevant to both believers and non-believers because mindfulness is what leads everybody to a greater sensitivity to context and perspective. Mindfulness means openness to the present moment in its fullness (Crane, 2017).

For non-believers, openness to the entire reality brings an opportunity to discover higher spiritual realms like greater peace and inner balance. For believers, this would be the result of being aware of God's presence in daily life and work, a presence that gives new meaning to every task but one that is now divine.

For someone with faith, mindfulness would mean actively noticing the development of the presence of God in their ordinary life, opening up to His gifts, being aware that every moment is a present from God. Mindfulness of God's presence and of His gifts or graces would be the first step in fostering a higher meaning, in this case, a supernatural meaning to daily work, to be able to perceive work itself as a divine gift.

In both cases, in a religious and in a non-religious context, mindfulness would be the door to be able to enter a higher meaning of daily work, but as we discussed in Chapter 5, one must quieten the external and internal distractions for this to be possible. In a noisy and busy world like the one in which we live, silence and meditation are being valued again. Attitudes of mindfulness, docility and dedication to spiritual insights are more frequent. For non-believers, these are sources of inner peace and joy; this is the case for believers, too, but in the company of God (see Figure 9.5).

As we saw in Chapter 6, this personal relationship of believers with a God that surpasses all human capacity and belongs to the realm of the mysterious, of faith, is also what defines religion. Without God's assistance, it

218 *Using the map of motivations*

would be impossible for human nature to enter into contact with Him in a mindful way and answer His calling with docility, dedication and celebration (see Figure 9.5).

It is in this context that the sense of a *higher calling*, of having a supernatural vocation, gives believers a higher meaning of human work and a higher type of motivation, which belongs to this realm of faith. The normal circumstances of each day allow each person of faith to grow in grace, holiness and self-giving to others and God and become occasions to serve, thank, worship and glorify Him with faithfulness, devotion, reverence, joy and peace, the perfection of joy (St Thomas, STh I-II, Q. 70, art. 3) (see Figure 9.5).

What others saw on a natural ethical level as an "inner calling" to improve the world is now perceived by believers on a *higher spiritual* level as a "divine calling" to be holy and help others to be holy. These two concepts of secular and religious callings are fully compatible with each other. In fact, for believers, the latter (natural calling) would be part of the former (higher supernatural calling).

For those with faith in God, the professional *inner calling* to happiness would be one aspect of the more general and universal *divine vocation* to happiness and holiness. God gives different talents to every person and a personal mission to use them in daily life and in work.

This universal calling to holiness is shared by the three Abrahamic traditions, and it is based on the opening pages of the Bible, where the vocation to sanctity is expressed in the Lord's words to Abraham: "Walk before me faithfully and be blameless" (Genesis 17:1). The Torah exhorts the Israelites to be holy and tells them how to do so: "Be holy because I, the LORD your God, am holy" (Leviticus 19:2).

	Extrinsic motivation Receiving	Intrinsic motivation Achieving	Transcendent motivation Giving	Extrinsic motivation Returning
	Towards a more meaningful HIGHER CALLING			
Spiritual Good Higher Spiritual Realm	Receiving with **Mindfulness**	Achieving with **Docility**	Giving with **Dedication**	Returning with **Joy & Peace**
Moral Good Ethical Realm	Receiving with Wisdom	Achieving with Responsibility	Giving with Exemplarity	Returning with **Reverence**
Pleasant Good Psychological Realm	Receiving with Gratitude	Achieving with Simplicity	Giving with Cheerfulness	Returning with **Devotion**
Useful Good Physical Realm	Receiving with Awareness	Achieving with Humility	Giving with Generosity	Returning with **Faithfulness**

Figure 9.5 Fostering higher meaningful work as a higher calling

For Muslims, the Qur'an calls to uprightness (al-salah), to conscientious devotion (al-taqwa), to goodness (al-husn) and to virtue (al-birr) (Qur'an 2:177). In the case of Christians, Jesus teaches his disciples to "be perfect, therefore, as your heavenly Father is perfect" (Matthew 5:48).

This universal calling to strive for perfection in Love, for holiness, assisted by God's grace, has always been part of the Christian faith and practice.[5] Regarding the importance of finding God in ordinary life and work, St Josemaría Escrivá, the "Saint of ordinary life",[6] devoted his entire life to remind people all over the world that work is a means of perfection, a way to sanctity (Escrivá, 1985, no. 10).

So far, we have analysed the different ways of achieving the highest possible level of motivations in organisations, resulting from the highest possible level of meaning that we give to our work. We have been able to build a *roadmap* that allows us to leave the *logic of fear*, move to the *logic of love* and find ways to work with greater love, with a more perfect love.

Now, it is up to each one of us to use the *map*, the *compass* and the *roadmap* to find out where we are right now and where we want to go. In other words, we need to reflect on the meaning we are giving to our work in this life's journey and decide if we want to look for a higher one. Next follows some final remarks about this book and this exciting personal task of searching for higher meaningful work in organisations.

In search of higher meaningful work and life

As I have discussed throughout the pages of this book, from a *humanistic* concept of management, motivations in organisations cannot be conceived as an automatic consequence of the simple application of incentive systems or motivational techniques. Human motivations are the result of the free human choice of each person working in the organisation.

For this reason, this book has offered a *humanistic* theory of motivations in organisations that integrates the most widespread *mechanistic* and *organicist* views into a broader *holistic* perspective, a dialogical approach that respects and complements the findings of the other theories.

In the future, it would be wonderful to have a text analysing to what extent managers can facilitate all these human motivations to grow and flourish in organisations, but this book had to come first. Moreover, it would also be desirable to have some text describing how organisations can align their organisational purposes with the motivations and personal purposes of all its members.

We need more *humanistic* explanations of management that consider all dimensions of human nature to govern people in a *holistic* manner. This book wants to be a complement to other works that have studied purpose in organisations but have not explored the moral or spiritual dimensions (Rey et al., 2019).

Being able to find similarities between one's own personal meanings and purposes in work and life and those of one's employer will help workers

220 Using the map of motivations

feel more motivated to support the missions of organisations. Moreover, it should help workers feel that their work makes their lives better overall by supporting their meaning in life (Nielsen & Randall, 2009; Steger et al., 2012; Steger, 2017).

It is important to clarify that not every organisational purpose contributes to the truly human good and the flourishing of the organisation's members nor to society as a whole. An organisation that does not contribute to the common good of society is an *ethically unhealthy organisation* (Bañón et al., 2012). Therefore, the study of the organisational purpose should always be accompanied by the analysis of the nature of the good pursued by those organisations.

Regarding the purpose of this book and having presented the *map of motivations*, its *coordinates*, the *compass* to use it and now the *roadmap*, the last thing I would like to do is leave it up to each reader to decide if they want to use the map and its various navigation tools. Maps are just that – maps. Their purpose is to help travellers reach their destinations.

Today, the maps are digital, and GPS systems help us get anywhere. In the end, however, it is always each person who decides where they want to go and has the means to reach their final destination. We all have to decide the meaning we want to give to our work and if we want to search for higher meaningful work.

Figure 9.6 shows the *roadmap* that we have finished outlining. It is a map that reflects the simple idea that motivations in organisations depend on the

	Extrinsic Motivation Receiving	Intrinsic Motivation Achieving	Transcendent Motivation Giving	Religious Motivation Returning
Spiritual Good *Higher Spiritual Realm*	Spiritual Growth		A Meaningful HIGHER CALLING	Love for the Other
Moral Good *Ethical Realm*	Moral Growth		A Meaningful CALLING Love for others	Growing in Love with order
Pleasant Good *Psychological Realm*	Psychological Growth	A Meaningful CAREER Love for ourselves		
Useful Good *Physical Realm*	A Meaningful JOB Love from others			

Figure 9.6 Roadmap for motivations: Searching for higher meaningful work

love that we are able to receive, achieve, give and return in our daily work. The dignity of work is based on love, a love that can grow high and wide.

Two people who work with similar responsibilities in the same organisation, in the same department and even sharing a desk may end up having very different motivations in their work. The reason is very simple: love at work depends on each of our decisions, and all things being equal, love can be as different as the meaning that each person decides to give to their work.

As we decide to move up and to the right on our *map of motivations*, we will be able to love higher and more transcendent goods in our lives and work. This means that we need to be *conscious* of our fears, *convert* and *change* (the three Cs). Every time we feel fear, we should be able to look higher, think bigger and try to love more (see Figure 9.6).

If we realise that the meaning of our work is only that of a mere *job*, we can always improve it if we gain professional enthusiasm and develop a good *career* but even more so if we discover our inner *calling* and, for those who have faith, if work becomes an occasion for a greater love for God, others and ourselves.

As I have said, people in similar conditions in an organisation may have very different motivations. However, anyone at any time can find up to sixteen different kinds of motivations (4x4) to love their work more. These motivations are all compatible and complementary, and for the most part, they depend on each of us.

Today, we are all eager to lead a healthy *physical* life (with balanced diets, regular exercise, going outside, staying hydrated, sleeping well, etc.). The same is true at the *psychological* level; there is a general interest in having a healthy psychological life (going offline, going dancing, getting a pet, stopping multitasking, laughing more, etc.). Unfortunately, little is said about leading a healthy *moral* and *spiritual* life. I still think that the moral and spiritual dimensions have been neglected in the workplace (Guillén et al., 2015), and we should do something to recover them.

I hope that a *humanistic* view of motivations like the one I have presented in this book can help us to think about how to achieve some healthier habits on the *physical* and *psychological* plane in our work and lives but also how to achieve some healthier habits on the *moral* and *spiritual* plane.

As I said at the outset, one of my main motivations for writing this book was to be able to help many people. I would love for some of the ideas in this book to help many find a higher meaning in their work, as they have helped me. With that purpose in mind, I have added Figure 9.7, which shows the content of this book displayed on the map of motivations itself.

This will be particularly useful if you want to use the map to diagnose your own motivations. The goal is to help you revisit or review any part of the book you deem appropriate. This "map of the map" will allow you to remember where each of the motivations was detailed, as well as the

222 Using the map of motivations

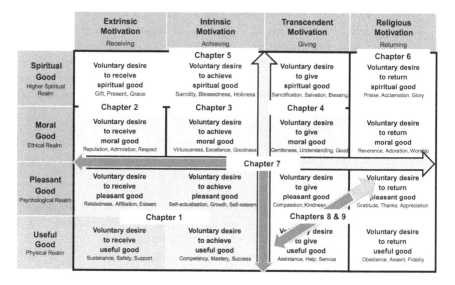

Figure 9.7 Content of the book: A "map of the map"

practical tips that you might want to try to put into practice (Chapters 1–6). You also will be able to find the map's navigation tools whenever necessary, including the coordinates (Chapter 7), the compass (Chapter 8) and the roadmap (Chapter 9) (see Figure 9.7).

To conclude, here are some questions that might help us consider how we could foster a higher meaning for our work. Following the roadmap that leads us to more meaningful work, let us ask ourselves to what extent we can be more motivated every day in our organisations, to what extent we can love our work more.

First, a final thought. To be honest, I must say that there is no secret or magic solution to finding a meaningful work-life balance because life is an adventure, a journey with all its risks and difficulties, including the tension between personal and professional spheres. Life's journey also has all its grandeur, though. We can grow if we learn to face our fears; if we face them with courage and look for higher and wider goods; if we keep thinking about our destination, our dreams and ideals day after day and, ultimately, if we continue to love our work and lives more each day. This is the real secret of human motivations in organisations, as the border police officer told me on my entry to the US.

Some questions for reflection

1 *How often am I aware of and appreciate the goodness of having a job, if I have one?*

2 *How often do I recognise the good I receive from others in my work with gratitude?*
3 *How often do I see my career as an opportunity to grow and to become better in what I do?*
4 *How often do I see every hour of work as an opportunity to contribute and to serve others?*
5 *How often do I try to transmit passion to others by showing enthusiasm for my work?*
6 *How often do I strive to convey a good example for others with my work?*
7 *How often do I attempt to attain and bring peace and joy to others through my work?*
8 *How often do I show others respect in my work, letting them know that they matter?*
9 *How often do I give others freedom to do their work in their way and respect their choices?*
10 *How often do I perceive my work as an opportunity to do the will of God and give Him glory (if I am a believer)?*

Notes

1 Many researchers have described this disordered or unreasonable kind of fear, but I normally recommend my students to read the popular book *The Happiness Trap*, which presents some findings of the cognitive behavioural therapy approach in this area and offers practical recommendations from acceptance and commitment therapy (Harris, 2014). It is interesting to see how all the modern psychological descriptions and treatments of unhealthy fear fit perfectly with the classic philosophical reflections made centuries ago.
2 Unfortunately, this is not the place to reflect on the hidden work of so many, nor the occupations of the elderly and infirm. That subject is worthy of another entire book, and I must focus here on motivations at work in organisations in general.
3 In this same book, the authors describe what they call "the four fatal fears", inherent in those who are looking for success in their professional careers. Unsurprisingly, the four fatal fears correspond exactly to the four fears reflected in the lower quadrant of our map, the one that conceives work as a *career* (see Figure 8.4). I normally recommend my business students read this book, as it is based on real-life case studies and the training programme successfully given over decades.
4 In an effort to pull together the many threads of meaningful work into a useful framework for fostering it within organisations, Professor Steger developed what he calls the SPIRE (Strength, Personalisation, Integration, Resonance and Expansion) model that focuses on some of the potentially important levers for building higher meaningful work, one conceived as a vocation or calling.
5 This universal calling to holiness has always been part of the Christian faith and was formally underlined more recently by the Catholic Church during its Second Vatican Council in the 1960s (Lumen Gentium, n. 41).
6 The Pope St John Paul II canonised the Founder of Opus Dei, Josemaría Escrivá on 6 October 2002. In his address, he called him "the saint of ordinary life". To learn more about work sanctification and the institution, see: https://opusdei.org/en-us/article/message/

References

Bañón, A. J., Guillén, M. & Gil, I. (2012). Ethics and learning organizations in the New Economy. In *Human Resource Management in the Digital Economy: Creating Synergy Between Competency Models and Information*. Hershey (Pennsylvania, EE.UU.): IGI Global. pp. 67–79.

Baviera, T., English, W. & Guillén, M. (2016). The 'logic of gift': Inspiring behavior in organizations beyond the limits of duty and exchange. *Business Ethics Quarterly*, 26(2), 159–180.

Crane, R. (2017). *Mindfulness-Based Cognitive Therapy- Distinctive Features*. London and New York: Routledge.

Duffy, R. D., Allan, B. A, Autin, K. L. & Douglass, R. P. (2014). Living a calling and work wellbeing: A longitudinal study. *Journal of Counseling Psychology*, 61, 605–615.

Escrivá, J. (1985). *Conversations with Monsignor Escrivá de Balaguer*. Manila: Sinag-Tala. A Public digital edition can be found at www.escrivaworks.org/book/conversations.htm.

Frankl, V. (1959). *Man's Search for Meaning*. Boston: Beacon Press.

Gardner, H., Csikszentmihalyi, M. & Damon, W. (2001). *Good Work: When Excellence and Ethics Meet*. New York: Basic Books.

Guillén, M., Ferrero, I. & Hoffman, W. (2015). The neglected ethical and spiritual motivations in the workplace. *Journal of Business Ethics*, 128(4), 803–816.

Hagmaier, T. & Abele, A. E. (2012). The multidimensionality of calling: Conceptualization, measurement and a bicultural perspective. *Journal of Vocational Behavior*, 81, 39–51.

Harris, R. (2014). *The Happiness Trap Pocketbook*. New York: Constable & Robinson.

Hicks, D. (2011). *Dignity: The Essential Role It Plays in Resolving Conflict*. New Haven and London: Yale University Press.

Hoffman, B. J., Bynum, B. H., Piccolo, R. F. & Sutton, A. W. (2011). Person – organization value congruence: How transformational leaders influence work group effectiveness. *Academy of Management Journal*, 54, 779–796.

Judge, T. A. & Piccolo, R. F. (2004). Transformational and transactional leadership: A meta-analytic test of their relative validity. *Journal of Applied Psychology*, 89, 755–768.

Littman-Ovadia, H. & Steger, M. F. (2010). Character strengths and well-being among volunteers and employees: Towards an integrative model. *Journal of Positive Psychology*, 5, 419–430.

Nielsen, K. & Randall, R. (2009). Managers' active support when implementing teams: The impact on employee well-being. *Applied Psychology: Health and Well-Being*, 1, 374–390.

Steger, M. F. (2009). Meaning in life. In S. J. Lopez (Ed.), *Oxford Handbook of Positive Psychology* (2nd ed.). Oxford, UK: Oxford University Press, pp. 679–687.

Steger, M. F. (2017). *Creating Meaning and Purpose at Work. The Wiley Blackwell Handbook of the Psychology of Positivity and Strengths-Based Approaches at Work*. Chapter 5, Eds. Lindsay G. Oades, Michael F. Steger, Antonella Delle Fave, & Jonathan Passmore. West Sussex, UK: John Wiley & Sons, Ltd.

Steger, M. F. & Dik, B. J. (2009). If one is searching for meaning in life, does meaning in work help? *Applied Psychology: Health and Well-Being*, 1, 303–320.

Steger, M. F., Dik, B. J. & Duffy, R. D. (2012). Measuring meaningful work: The Work and Meaning Inventory (WAMI). *Journal of Career Assessment*, 20, 322–337.

Rey, C., Bastons, M. & Sotok, P. (2019). *Purpose-driven Organizations. Management Ideas for a Better World*. Cham: Palgrave Macmillan.

Walker, A. G., Jones, M. N., Wuensch, K. L., Aziz, S. & Cope, J. G. (2008). Sanctifying work: Effects on satisfaction, commitment, and intent to leave. *International Journal for the Psychology of Religion*, 18(2), 132–145.

Wilson, L. & Wilson, H. (1998). *Play to Win. Choosing Growth Over Fear in Work and Life*. Austin, TX: Bard Press.

Index

Page numbers in *italics* indicate figures.

Abigail Adams Institute (AAI) 44, 65n2
Abrahamic faiths 102, 108, 121, 125, 145n3, 171, 174, 176, 218
Adams, John Stacey 31
agnostics 100, 117
applied sciences, understanding human motivations 152, *152*
Aquinas, St. Thomas 52, 177n1
Aristotle 44, 47, 52, 56, 59, 107, 177n1; comparing Maslow's hierarchy with conceptions of good 25–29; dialogue with Maslow and Herzberg 22–25; extrinsic and intrinsic motivations 160; on friends 154–155; ideas on human nature and moral goodness 44–46; kinds of goods 25–29, 50; on love 151, 155, 165–166; moral good 31; motives for acting 25
atheists 100, 106, 112, 117, 120, 125, 127–129, 131, 139, 143, 150
Augustine of Hippo (Saint Augustine) 120, 122, 159, 160, 166
autonomy, concepts of 27

behaviourism 9
Benefiel, Margaret 114
bonum est diffusivum sui (the good diffuses itself) 188
Boston College 104
Buddhism 101, 108, 121
business ethics 58

calling: calling orientation model 191–192; concept of 192; concept of higher 193; inner 189, 193; meaning of work as 188–192, *190*; meaning of work as higher 192–195, *194*; transcendent motivation 78; word 193
Catholic faith 124, 134, 141, 165, 223n5
Christianity 102, 121, 125, 135, 145n3
Colorado University 183
compass for motivations 177; map of motivations and 198–199; meaning in life and motivations 179–181; meaning of work and motivations 181–183; meaning of work as a calling 188–192; meaning of work as a career 186–188; meaning of work as a higher calling 192–195; meaning of work as a job 183–186; searching for meaningful work-life balance 195–198; *see also* roadmap for motivations
Conant, Douglas 34
Confucianism 101, 117n2
conscientiousness 46, 49, 96
content theories of motivation 13, 20n2
Covey, Stephen 34

Dawkins, Richard 69
dignity, ten elements of 38
Dostoevsky, Fyodor 143
Duhigg, Charles 55

EBEN (European Business Ethics Network) 42, 215
effectiveness 58, 185
efficiency 58, 185
Enron 69
Enron: The Smartest Guys in the Room (documentary) 91n1

equity theory, Adam's 31–32
Escrivá, Josemaria 219, 223n6
esteem needs 8; comparing motivation theories *11, 12, 13*
ethical: level 52; order 51–52; realm 50, *53*
ethically unhealthy organisation 206, 220
ethics 27, 58–59; business 50, 58, 69; understanding human motivation *152*, 153
external goods 27
extrinsic moral motivations 30–33, 43, 48; accuracy of 39–40; examples of 37; human dignity and trust 33–35; practical tips for 36–39; ten elements of dignity 38
extrinsic motivations 70–71; attitude of gratitude 210; Herzberg 3–6; love as summary of human motivations in organisations *150*; negative, 204; for pleasant good 27; practical tips 17–18; for useful good 26
extrinsic pleasant motivations 28, 186, 208
extrinsic spiritual motivations 106–108
extrinsic spiritual needs *107*
extrinsic useful motivations 28, 86, 174, 184

Farther Reaches of Human Nature, The (Maslow) 44
Fastow, Andrew 69
fear: from logic of, to logic of love 203–205; map of negative motivations *204*
Ferrero, Ignacio 94, 95
Five Factor Model 46
Fordham University 120
formal sciences: understanding human motivations 152, *152*
fortitude 59
Four Loves, The (Lewis) 157
framework: accuracy of 19–20; map of motivations 14–15
Frankl, Viktor 77, 207, 209
freedom 49, 168, 213; ethical 53; fake 55; human 117, 121, 176; kinds of 54; moral 54–55, 58, 70; personal 137; psychological 54, 55; religious 123, 141, 142–143, 160–161, 171; seeking meaning in work 199; of thought 103, 171; of will 77

free moral character, intrinsic moral motivations demanding 57–59
friendship: love of 154–155; as moral good 159–160
Fundamentals of Management class 21

Gandhi, Mahatma 112
Gardner, Howard 62–63
gift, logic of 78, 79, 168, 216
gift-giving, logic of 73, 78
Giles, Sunnie 34
Give and Take (Grant) 77
giving motivation 71; *see also* transcendent motivations
God: belief in 99–102, 108–111, 117; contemplation of 143–144; discovering God's love 124–127; faith in 115–116, 123, 171; higher calling of 217–218; Love of 111, 171; natural and supernatural good from 161; personal relationship with 96, 102, 112, 121–124; prayer and 112, 113, 115; spiritual goods as gifts from 102; spiritual joy and 105; spiritual motivations *114*; willing to return moral good to 134–136; willing to return pleasant good to 133–134; willing to return spiritual good to 136–139; willing to return useful good to 130–132, *132*; *see also* religious motivations; spiritual motivations
Golden Rule 173–175
González, Tomás 33, 42
good, kinds of 25–29
GoodWork Project 62
Grant, Adam 77, 78, 89
growth, concepts of 27

Hancock, Jennifer 145n2
Happiness Trap, The (Harris) 223n1
Harvard Business School 65n5
Harvard Divinity School 108
Harvard Kennedy School 94, 172
Harvard Medical School 63
Harvard University 3, 20n1, 40n1, 104, 149, 191
Herzberg, Frederick Irving 4, 18; Aristotle and 22–25; comparing motivation theories *11, 12, 13*; extrinsic and intrinsic motivations of 3–6; two-factor theory 32
HEXACO model of personality 46

Index

Hicks, Donna 30, 33, 34, 35, 38, 209
hierarchy of needs, Maslow's 7–10, 23–25, 172
higher meaningful work: searching for 201–202; search of, and life 219–222; search of, in calling 212–216, *214*; search of, in career 208–212, *210*; search of, in higher calling 217–219, *218*; search of, in job 205–208, *208*; *see also* work
higher spiritual realm 52, 98, 102, 105, 109, 111, 116, 123, 151, 217
Hinduism 101, 102, 121
Hodson, Randy 34
Hoffman, W. Michael 94, 95
honest good 26
human behaviour 10, 20, 65, 90–91; amorality of 48, 90; drivers of 17, 24–25, 82, 128; extrinsic motivations of 74; framework of 69; predicting 51–52; realms of 84; religion and 121
human dignity, extrinsic moral motivation 33–35
human generosity, transcendent motivations or 74–78
human goods: achieving truly, in organisations 161–166; definition of motivations for Aristotle's type 28; giving truly, in organisations 166–169; Maslow's hierarchy *vs* Aristotle's types of 26; receiving truly, in organisations 157–161; returning truly, in organisations 169–172; spiritual motivations as highest 95–97; truly 199n1; *see also* organisations
human ideals, intrinsic moral motivations manifesting 59–62
humanistic management 120, 127, 145n1, 153, 169, 172–173, 189, 191, 202
human motivations 202; framework of 70; love as summary of *128*; overcoming self-centered vision of 69–71
human nature: anthropological dimensions of 104; Aristotle investigating 154; hierarchical order of human goods and 53; moral goodness and 44–46; moral philosophy 56; realms of 157
human organisations: logic of love in 153–157, *156*; *see also* organisations
human sciences: disciplines understanding human motivations *152*; logic of love in 151–153
hygienic factors 4

idealism 91n3
IESE Business School 72
injustice 21, 35, 54
Institute for Ethics in Communication and Organizations (IECO) 40n1, 117n1
internal goods 27
International Association for Humanistic Management (IHMA) 120, 121, 125, 141, 145nn1–2
intrinsic moral motivations 40, 43, 48; accuracy of 64–65; defining *47*; demanding free moral character 57–59; human desire to do good 47–49; as manifestation of human ideals 59–62; participants' ideals and 61; practical tips for 62–64; shaping moral virtues and moral conscience 55–57
intrinsic motivations 70–71; Herzberg 3–6; love as summary of human motivations in organisations *150*; negative 205; for pleasant good 27; practical tips 17–18; for useful good 26
intrinsic pleasant motivations 28, 187, 208
intrinsic spiritual motivations 108, 109–111
intrinsic useful motivations 28, 187, 208
Islam 102, 121, 125, 135, 145n3

Japanese Shinto 102
Judaism 102, 121, 125, 135, 137, 145n3
Jung, Carl 77
justice 21, 30, 60, 97; equity or 31; fairness or 19, 26; God and 131, 134; virtue of 59, 64; workplaces and 157

Kennedy, John F. 188
Kreeft, Peter 110, 124

Langer, Ellen 115
Lay, Kenneth 69
Leading with Dignity (Hicks) 34
Lewis, C. S. 157
life and work, logic of love in 149–151; *see also* work

logic of love 149; friendship and 154–155; Golden Rule and 173–175; in human organisations 153–157, *156*; in human sciences 151–153; in life and work 149–151; from logic of fear to 203–205; map of motivations and 176–177; order of love and order of loves 172–176, *176*; term 153

love: achieving love at work *162*; discovering God's 124–127; friendship and 154–155; giving love at work *168*; Golden Rule and 173–175; logic of 130; order of 172–176; others-love 166; religious motivations all about 127–130; returning love at work *170*; self-love 162, 164–167, 212; summary of human motivations *128*; summary of human motivations in organisations *150*; term 153; *see also* logic of love

McLean, Bethany 91n1
Majeres, Kevin 63
Man's Search for Meaning (Frankl) 207
map of human motivations 3, 20, 40, 104: diagnosing personal drivers 163; expanded *72*, *74*, *78*; humanistic 117; logic of love in 150; order of love *172*, *175*; physical, psychological and ethical levels 46, *47*, 50 religious spiritual motivation and 104, 112, 136, 141, 150, 170; truly human good in 162–163; work as calling 189; work as higher calling 193–195; work as career 186–187; *see also* map of motivations

map of motivations 8, 9, 36, 56, 65; accuracy of 19–20; adding religious motivations *129*, 130; building 10–14; coordinates for *175*; coordinates of *156*; hierarchical levels of 151, *152*; logic of love in *156*; map coordinates for motivations *175*; Maslow's hierarchy and Aristotle's human good *26*; meaning in life and *180*; meaning in work and *182*; religious moral motivations *135*; religious motivations *140*, 141; religious pleasant motivations *133*; religious spiritual motivation *137*; religious useful motivations 131, *132*; spiritual and religious *105*, 117; using 14–17

map of negative motivations, logic of fear *204*

Marcel, Gabriel 161

Maslow, Abraham Harold 7, 20n2, 86; Aristotle and 22–25; being values (B-values) 97, 107, 111, 122; comparing Aristotle's conceptions of good with hierarchy of 25–29; comparing motivation theories *11*, *12*, *13*; hierarchy of needs 7–10, 23–25, 172; idealism 91n3; idea on moral dimension of motivations 42–44; ideas on human nature and moral goodness 44–46; meta-needs 97–98, 104, 107; spiritual motivations and 97–99, 122

meta-motivations 91n3, 93, 98

mindfulness 94–95, 101, 106, 111; concept of 217; of God's love 217, *218*; higher levels of 110; promoting ethical behaviours 114–116

mirror neurons 82

MIT (Massachusetts Institute of Technology) 104

moral conscience 55, 57–58, 189

moral freedom 54–55, 58, 70; *see also* freedom

moral good 26, 29, 30, 32, 50; extrinsic moral motivation *37*; friendship as 159–160; human nature and human goods *53*; intrinsic moral motivation *47*, 57–58; in organisations 157, 158, *158*, 160, 162, *168*, *170*; participants' intrinsic moral motivations or ideals *61*; transcendent motivations 83–85, *84*

morality, human motivation theories neglecting 21–22

moral motivation: Aristotle's types of human good *32*; higher than useful and pleasant motivations 49–55; role in rebuilding trust 35–36

moral principles 54–55

moral realm 20, 49–50

moral relativism 46, 54–55

moral virtues 42–43, 59, 83; attaining 58, 64, 165; intrinsic moral motivations shaping 55–57; specific 63–64; work and 213, 216

Mother Teresa 75, 112

motivation(s): Aristotle's types of human good *28*; content *vs* process theories 20 n2; hierarchical order of human nature and human goods *53*; meaning of life and 179–181; meaning of work and 181–183; philosophical distinction from motives *24*; three Cs (consciousness, conversion and change) 197, 206; *see also* compass for motivations; roadmap for motivations

motivation theories: comparing Maslow's, Herzberg's and other *13*; comparing Maslow's and Herzberg's *11*, *12*; diagnosis of students' motivations *15*; neglecting moral dimension of 21–22; recovering neglected moral dimension 29–33

motivator factors 4

Muslim 102, 124–125, 137, 219; *see also* Islam

natural sciences, understanding human motivations 152, *152*

nature 51; human reality by *50*; laws of moral 51–52; love for others 166, 168; *see also* human nature

neuroscience 31

New England Alumni Association 94

Nicomachean Ethics (Aristotle) 25, 154, 164

Nietzsche 126

Noahide Code 125

non-religious spiritualities 100

Notre Dame University 82

Optimal Work project 63

order of love 155, 159, 175, *175*, 176

order of loves 175, *175*, 176

organisations: achieving truly human good in 161–166; giving truly human good in 166–169; logic of love in human 153–157, *156*; logic of love in life and work 149–151; love as summary of human motivations in *150*; receiving truly human good in 157–161; returning truly human good in 169–172; three Cs (consciousness, conversion and change) 197, 206

others-esteem 12, *12*

Parmenides 107

Pérez-López, Juan Antonio 50, 52, 65n5, 72

personalisation 214, 215, 223n4

physical nature 54

physical realm 49, 158; *see also* useful goods

physiological needs 8, 28, 49; comparing motivation theories *11*, *12*, *13*; Maslow 8, 13

Pink, Daniel 73, 75

Plato 44, 47, 56, 59, 107, 177n1

Play to Win! Choosing Growth over Fear in Work and Life (Wilson & Wilson) 209

pleasant goods 26, 27, 29, 49, 50; extrinsic moral motivation *37*; human nature and human goods *53*; intrinsic moral motivation *47*, 57–58; in organisations 157, *158*, 159, 160, *162*, *168*, *170*; participants' intrinsic moral motivations or ideals *61*; transcendent motivations 80–83, *81*

Power of Habit, The (Duhigg) 55

practical wisdom 59, 100, 107, 213

process theories, motivation 20n2

psychoanalysis 9

psychological freedom 54, 55

psychological level 52, 159, 164, 221

psychological nature, laws of 54

psychological realm 51, 54, 65; *see also* pleasant goods

psychology 9, 46, 71, 83, 96, 216

Quality Management 33; Total (TQM) 42, 65n1

Real Colegio Complutense (RCC) 20n1, 93, 94, 116, 117n1

reciprocity 77, 89, 173

religious moral motivations: examples of 140, *140*; map of motivations *135*; willing to return moral good to God 134–136

religious motivations: accuracy of 144–145; all about love 127–130; Book of Psalms 129; concept of 126; discovering God's love 124–127; evidence of 139–142; examples of *140*; human *129*; human reality 120–121; love as summary of human motivations in organisations *150*; love as summary of human motivations *128*; map of motivations *129*, *130*; negative 205; personal relationship with God 121–124;

practical tips for 142–144; *see also* spiritual motivations
religious pleasant motivations: examples of 140, *140*; map of motivations *133*; willing to return pleasant good to God 133–134
religious spiritualities 100; in a broad sense 101; in its narrowest sense 102
religious spiritual motivations: definition of 137; examples of *140*, 141; map of motivations *137*; willing to return spiritual good to God 136–139
religious useful motivations: examples of 140, *140*; willing to return useful good to God 130–132, *132*
roadmap for motivations 145, 195, 198–199; in search of higher meaningful work and life 219–222; in search of higher meaning in a calling 212–216, *214*; in search of higher meaning in a career 208–212, *210*; in search of higher meaning in a higher calling 217–219, *218*; in search of higher meaning in a job 205–208, *208*; from logic of fear to logic of love 203–205; map of the map *222*; searching for higher meaningful work 201–202

safety needs 8, 28, 49; comparing motivation theories *11*, *12*, *13*
St. Teresa of Calcutta 75
sanctification of work 194, 223n6
science, term 152
Second Vatican Council 223n5
self-actualisation 8, 43; comparing motivation theories *11*, *12*, *13*; concepts of 27; growing tip of humanity 44
self-actualisers 44
self-esteem 8, 12
self-fulfilment 8, 10, 25, 43
Selfish Gene 70
Selfish Gene, The (Dawkins) 69
self-love 162, 164–167, 212
self-transcendence 72
self-transcendent motivation 87
Shintoism 101
Sikhism 101
Skilling, Jeff 69
Smith, Adam 74, 75
social needs 8; comparing motivation theories *11*, *12*, *13*

social sciences, understanding human motivations 152, *152*
Socrates 44, 46, 47, 107, 177n1
Spanish Higher Education system 20n1
SPIRE (Strength, Personalisation, Integration, Resonance and Expansion) model 216, 223n4
spiritual goods 94; defined 95; highest of human goods 95–97; in organisations 157, *158*, 159, 160, *162*, *168*, *170*; willingness to acquire 109–111; willingness to give 111–112; willingness to receive 106–108
spiritual intelligence 114
spiritual motivations 91; accuracy of 116–117; concept of 94; different conceptions 99–103; evidence of 112–113; examples of *114*; extrinsic 106–108, *107*; intrinsic *109*, 109–111, 113; mapping territory of *105*; in Maslow's latest enquiries 97–99; neglected 93–95; practical tips for 113–116; pursuing highest human goods 95–97; spiritual good defined 95; transcendent 111–112, *113*; universal recognition and respect 103–106; willingness to acquire spiritual good 109–111; willingness to give spiritual good 111–112; willingness to receive spiritual good 106–108; *see also* religious motivations
St. Augustine of Hippo 155, 177n1
St. John Paul II (pope) 223n6
Steger, Michael F. 183, 216, 223n4
students' motivations, diagnosis using 2x2 map *15*
Subhanallah 137–138
suicide 183

Taoism 101, 102, 117n2, 121, 123
TED Talk, Pink's "The puzzle of motivation" 73
temperament, Cloninger's general model of 77
temperance 59
theology 120, 124, *152*, 153, 171
Theory of Moral Sentiments (Smith) 74
Theresa of Jesus 211
Total Quality Management (TQM) Programme 42, 65n1
transcendent moral motivations: human willingness to give moral

good (to do good) 83–85; mapping the territory *84*
transcendent motivations 71, 215; accuracy of 90; defining 72; examples from participants' *88*; human generosity in academic debate 74–78; human willingness to give 71–74; logic of gift-giving 73; love as summary of human motivations in organisations *150*; love for others 167–169; map of motivations 85, *87*; moral good 83–85, *84*, *87*; negative 205; in ordinary and professional life 85–88; pleasant good 80–83, *81*; practical tips for 88–90; useful good 78–80, *79*, *88*
transcendent pleasant motivations: human willingness to give pleasant good (to please) 80–83; mapping the territory *81*
transcendent spiritual motivations 108, 111–112
transcendent useful motivations: human willingness to give useful good (to serve) 78–80; mapping the territory *79*
transcenders 71, 75, 85, 111, 166
trust: extrinsic moral motivation 33–35; role of moral motivation for rebuilding 35–36

United Nations, Universal Declaration of Human Rights 103

universal needs, spiritual motivations 103–106
University of Valencia 33, 42
Unselfish Gene 70
useful goods 26, 49, 50; extrinsic moral motivation 37; human nature and human goods 53; intrinsic moral motivation 47, 57–58; in organisations 157, *158*, 159, *162*, *168*, *170*; participants' intrinsic moral motivations or ideals *61*; transcendent motivations 78–80, *79*

Wealth of Nations, The (Smith) 74
Wharton Business School 77, 78
White, Thomas 45, 46, 65n3
work: achieving love at *162*; giving love at *168*; meaning of, and motivations 181–183; meaning of, as a calling 188–192, *190*; meaning of, as a career 186–188; meaning of, as a higher calling 192–195, *194*; meaning of, as a job 183–186, *185*; receiving love at *158*; returning love at *170*; sanctification of 194; searching for higher meaningful 201–202; searching for meaningful work-life balance 195–198, *196*; in search of higher meaningful 219–222; three C's (consciousness, conversion and change) 197; *see also* higher meaningful work; organisations
World War II 103